Aboriginal Conditions

Edited by Jerry P. White,
Paul S. Maxim, and Dan Beavon

Aboriginal Conditions:
Research as a Foundation for Public Policy

UBCPress · Vancouver · Toronto

09 08 07 06 05 04 03   5 4 3 2 1

Printed in Canada on acid-free paper ∞

National Library of Canada Cataloguing in Publication Data

Main entry under title:
  Aboriginal conditions : research as a foundation for public policy /
  edited by Jerry P. White, Paul S. Maxim, and Dan Beavon.

  Includes bibliographical references and index.
  ISBN 0-7748-1021-1 (bound); ISBN 0-7748-1022-X (pbk.)

  1. Native peoples – Government policy – Canada. 2. Native peoples – Canada – Social conditions. I. Beavon, Daniel J.K. II. White, Jerry Patrick, 1951- III. Maxim, Paul S., 1950-
E78.C2A14 2003   305.897'071   C2003-910997-6

Canadä

UBC Press gratefully acknowledges the financial support for our publishing program of the Government of Canada through the Book Publishing Industry Development Program (BPIDP), and of the Canada Council for the Arts, and the British Columbia Arts Council.

This book has been published with the assistance of the J.B. Smallman Publication Fund, Faculty of Social Science, University of Western Ontario.

UBC Press
The University of British Columbia
2029 West Mall
Vancouver, BC V6T 1Z2
604-822-5959 / Fax: 604-822-6083
E-mail: info@ubcpress.ca
www.ubcpress.ca

Contents

Tables and Figures

Tables

Figures

Acknowledgments

This book would not have been possible without the work of Terri Tomchick, who worked daily with Jerry White, and the research support of Rena Bivens, Ania Barszczuk, Peter Wilk, Erin O'Sullivan, Nick Spence, Curtis Jones, and all those connected with the First Nations Cohesion Project in Ottawa and at University of Western Ontario.

The authors would like to thank the Social Science and Humanities Research Council of Canada for funding the First Nations Cohesion Project at the University of Western Ontario. All author royalties are being donated to the Aboriginal Achievement Awards of Canada.

Jerry White thanks Karen White for all she has done.

Introduction:
The Focus of Aboriginal Conditions
Jerry P. White

This book concerns the challenge that faces social scientists outside the government, researchers in the government, policy makers, and the Aboriginal community.[1] Can we come together to develop better understandings of the problems and processes that create the Aboriginal condition?[2] Can we create the cooperative relations that will foster evidence-based policy making and thereby make improvements in the conditions that face Aboriginal Canadians? For decades scholars in academic settings have debated whether they can or should play an expanded role in the policy process. Sometimes academics argue over objectivity and sometimes over the need to conduct rigorous science and maintain independence. Government officials and policy makers bemoan what they perceive as academic "ivory towerishness," or wrap themselves in their thoughts of how practical, important, and impervious to involvement their world is. The people who are the subject of research have been silent for a long time, and have been left out except as subjects. Just as Aboriginal Canadians demand more control, more say, more access, and capacity for self-study, policy makers and researchers alike are discussing and experimenting with more open interaction. Now is the time to build a research-policy nexus.

What Is a Research-Policy Nexus?
Our book is born from the new attempts to have researchers, both in and out of government, work in cooperation on problems and issues. This involves discussing and sharing research agendas, facilitating data access, and assisting in analysis through mutual critique and review. We draw our problematic from current conditions that face Aboriginal Canadians. We are trying to engage members of the Aboriginal community, as students, researchers, and policy makers in the quest for a better understanding of the conditions facing Aboriginal people. The dialogue and discourse between researchers, both in and out of government, are the foundation of a research-policy nexus. When

superior-quality research is produced and used in making policy, the structure is complete. In the case of the Aboriginal question, there are additional dimensions, including the need to involve and train Aboriginal researchers and policy makers in these activities.

The First Nations Cohesion Project at the University of Western Ontario's Sociology Department and the Strategic Research and Analysis Directorate of the Department of Indian Affairs and Northern Development have developed the foundation of a research-policy nexus. Through the anticipated involvement of other federal departments, universities, and Aboriginal organizations, this nexus will continue to expand. This book, which is aimed at researchers and policy makers, is one of many positive outcomes expected to result from this process. In November 2002, INAC and the University of Western Ontario organized the Aboriginal Policy Research Conference. The nearly 700 delegates came from the federal government and academic and Aboriginal organizations to spend three days discussing research and policy. Co-chairs Dan Beavon and Jerry White launched a series of initiatives to build the research-policy nexus. The message is simple: it is important to develop linkages between policy and research, and between policy makers and researchers. In our case, these linkages will be built in the course of common work and research on key issues relevant to Aboriginal conditions.

Understanding and Confronting Aboriginal Conditions: The Need for a Research-Policy Nexus

The world today is composed of peoples bound together in groups that share some characteristics that create bonds between them. These groups coalesce for a variety of reasons. More often than not, the bonds of cohesion have some relationship to cultural and physical similarities. Social scientists have spent countless research hours studying these ethnic and racial ties. It is important to note that ties that bind groups together also create differences between groups. These differences between collectivities can often involve the development of hierarchies and inequalities. Socio-economic conditions, sometimes measured and sometimes assumed, are used to rank peoples. At the root of some of the most complex social problems is the differential development of ethnic groups and the social ranking that come with these variations. Public policy in this era of human development is confronted by these social problems and the questions that arise from them. Any hope of pushing forward the resolution of these issues rests on developing a research-policy maker interaction.

It is our observation that, now more than ever, answering a simple pair of questions is the foundation of public policy: "What is the situation?" and "Why has it developed?" By answering these questions, we will take the first steps in the process of crafting policy that addresses social problems. Making public policy that addresses the socio-economic difficulties and the resultant health and social conditions that face Aboriginal peoples requires a refined scientific investigation of the true conditions facing the Aboriginal population in Canada.

Why Can't Universities and Government Work Together More Closely?

Unfortunately, in this era of complex social problems, the policy maker and the social scientist all too often find themselves separated, even at odds. Scientists are housed in academic institutions or private consulting agencies that are seen by the policy maker as "outside." Scientists and social researchers are seen as less constrained and less aware of the important confines of the world that limit discretion in public action. For many of the policy makers whom we interviewed, the advice of outside researchers can be suspect. In the words of a Privy Council functionary: "It isn't that we can't use the information. We often don't have the resources to develop it ourselves. The problem is that once you open the door and the information is on the table it can't be ignored. What if it's off the wall? I have been caught in problems where the academics make proposals that simply could never fly and I'm stuck trying to figure out how to do damage control."

This problem is often expressed through the characterization of academics as "ivory tower," and leads policy makers to view academics as too out of touch with the realities of policy making to carry out policy-directed research. The need for policy-relevant research has never been greater, however. Riddell (1998) notes, in his study of federal research capacity, that 40% of the departments studied believe that their current research resources are totally inadequate to carry out the necessary policy research. Policy bodies are shedding long-term research and divesting themselves of their internal scientists in favour of policy analysts. They seek short-term applied information to the detriment of general research. A manager comments: "It is easier to get money for consultants than for hiring. It's easier to expand your analysts than to set up internal research capability." Interestingly, this contracting out can sometimes lead to avoiding departmental responsibility for the research findings, thereby gaining governmental access to the information while avoiding the political backlash that may occur.

It is no secret that, driven by deficit reduction in the early 1990s, governments became preoccupied with cost-containment issues. Policy issues in general and social science research in particular took a back seat. One casualty was the decline in the overall internal policy research capacity of governments and the abovementioned reliance on external researchers for policy-relevant knowledge.

The loss of internal research capacity has forced the federal government to contract out research questions when faced with acute issues. These projects are of less interest to university researchers for several reasons, however. First, the time frames for these projects make them less attractive to general research scientists. For a university social scientist, research pieces that are not embedded in larger contexts are of much less interest. These piecework investigations cannot challenge policy or raise serious questions because they lack a wider rubric.

Second, in the academy, those who do consultant work are considered second-class citizens, and publishing the results of consultant work is considered second- or third-class activity, if it is recognized as meritorious at all. Within universities some administrators have clung to the view that the only scholarship that is worthwhile is that done by the single academic working on their own within their most specialized area. Marc Renaud (1998), president of the Social Sciences and Humanities Research Council of Canada (SSHRCC), calls this "arcane thinking," where research is divided between applied/commissioned and interest/curiosity-driven. Multidisciplinary work, which is often the core of middle theory and more applied social science, has been promoted by some while being discouraged by others. An academic at the University of Western Ontario comments: "Some have never accepted that multidisciplinary work is reputable social science even in the face of senior administration promotion of such activity. If you stick to your small box and publish esoteric university press editions you get rewarded with salary points, if not, you don't."

This story is repeated in many institutions. General research, driven by the imagination of the scholar, is commendable; it is certainly very important to the development of science and society. However, it is not the only true science. It is not the only research that is important. Those who believe so create roadblocks to the development of relationships between science and policy making. They undermine evidence-based decision making.

The policy community within the federal government reports a series of problems with university research from their perspective: "Universities simply get an 'F' in terms of communicating research findings. Frankly, the research often needs to be cast in a frame that speaks to policy. They do not do that. Why can't they distill competing research results and make choices easier for policy types?"

These problems are reinforced through a structural resonance created by government actions. The government divestiture of internal research has, in effect, done collateral damage. The external research community has fewer people *within* the government to liaise with, and within the federal government there are fewer people who show an interest in the research being carried on outside the government. These missing people would have been potential conduits for external research to reach decision makers.

For their part, researchers and scientists are seen by policy makers as being less interested in policy-applicable research. Therefore, few departments take any time to inform outside researchers of their research plans and agendas. This was seen as a problem in the past by Drummond (1997). At that time, less than "half of the departments studied have formal processes to inform selected members of the external community" (Drummond 1997), and our informal interviewing indicates that this had not changed as of 2002.

Another demonstration of this problem of underdeveloped interconnections has been the complaint that monies put into the research funds of bodies such as the Social Sciences and Humanities Research Council of Canada or even the Canadian Institutes of Health Research (CIHR) have generated little policy-relevant work. The personal projects of scientists have had only oblique application to important issues facing the policy community, or no application at all, according to audits. The Department of Indian Affairs and Northern Development audited the SSHRCC research projects over a ten-year period: "We came to the conclusion that there was less than 1% of the research output that had any policy relevance. We essentially got very little from our contribution to these general research funding bodies."

What Is Being Done?

The concerns and beliefs that little "valuable" or policy-relevant research is being funded through the SSHRCC is an illustration of the distance or discordance between policy makers in government and the scientific community. The response by the SSHRCC has been to hold special competitions to fund larger projects that are "policy-relevant" and that build "partnerships between policy makers in the federal government and university-based research scientists." The strategic funding of cohesion research projects, one of which was the First Nations Cohesion Project at the University of Western Ontario, is an example of this initiative. This funding has not only generated policy-relevant research but also created cooperation between researchers in the government and university-based scholars. This book is the result of this type of cooperation.

The SSHRCC has tried to play a role in developing more cooperation. SSHRCC president Marc Renaud has addressed this problem, arguing that there is a prevalence of simplistic, binary thinking where research is either curiosity-driven research or policy-driven. He suggests that we have to get past this through dialogue between producers of research and users of research. Renaud has committed the SSHRCC to promoting a number of joint initiatives, between the SSHRCC and the federal government, that demonstrate the value of collaboration and multidisciplinarity (Renaud 1998).

Another indication of the move toward more policy-driven research was the establishment of the Policy Research Initiative (PRI) in the federal government in 1996. The focus of the PRI is to develop "new activities and new partnerships in the constant pursuit of building a stronger capacity to identify, understand and address longer-term policy issues facing Canada" (Policy Research Initiative 2001). It has expanded from being an intra-government initiative to identify and fill research gaps to trying to advance a more aggressive, forward-looking policy research agenda aimed at strengthening policy research capacity in and out of government. It also claims an interest in facilitating an overall culture change in terms of how research is understood and developed (Policy Research Institute 1998). According to the PRI's own reports, the first phase of this initiative looked at the key policy pressures facing Canada, then moved to the construction of a network of "30 federal departments and agencies, provincial governments, numerous think tanks and many universities" (Policy Research Institute 2001).

The reason it began internally was not purely pragmatic. It assessed that "the science and policy communities in the federal government operate as two solitudes. For greater effectiveness and efficiency in decision making, the two communities need to work together more closely" (Doern 1999). The PRI has attempted to determine what blocks departments from developing research capacity. It sees a problem with senior leaders who have little interest in long-term research that spans departments. These leaders are preoccupied with their political agendas and budget garnering. Our interviews indicate that "most of the resources [are] being directed toward short-term priorities and day to day operations." Data issues rank high in the lack of research development. To use data, one needs to know what exists and how to get it. This is compounded by issues of privacy, which impair micro-data access or data linkages that are critical to evidence-based decision making. Finally, there are concerns about the existence of a culture in which dialogue is not encouraged. Researchers in government comment: "I don't get the opportunity to discuss my research with senior people. Sometimes you don't even hear what they thought of it."

Some of the same problems can impact the university and private research community. It is often difficult to gain access to the types of data that can push both general science and policy-related inquiry ahead. The advantage of government researchers is that they have access to departmental data holdings and they can sometimes use the bureaucratic hierarchy to pressure external organizations to provide, release, or collect data (for example, Statistics Canada). The university researcher has less access and less weight in these matters. This can lead to an inability to explore questions that are current and policy-relevant, and also discourages the pursuit of funds aimed at middle theory and policy-related issues. University researchers are not rewarded for seeking answers or for working to establish better data. They are rewarded only for finding answers. Spending six months seeking out data access just to begin an analysis can be very costly to an academic's career.

The political problems associated with data are often left without comment. The Human Resources Development Canada (HRDC) scandal of 2000, over their data holdings and data linkage, sends chills through agencies like Statistics Canada. This magnifies the ongoing problem where anything that impacts or may impact the Census of Canada can be derailed. The many initiatives to "liberate data" are positive in this regard. An example of one such progressive move is Statistics Canada's acknowledgment of the importance of creating census data access points at universities and the agency's subsequent creation of several research data centres.

The PRI has been successful at stimulating significant interest in policy research, and sees the beginning of a conversion of that interest into increased demand (Policy Research Initiative 1999). However, the interviews we conducted appear to indicate that resources get allocated only where the political agenda and research agenda cross. This is to be expected, but again it will not provide a long-term shift in the research-policy nexus and create the research discourse that we see as necessary.

The PRI-sponsored journal *Isuma* has published quality work and, until its shutdown in 2003, proved to be an important bridge between policy makers and researchers. Creating openness where research findings are published and accessible, and encouraging debate between policy researchers in government and academic researchers, is important to the development of a research-policy nexus and discourse. The PRI has shifted its attention to asserting joint publishing ventures with university-based scientists, such as the upcoming book on urban Aboriginal conditions.

The University of Western Ontario's First Nations Cohesion Project is a practical example of an endeavour to create an interaction like the one called for by the PRI and President Renaud of the SSHRCC. The PRI has proposed that a "common space" be developed where academics, policy researchers, and policy makers "continue their own work but dedicate a small amount of their activity to a shared effort at greater community cooperation intended to encourage agenda-sharing, promote coordinated research on medium-term, horizontal issues, facilitate information and data exchange, foster personal and professional exchanges, and promote linkages across the research and policy community" (Policy Research Initiative 1999). In our case, tackling issues related directly to many Aboriginal conditions, the policy makers and researchers include those in the Aboriginal community themselves.

How Might the Government Play a Role in Encouraging the Process?

As a start, there are university shortfalls that need be addressed. The lack of funds to pay the full cost of research is a critical problem for universities today. Paul Davenport, president of the University of Western Ontario and former chair of the Ontario Association of Universities, comments: "It is crucial that the federal government funds the total cost of the research it wishes to encourage in universities. Currently universities must tax other parts of their budgets to fund the overhead and space costs of their federal research grants. If we are to maintain excellence and increase capacity, we need federal funding for these 'indirect costs' of research, which have been funded in the US for decades" (Paul Davenport, personal communication, October 2001). Since Davenport made this statement, the federal government has begun funding about one-third of the indirect costs of research on the federal grants.

Is it possible that the government could begin with the transfer of funds to cover research infrastructure in proportion to the policy-related research done in an institution? This can be justified given that the universities are really assuming costs that are shed by the government departments. We would have to protect the flow of funds to general scientific work and social science funding that is not policy-relevant. However, this would be a giant step toward building the interest in and the capacity to develop the research-policy nexus we need in Canada.[3] In 2003 some funding for indirect costs has found its way to universities.

The Purpose of This Book

This book speaks to three important constituencies and therefore has three purposes. We speak to other scientists, and our aim is to present findings from very recent research and thereby push forward the research agenda on issues of relevance to Aboriginal Canadians. We hope this research will generate scientific interest, lead to the development of more investigation, and contribute eventually to positive social development. It also serves as a notice to those in the academy who feel that multidisciplinary work and policy-relevant research are less developed and less important.

We speak to policy makers with the aim of promoting evidence-based policy making, to encourage a greater link with the scientific and external research community, and to demonstrate what type of research is necessary as a foundation for public policy. We also want to speak as scientists to the Aboriginal communities about research and how to proceed on issues of data collection and analysis. Our book is a call for more cooperation between scientists and Aboriginal organizations. Like our work on First Nations Cohesion, which has targeted the building of Aboriginal capacity to collect and analyze data, our book is also aimed at building capacity in the First Nations community.

Can researchers in and out of government work together to develop important joint projects? Can we create the nexus of research and policy that will make strides in confronting the roots of the Aboriginal condition? We believe that it is very possible.

Speaking to Scientists, Researchers, and Policy Makers

This book is about bringing together scientists in university settings, consultant groups, and researchers in government. We present some of the most rigorous and up-to-date research on the Aboriginal condition in the hopes that it will have three effects. The first is to advance the most developed research we can on a range of conditions facing First Nations and other Aboriginal peoples. Many nations and ethnic groupings make up the Aboriginal population of Canada. Each nation shares cultural and social characteristics, but as a population they represent a grand diversity. Each nation has a history, has currently or in the recent past shared a language, and certainly experiences a social existence that places them in a hierarchy of disadvantage. With this diversity, one may expect a dramatic diversity of social and economic conditions. However, we find that all First Nations share certain characteristics. These can be measured in terms of socio-economic characteristics such as income and educational attainment, in terms of health when we compare life expectancy, and in terms of social disruption when we assess imprisonment rates, child welfare, or even suicide rates. There are obvious implications for scientists. We should be dedicated to uncovering why this is so, and to finding solutions to social problems. As the chapters unfold, we paint a picture of the basic demography of First Nations and some characteristics of other Aboriginal peoples. We look at the income characteristics, migration, and population patterns. There are discussions of cultural conditions such as language maintenance and how traditional language maintenance is related to socio-economic development. We also explore community capacity and the level of human development and well-being. In short, we try to open many fronts of research and policy inquiry and hope that this will stir an interest in pursuing these and other issues even more systematically.

The second purpose is to send a message to policy makers. If you wish to make policy on more than ideological and subjective grounds, then you need to help produce and use high-calibre research findings. It is simply not enough to delve superficially into issues or be driven by political agendas that have little grounding in the current situation. It is not entirely unfair to say that too often policy has roots in the anecdotal understandings of those who make it, or it is informed by the political constraints that parties, ideologies, or day-to-day exigencies dictate. This is a fact of life, and while we can recognize it, we need not be totally constrained by it.

This may seem to some like a call to have "objective science" rule our policy-making world. We know that it is an error to fall into the "technocratic wish" that appeals to objective measures to resolve all contentious issues and/or clothe their resolution as scientifically logical and natural.[4] Science, and the research findings that flow from scientific work, is not entirely objective. Scientific work may often be composed of subjective choices that are debated among scientists themselves, and often the norms are just the brokered agreement. Objective truth is historically contingent. However, we are of the firm opinion that we must start with a clear view of today's reality, however flawed by the era we live in or the level of understanding we have.

Can there be scientifically based public policy? Formani (1990) says that the dream of scientifically based public policy, which has grown ever since the Enlightenment and perhaps reached its apogee toward the close of the twentieth century, is a "myth and a theoretical illusion." We both agree and disagree. While we do not advocate that the latest statistical techniques prove causation and therefore should be treated as biblical in their intent, we do say that the *more* decisions that are made based on the *best* evidence available, the *more* likely we are to have *better* decisions.

We would also argue that outside of the incompetent or dishonest, all policy makers have an interest in narrowing the gap between policy promises (intentions) and policy outcomes (consequences). The question is whether one can narrow the gap in the unfulfilled expectations and between the intended and unintended outcomes. We would answer in the affirmative.[5]

This debate will continue long after this book has been forgotten. It began centuries ago. It was Francis Bacon who argued for an understanding of the world free from theologically distorted realities. However, we hope that this dialogue and research move us closer to where we want to be.

We are neither the positivists of the policy science movement (Lazerfeld 1975) nor postmodernists. We are structuralists, and our view of the role of scientific research (social and natural) is grounded in the recognition of the changing role of the state after the Second World War. From that time, there was a growing interest in developing the scientific knowledge of societal conditions and a growing understanding of the benefit of engineering change in those conditions. This was because the welfare state, developing and expanding during this period, demanded that understanding. This need for research in the governmental policy process has expanded the research agenda and promoted the development of many branches of research.[6]

The research that has been done into policy making and the science behind it indicates that where the *aims of policy* are widely accepted and the *best path is unclear,* the role of the research is enhanced dramatically (Galster 1996, 238), whereas it is much less so in debate where different ideological and political interests are marshalling research to support their policy preference (Galster 1996, 239).[7] This would make those with power who hold to the existing paradigm more open to allowing research evidence into the public policy discourse. The funding made available within a paradigm, as in the SSHRCC example above, circumscribes a paradigm shift by setting key strategic funding areas *within* the logic of the paradigm. We currently hold a view that stresses the movement to an abridged sovereignty for First Nations while accepting difference, but promoting equality. We are open to change, however. The questions of Aboriginal community capacity to handle devolution should be important now, as there is both the ideological and practical movement toward the devolution of programs. Interest should also extend to the socio-economic differences with non-Aboriginal society and the ways to reduce those differences. This research agenda suits the paradigm in which we currently operate. While we acknowledge that social scientists should also be seeking out the dead ends within a paradigm and solving those problems, our purpose here is to advance the research-policy nexus, not dramatically shift paradigmatic perceptions. The social demographer can certainly determine whether "reserve populations" are increasing along with urban Aboriginal populations and make that known to help readjust public policy, or point to policy changes around who is an Indian and forecast the implications. The sociologist can point to the inequality in income and some indications of the causes as a guide to building equality. The choice of research that we present in this volume is not arbitrary, but is circumscribed by the space we have and the many good pieces of research being produced by our partners to date.

Speaking to the Aboriginal Communities

The third purpose of this volume is to speak to Aboriginal peoples. The politics involved in Aboriginal groups working with policy makers is beyond our scope of involvement. However, the involvement of First Nations and other Aboriginal peoples in the research process is properly within our capacity and our agenda. There have been, and can be, evolving co-research projects such as the Aboriginal Peoples Survey. There has been, and will continue to be, a need for building and expanding Aboriginal research capacity and consultation on research agendas. We hope this volume will contribute to this legacy and provide a solid foundation on which future Aboriginal researchers will build.

Currently, there is a developing interest and dialogue in Aboriginal organizations concerning control over research and making it serve Aboriginal interests. This comes out in many ways, such as the demand by the Assembly of First Nations for control over data relating to Aboriginal peoples' health issues and the application of OCAP principles.[8] The recently formed National Aboriginal Health Organization (NAHO), which has members that represent the major Aboriginal groups in the country, has in recent times pursued the idea of creating an Aboriginal Data Institute (ADI) that Aboriginal organizations would not only have jurisdiction over but also use to assess the Aboriginal condition and shape their policies and proposals for public policy. Such an institute would have Aboriginal input and direction over the collection and analysis of research data. Similarly, the federal government is actively exploring the creation of a First Nations Statistical Institute. We are stakeholders in the collection and analysis of data, and we certainly recognize that Aboriginal peoples and their organizations are stakeholders. We want to help develop Aboriginal expertise in the collection and analysis of data. The data that underlie the analysis of issues and research questions addressed in this book were, in part, collected by Aboriginal people. In fact, some of the authors and editors of this book are themselves Aboriginal, while others are not.

The message we wish to give is that political control is one thing, but real control comes with the development of more Aboriginal scientists and more strategic partnerships with non-Aboriginal scientists to find real answers to real problems. We wish to be part of the creation of that capacity and eventually see the functioning of a top-quality Aboriginal Data Institute and more high-calibre Indigenous scholars teaching and doing research in Canadian universities. Moreover, we do not want to insinuate that Indigenous scholars should undertake only Aboriginal research. As academics they should be free to pursue whatever curiosity-driven research strikes their interest, including research on the non-Aboriginal population within Canada. Hopefully, some of these Indigenous scholars will use their greater cultural understanding and personal histories and join with us to address many of the data and analytical gaps that plague the Aboriginal policy domain. This is a necessary part of the research-policy nexus, and as such is a key aspect of the purposes of this book. We dedicate this book to that quest. That is why we called it *Aboriginal Conditions: Research as a Foundation for Public Policy*.

Outline of the Book

This book is divided into four parts. The first part presents a theoretical model that places communities at the centre of scientific inquiry. Utilizing the social capital and social cohesion approaches that are central to social science at this time, a paradigm for future study of First Nations is presented.

The research enterprise of all the contributions is not defined by this model, but it provides a paradigmatic backbone that we return to in the conclusion to the book. Chapters 2 through 10 look at some of the core issues that require clarification in order to build a common paradigm.

The second set of studies is designed to show how our understandings of who is Aboriginal, and how we define the First Nations peoples, is fragile. How can we make policy when we are not sure who are in the target populations? We illustrate the problems inherent in population projections, how government policy has reshaped who is a First Nations person, and finally how identity shifts are taking place within and outside the Aboriginal population.

Part 3 picks up two strands from the earlier chapters. There are two studies of language. Chapter 6 looks at the relationship between identity and language, setting out to see whether maintaining language has any effect on socio-economic development. Chapter 7 examines how traditional languages are in decline and the effect that this might have on identity. Language is a core element in national and community identity and relates to cohesion and the production of social capital. Language can also divide peoples and impact on economic integration. Having a clearer picture of the status and impact of language is important to policy making.

Finally, in Part 4 we look at the issues of development, inequality, and community capacity. First Nations human development is measured utilizing the United Nations Development Program Human Development Index. We then compare the well-being and development of First Nations with other countries and with the rest of the Canadian population. Part 4 also includes a chapter that explores income inequality. However, it looks not only at the income inequalities between Aboriginal and non-Aboriginal groups within Canada but also at the inequalities within the Aboriginal groups themselves. Finally, we conclude with the policy lessons that can be drawn and outline the next stage of research that we see arising from this collection of studies.

Notes

1 Throughout this book we use the terms "Status Indian" and "Registered Indian" interchangeably. Authors also refer to this group of Aboriginal people as "First Nations" people. These are persons who have rights through the acts of Parliament and qualify to be recipients of rights and privileges accorded those who are registered with the Department of Indian Affairs and Northern Development (DIAND). This department is sometimes referred to as Indian and Northern Affairs Canada (INAC).

2 By "the Aboriginal condition" we mean that on almost every socio-economic or health indicator, Aboriginal people lag or do worse than non-Aboriginal people within Canadian society.

3 The creation of the Canadian Foundation for Innovation is also a very positive step.

4 Many scientists have argued that science cannot be value-free or thoroughly objective. Connie Ozawa (1991), in opposition to what she calls the logical positivist empiricist paradigm, argues that science can never reach its goal of objectivity, but she concedes that scientifically wise decisions are better than uninformed decisions. Research has many components and each of the components is differentially affected by, and susceptible to, ideological and political determination and conditioning (Fisher and Forester 1987). The *process* of scientific inquiry can often be more objective than the *choice of the target*. The *question* one asks is more ideologically conditioned than the methods one employs to do one's research to *answer* that question. Feminist scholar Simon (1996, 118) argues that a person's religion, gender, political orientation, or race may affect what problems they wish to do research on, but they do not necessarily influence, nor should they influence, the research design and scientific assessment of the findings.

5 The quest for a realistic, explanatory, and more objective view of problems and issues is compromised by the process of gathering knowledge. Knowledge gained through rigorous scientific investigation may be fragmentary, and when pulled together, it is done so by someone who mediates the findings (Ozawa 1991, 11-12). This mediation conditions the research ideologically, argues commentators such as Dickson (1984). However, whether fragments or large puzzle pieces, research based on good rigorous methods has the advantage of being open to critique. It is assessable and accessible by other scientists and even those with less training. The existence of evidence with more transparent explanation of how that evidence was amassed creates a much more fertile ground for a policy discourse than non-evidence-based decision making.

6 The promotion of research can sometimes take the form of manipulation through state funding of strategic initiatives or through the private sector engaging researchers to "find" results. We believe that at the crossroads of all these positions there still lies the capacity to base policy on reason and firm research foundations. Research that is part of the public policy discourse is open to refutation.

7 Kuhn (1970) may provide some insight here. If the debate is in motion as to what the dominant paradigm should be, then the research will be marshalled by those wishing their vision be dominant. As such, the debate within the policy discourse may be highly truncated by ideology. For example, in the case of Aboriginal policy, the paternalist paradigm gave way to the integrationist, and now we have a more *separate but equal* approach (Royal Commission on Aboriginal Peoples 1996). Each of these overarching policies have many specific implications. The dominant approach, or understanding, then influences all policy after a dominant paradigm is put in place; ideology takes a reduced role and scientific research can be more influential.

8 OCAP stands for Ownership, Control, Access and Possession, and refers to Aboriginal juridisdiction over research data at all levels.

References

Dickson, D. 1984. *The New Politics of Science*. New York: Pantheon Books.

Doern, G. Bruce. 1999. *Science and Scientists in the Context of Politics and Federal Decisions*. Policy Research Initiative working paper. Ottawa: Policy Research Initiative.

Drummond, R. 1997. Drummond Report: Relations with the External Policy Research Community. Ottawa: Umbrella Group on Policy Management, Sub-Group on Relations with External Policy Research Community, Privy Council Office.

Fisher, B., and B. Forester. 1987. *Confronting Values in Policy Analysis: The Politics of Criteria*. Beverly Hills, CA: Sage.

Formani, R. 1990. *The Myth of Scientific Public Policy*. London: Transaction Publishers.

Galster, G. 1996. *Reality and Research: Social Science and US Urban Policy since 1960*. Washington, DC: Urban Institute Press.

Kuhn, Thomas. 1970. *The Structure of Scientific Revolutions*. Chicago: University of Chicago Press.

Lazerfeld, Paul. 1975. Policy sciences movement: An insider's view. *Policy Sciences* 6: 56-79.

Ozawa, Connie P. 1991. *Recasting Science: Consentual Procedures in Public Policy Making*. Boulder, CO: Westview Press.

Policy Research Initiative (PRI). 1998. *Outlook Document: The Policy Research Initiatives Business Plan*. Ottawa: PRI.

–. 1999. *Improving Relationships within the Policy Research Community*. CPRN/PPF Report. Ottawa: PRI.

–. 2001. <http://www.ottawapolicyresearch.gc.ca/>

Renaud, Marc. 1998. The Policy Research Initiative and the challenge of multidisciplinary approaches. President's speech, Congress of the Social Sciences and Humanities, 2 June 1998.

Riddell, Norman. 1998. *Policy Research Capacity in the Federal Government*. Report prepared for the Policy Research Secretariat. Ottawa: PRI.

Royal Commission on Aboriginal Peoples. 1996. *People to People, Nation to Nation*. Ottawa: Minister of Supply and Services Canada.

Simon, Rita. 1996. The role of social science data in public policy issues. In *From Data to Public Policy: Affirmative Action, Sexual Harassment, Domestic Violence and Social Welfare*, edited by Rita Simon. New York: Women's Freedom Network and University Press of America.

PART 1

Thinking Outside the Box: Building Models Based on Communities
Jerry P. White

We are often trained to think about the subject of research as either the individual or the entire collectivity. For example, when we look at human capital among Sri Lankans entering Canada, we take the education and training levels of the individuals and aggregate them to create a picture of all Sri Lankan immigrants. Speaking hypothetically, let us say we find a deficit in comparison with other immigrant populations. We develop a policy where we target the entire population. We build our understandings on the cumulation of individual data and we aggregate to some natural target population. Can we think of other ways to conceptualize our problems?

In the Aboriginal population, we know that there are many nations, many cultural and linguistic roots – in short, many particularities. Yet when we look at the population attributes, the demography, and the socio-economic characteristics, we see many intra-Aboriginal similarities. These similarities have led many researchers to concentrate on Aboriginal versus non-Aboriginal comparisons. More recently, some research has looked at the differences between First Nations, Non-Status, Métis, and Inuit populations versus non-Aboriginal peoples (George et al. 1996; Bernier 1997). What is proposed in Chapter 1 is to look at the results of our labours, both university and state policy, recognize our achievements, but acknowledge that we are operating inside a box. That box is reducing the policy options by limiting the research questions and models. In Chapter 1, White and Maxim argue that some of the particularities of Aboriginal conditions can be better understood if we think of the Aboriginal people not as individuals but as grouped in communities. Researchers need to recognize that communities have inherent qualities of their own, and characteristics that are different from the sum of their parts. These characteristics can give us insight into both the outcomes of those collectivities *as communities* and the lives of the persons who live within them. Just as a watch is more than the sum of all its springs, gears, or chips, the community is more than simply the sum of its inhabitants.

The use of communities as a unit of investigation and policy is not a revolutionary idea. As far back as the 1920s, sociology was centred on the study of communities. Since the days of the Chicago school, there has been a current in North American sociology looking at the behaviour of communities. The earliest writings argued that successful minority groups moved out from their settings as they grew in affluence (Park 1926, 9). This thread developed into theories equating social distance with physical separation, and finally proposing that separateness/segregation and economic difference are correlated (Massey 1981). Whether it be criminology or urban sociology, there has been a long history of ecological studies and theories developed using communities as the base (see, for example, Morris 1957 and Ogburn 1935).

This research approach was largely abandoned, however. We might point to an influential article by W.S. Robinson in 1950 that contributed to the directional shift away from community research. The ecological fallacy, as he called it, was to scare people away from looking at ecological correlates. Robinson convincingly warned of the problems associated with imputing aggregate characteristics back to individuals. He was right, within the narrow case he was making, but what happened was the abandonment, by many, of the thinking that went along with conceptualizing about communities. Technologies also reinforced this movement away from communities and toward individual data analysis. As we were able to look at the huge individual-level data sets from the census and other surveys, we had less need to conceptualize about aggregations other than total population patterns. Computing software allowed us to talk about the average education of African American males in the United States and the average income of those identified as Aboriginal in Canada. Graduate students at our university, the University of Western Ontario, can research complex questions in large populations utilizing data and software programs available at the click of a mouse. This type of technical ability has pushed us away from community studies.

In Chapter 1, White and Maxim simply ask that we look at models that are constructed from a knowledge and perspective of community. They believe that the cohesion of communities has an influence on the population outcomes of that community, and that the cohesion of a community and its population outcomes are related to the levels of social, physical, and human capital that a community has at its disposal. The authors take us briefly through the debates over definitions to arrive at a conceptual model that they see as being potentially operational and that can and will, when data are available, be measurable.

It is difficult to look at these types of models because we do not have ready examples of communities where we have experimented with the factors that

White and Maxim point out are the key independent variables. They do raise illustrations, some hypothetical and some all too real. One illustration is the case of Port Harrison (now called Inukjuak). The Canadian government relocated families from Port Harrison to Resolute Bay and Grise Fiord. The results of these actions, in hindsight, caused significant social harm to the people. We want to think of the problem as a community problem, not one that affected many individuals. When this relocation took place, the community, as a community, was changed. The relationship between the skills and the resources was altered. The outcomes were devastating for the community and its citizens. There was a decline in cohesion and subsequent social breakdown. The authors also draw on the example of Davis Inlet to illustrate some of the processes at work. In this instance, a similar movement of a community led to social breakdown. The authors comment: "If we examine some of the social and health population outcome patterns of Davis Inlet, we see that the tiny community has been plagued by alcoholism, gas sniffing, physical and sexual abuse, and suicide. The pinnacle may have come in 1992, when five brothers and sisters, along with an infant cousin, died in a house fire while their parents were out drinking. At that time, an estimated 75% of the 168 adults of Davis Inlet were alcoholic."

Policy implications are manifest. If communities are a key to population outcomes, then policy might best be aimed at communities and be differentially applied to the specific needs in terms of human, social, and physical capital resources. It also implies that there are complex interactions that make simple single-variable solutions inappropriate. White and Maxim argue that we need to construct a community-level database that allows us to examine communities and their characteristics and assess the intra-community dynamics. Such a database will permit the scientific investigation of the patterns displayed across communities. Such a database is being built at the University of Western Ontario with a view toward creating a cooperative data institute that would be accessible by government research and policy stakeholders, Aboriginal research organizations, and university-based research scientists.

References
Bernier, R. 1997. *The Dimensions of Wage Inequality among Aboriginal Peoples*. Research Paper Series No. 109. Ottawa: Analytical Studies Branch, Statistics Canada.
George, P., P. Kuhn, and A. Sweetman. 1996. Patterns of employment, unemployment and poverty: A comparative analysis of several aspects of the employment experience of Aboriginal and non-Aboriginal Canadians using 1991 PUMF. In *People to People, Nation to Nation*, the Royal Commission on Aboriginal Peoples. Ottawa: Minister of Supply and Services Canada.
Massey, D.S. 1981. Social class and ethnic segregation: A reconsideration of methods and conclusions. *American Sociological Review* 46: 641-50.

Morris, T.P. 1957. *The Criminal Area: A Study in Social Ecology.* London: Routledge and Kegan Paul.

Ogburn, W.F. 1935. Factors in variation in crime among cities. *American Journal of Sociology* 30: 12-20.

Park, R.E. 1926. The urban community as a spatial pattern and moral order. In *The Urban Community,* edited by E.W. Burgess. Chicago: University of Chicago Press.

Robinson, W.S. 1950. Ecological correlation and the behavior of individuals. *American Sociological Review* 15: 351-57.

1
Social Capital, Social Cohesion, and Population Outcomes in Canada's First Nations Communities

Jerry P. White and Paul S. Maxim

Communities are social constructions built through the interaction of human actors with each other and with their environment. As such, a community is both a physical entity and a relationship. Organizations, institutions, structures of custom, and patterns of everyday life are products of our interrelationships in our communities. These interrelationships can produce cohesion and solidarity or discord and disunity. Whether we believe that it is the sameness of life that produces cohesion (as in Durkheim's mechanical society), or the class consciousness that defines world views, solidarity affects people's well-being and their social and economic achievements.

The sociology of this century has demonstrated a fascination with cohesion and the lack of it in the human community. From the anomic post-structural angst of anti-positivism to the Colemanesk social capitalist constructions of trust, the problems that we as sociologists focus on are similar. What are the features of our communities that explain the human condition? Can we come to understand them and even predict their effect?

This chapter is a contribution to this attempt to understand cohesion and its role in human affairs. We are concerned in general with determining what factors in the makeup and functioning of communities contribute to differential population outcomes. This project is anchored in the sociology of policy and purpose, even as it addresses this theoretical issue. We are centrally concerned, as social scientists, with what makes the population outcomes of the First Nations peoples unique. The First Nations communities in Canada share a demography that sets them apart from non-Aboriginal communities. Despite being particularistic by culture and geography, they share commonalities across the country. We believe that the key to this enigma lies in the very nature of the communities and how different social and physical resources interact to effect the cohesion of these collectivities.

It is the University of Western Ontario First Nations Cohesion Project (FNCP) that has spawned this work. This project addresses how variations among available forms of capital (including social, human, and natural/physical capital) and the cohesiveness of First Nations communities generate differential population outcomes. Those outcomes include variations in life expectancy, differential educational attainment, income inequality, rates of infant mortality, patterns of migration, levels of morbidity, and a range of other unique patterns of factors within those communities. In this chapter, we present our working hypotheses in the form of a model. We outline the components of the model and some of the assumptions underlying it.

Underlying Understandings and Assumptions

The Hypotheses and the Model

Our theoretical model includes several components: (1) a multifaceted dependent variable – population outcomes; (2) three independent variables – social capital, human capital, and physical capital; and (3) one intervening variable – social cohesion. Figure 1.1 outlines the model.

The model presupposes a unitary direction for the influence of variables; we believe, however, that there are non-recursive paths that will appear in the actual functioning of the system when we get to the stage of actual measurement. We already know that there is a non-recursive relationship between human and social capital (a parent-teacher association enhances school operations) and a weak but observable relationship between investment in a community (physical capital) and the development of human capital (e.g., capital investment in businesses leads to training on the job, company tickets, and even full apprenticeships).

We see physical capital and human capital influencing the community both directly and in conjunction with social capital. We hypothesize that variations in social capital will affect social cohesion and, through this influence, have an effect on various population outcomes. Empirical research on social capital indicates that it has an impact on health (Putnam 2000), general mortality

Figure 1.1 Population outcomes model

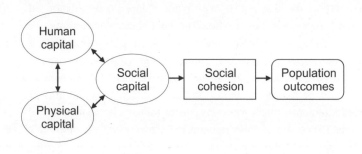

(Ichiro et al. 1997), infant mortality (Bendahmane 1994), morbidity in vulnerable groups (Aday 1997), fertility (Lilliard and Waite 1993), economic performance (Grootaert 1998, 1999; Knack and Keefer 1997), and a range of other population and health outcomes (Sandefur and Lauman 1998). It is also related to human capital, as we indicate in the model (Teachman et al. 1997; Coleman 1988). The primary influence we see is human capital enhancing the capacity to have stronger levels of social capital, but we also recognize the strong possibility that higher levels of social capital may enhance the acquisition of human capital. For example, a parent-teacher association often contributes to the functioning of the school on a reserve. We believe that it is possible to measure social capital at the community level and refine an index based on critical variables identified in existing research (Krishna and Shrader 1999). The Aboriginal Peoples Survey (APS), the Census of Canada, the DIAND (Department of Indian Affairs and Northern Development) Survey of Community Characteristics (DSCC), and the linked Indian Registry/Vital Statistics, when developed into an integrated data set that describes communities, will allow us to construct this index through variables concerned with, among others, the existence of community associations, membership participation, proportion of single-parent families, language retention, and trust in community political leadership.[1] Graduate students attached to the project have tried to model social capital using the APS, with interesting results (see Enright 2001), and tested the socio-economic effects of language retention (see O'Sullivan 2001).

In the simplest terms, communities that can draw on civic involvement, positive norms, and trust and trustworthiness while having education and training-based skills combined with the requisite financial and physical resources will be better-functioning communities. An aspect of such a community is how well its constituents adhere to the collective. We call this *cohesion* and, as we detail below, it involves how a community manages its diversity and resources through established institutions for the benefit of its members. We propose that cohesive communities are those that create or have webs and networks of sites that produce social capital and enhance other forms of capital.

Population Outcomes: A Multifaceted Dependent Variable
We begin with the understanding that the social and demographic developments of most of Canada's First Nations communities are heading in different directions from those of the broader society:

- The First Nations population is young (with a median age of 25 compared with 35 years for all Canadians); 53% of reserve populations are under 25 years of age.

- First Nations populations are growing rapidly, with projected increases, between 1997 and 2005, of 1.7%, compared with 1.1% for the general Canadian population (DIAND 1997).
- First Nations people are both a rural and an urban people, with 40% living outside reserves (Royal Commission on Aboriginal Peoples 1996, Chapter 5 of this volume). Migration data show that reserve populations are increasing (Beavon and Norris 2000), while non-reserve populations are also growing (Clatworthy 1995). First Nations communities churn with migration rates close to 60% between minor census periods (e.g., 1986-91) (Chapter 4 of this volume).
- The gap in life expectancy between First Nations people and all Canadians is seven years, with First Nations men at 66.9 years and First Nations women at 74 years (compared with 74.6 and 80.9, respectively, for all Canadians).
- Birth rates are twice the national average. Infant mortality rates, while falling from 28 to 11 per 1,000 live births between 1979 and 1993, remain nearly double the national average (Royal Commission on Aboriginal Peoples 1996).
- Suicide rates for youth are eight times the national average for females and five times the national average for males (Health Canada 1997).
- Addictions and solvent abuse are reported as serious community problems by 62% of First Nations people over 15 years of age (Royal Commission on Aboriginal Peoples 1996).
- Cancers in women, particularly cervical and breast cancers, have higher than average occurrence (Health Canada forthcoming).
- Four percent of First Nations children were in the custody of child and family services agencies in 1996-97 (DIAND 1997). Some 39% of adults report family violence, 25% report child abuse, and 15% report rape as problems in their communities (Statistics Canada 1991).
- Rates of incarceration for First Nations persons are over five times higher than the national average (Solicitor General of Canada 1997). In some jurisdictions, such as Saskatchewan and Manitoba, Aboriginals account for nearly 60% of all jail and prison admissions. Some of these realities are presented in Chapter 3 of this volume.

These population dynamics vary by First Nation, but they form patterns that make all First Nations distinct from the non-Aboriginal populations around them. Despite a diverse geography and varied language and culture, the patterns are undeniable and therefore beg the scientific question, "What are the factors that are leading to these patterns?"

Our aim here is to begin the process of modelling that will eventually uncover some explanations for these phenomena. This process is hampered by numerous problems with the available data on First Nations. Measuring population outcomes for First Nations communities is a difficult proposition. One of the main data sources is the Census of Canada. This is a rich source of information, but it has some problems in terms of the data on First Nations. In 1991, seventy-seven First Nations communities were considered by Statistics Canada to be under-enumerated, and these communities were excluded from the census database. Parent (1995) has estimated the number of individuals excluded at approximately 37,000. Parent (1995) also warns that the undercount on reserves *included in the census* may be relatively higher than for Canada as a whole, but there are no reliable estimates.[2]

It is also difficult to track particular communities from census to census because names change and new communities are created. We have created a map of communities for Canada and a method of ensuring concordance between census periods. This is one of many pieces of data needed to fully test our model. The testing of the model we are proposing will require construction of a major data set that will include a range of existing data sets, such as the Community Program Data collected by DIAND, the Aboriginal Peoples Survey (APS) 1991, the DIAND Survey of Community Characteristics (DSCC), the mother and infant data, from provincial Vital Statistics mortality data, the national cancer data set, and several others. All the data will have to be aggregated to the community level to enable analysis while protecting confidentiality. These multifaceted data will be attached (not linked) to the available census data. We have taken the 1986, 1991, and 1996 census data for First Nations and aggregated them by community, which will create the kind of community database that will enable analysis of the model.

We are currently creating this multifaceted data set, which will allow us to address a wide range of social and demographic issues. Three categories of population outcomes will be studied in our initial research, including variations in mortality; patterns and variation in morbidity, particularly cancer; and mother-daughter health and fertility patterns. We will also examine new vistas in male and female fertility, as well as spacing, rates, and issues of infertility. These questions, while of utmost importance in themselves, will be looked at through the lens of the model. We will also continue our look at issues pertaining to socio-economic and socio-cultural development.

The model presupposes that these outcomes are related to physical, human, and social capital interrelationships that spawn cohesion. This hypothesis is innovative, but far from entirely original. Income inequality and the distribution of mental and social disorder is well known in the epidemiological literature: "Lower SES [socio-economic status] is associated with lower life expectancy, higher over-all mortality rates, [and] higher rates of infant and perinatal mortality. In fact, SES is correlated with all the major cause of death categories in the ICD, as well as other health outcomes, measures of life expectancy, physical and mental" (Link and Phelan 1995, 81). While it is acknowledged that the proximate conditions of life that are correlated with poverty are no doubt involved in explaining the variance, lifestyle, and less enriching physical and social environment, there is, as Benediktsson (2000) notes, much evidence to show that these features do not explain the differences in health outcomes and that despite absolute increases in wealth, health outcomes have not increased as rapidly. What other forces are at work?

There remains a clear set of pointers indicating that deprivation, poverty, and even unemployment have effects on population outcomes. Avison et al. (1999, i) found in their study of unemployment and the mental health of families that women who experience job loss have significantly higher rates of diagnosed disorders. This finding agrees with other studies, such as those of Brenner (1979), who found relationships between unemployment and both mortality and diagnosed mental disorders in Britain, and Catalano (1991), who found that income disparity and economic insecurity have effects on health in the US. Extensive work has been done by Wolfson on both the US and Canadian experience. Wolfson et al. (1992) find a significant association between income inequality and mortality. They note that there are important reasons to consider a broad range of factors, including economic well-being, income polarization, and disparity, when reviewing determinants of health.

The social cohesion perspective, typified by R.G. Wilkinson (1996, 1997, 1998), argues that structural forces related to income inequality and relative and absolute poverty are related to poor population outcomes. This relationship has been tested at several levels of analysis, including international, regional, and between communities, with the finding that societies with less income inequality are healthier on the whole (Benediktsson 2000, 12). Whether the analysis is at the international level (Wilkinson 1998), intra-nationally between regions (Kaplan et al. 1996; Kennedy et al. 1996; Kawachi and Kennedy 1997), or at the community level (Narayan 1999), the findings point to a pattern where the more unequal the income distribution, the poorer the health outcomes. There seems to be relatively conclusive evidence that there is something structural that is related to the cohesiveness of the community (Kawachi and Kennedy 1997; Kennedy et al. 1996; Narayan 1997; Wilkinson 1996, 1997, 1998). The World Bank Research Group on Social Capital has developed a number of studies indicating that a range of factors involving income and community organization impact on health and general population outcomes (Grootaert 1998, 1999; Narayan 1997). While they use the term "social capital," they are looking at a variable that has the characteristics of both social capital and social cohesion. Our research is innovative in that we separate these into two distinct concepts. We will explore the intra-variable relationships between these variables and the interrelationship between the variables and population outcomes below.

Social Capital, Human Capital, and Physical Capital: Three Independent Variables

Social Capital

The concept of social capital has become central to research agendas in both North America and Europe (see Veenstra 2001; Putnam 2000; Bourdieu 1990; Coleman 1990; World Bank Social Development Network 1998), and dates back to the 1980s in sociological discourse (Coleman 1988; Granovetter 1985). Social capital is a resource that is created in the relationships among persons and groups that engender trust and mutual obligations that can be drawn upon in order to develop and act effectively (Callahan 1996). It is inherent in the structure of relations between and among actors, and is made up of obligations, expectations, information channels, norms of reciprocity, and effective sanctions that constrain or encourage certain types of behaviour (Callahan 1996; Wall et al. 1998). Coleman developed this concept in the context of defining it according to its function. He saw it as a variety of entities, with two elements in common: (1) they consist of some aspect of social structures facilitating the actions of individual or collective actors, and (2) they are productive, that is, they make achievement possible (Coleman 1988, 98). Coleman also noted that it is less fungible than other forms of capital. It is less tangible than both physical and human capital in his estimation, but nonetheless exists because it can be called upon and used to enhance productive activity (Coleman 1988, 100). We concur to a degree with Coleman, but wish to push the concept further to facilitate its measurement and also increase the predictive ability of our model, which employs social capital as a central variable.

Social capital stands for the ability of actors to secure benefits by virtue of their association in a structure, what Portes (1998, 6) has called membership in social networks. We are hypothesizing that the development of human capital and the establishment of a physical resources infrastructure need to be complemented by social capital, which in turn allows institutionalized development in order to reap the full benefits of all these investments. The redemption of social capital brings it into being and gives it a use value. Its exchange value is simply its ability to be redeemed. This is best understood as a process of commodification where the capital becomes a resource that can be exploited in a social network. That network could have at any of its nodes organizations such as companies or collectivities. As will be seen below, the crystallization of that network into an institution creates social cohesion.

Social capital, in our model, can best be understood as being potentiated along three dimensions. The first is virtually identical to the Putnam/Coleman notion of existence and participation in community (civic) organizations. The second is the construction of trust and trustworthiness, and the third is the development of norms of cooperative behaviours and reciprocal obligations. If we examine these one by one, the concept of social capital becomes clearer and the measurement possibilities – the evidence of social capital – develop a focus.

The concept of trust has been considered central to social capital since the first writings on the subject (Coleman 1988). We start by looking at the functioning of trust. We read in Coleman's *Foundations of Social Theory* (1990) about Jerusalem and the mother of six who moved there because it was safer for her children to play there. This is a clear descriptive, but let us look at some more complex examples to develop the concept. There are many tangible examples of this relationship between people. For example, the Danes have a high-trust society. Mothers (and fathers) park their children outside shops in their buggies while they enter the stores to shop. The level of trust allows the shopping to be more efficient and is an indication of the existence of social capital that we can see as it is redeemed. However, the *New York Times* of 22 May 1997 reported that this practice led to the arrest of a visiting Danish woman. She attempted to redeem the social capital built up in Denmark in New York by parking her stroller and entering a store. This was a non-redeemable environment because it was a low-trust environment. The norms of social control in the United States actually worked against this woman. Such a norm might work in favour of children in some cases, as it sanctions abuse in the non-trust society, but in the case of the Danish visitor it operated differently. The social capital did not exist. Why can we say that? It could not be redeemed. It did exist in Denmark, and the evidence is that it could be redeemed. In both cases, that is, in Denmark and New York, the individual tried to redeem. In both cases *they* perceived it to exist; in only one case, however, did it exist as it was perceived. In the US, we saw a norm of social control redeemed by an unknown person. By this we mean that someone called the police when they perceived that a woman was abandoning her child. The norm that was redeemed was one shared and developed in that society as a sanction against abuse. In the US, the parent is responsible for protection of the child because there is a much reduced level of social trust, that is, less faith in the general community as a caretaker. Both are forms of social capital, but they are unique in that they are created in the differential social interactions and relationships of actual life. Are they equal but different? No – the US form of social capital is diminished as it is less universal (not everyone would report the abandonment) and based on lower forms of cooperation (reliance on authorities to discipline). This means that it is less social capital, not a different type or form of social capital. Social capital is a resource just as the other forms of capital are resources. It is important to reject the notion of a "negative social capital" or "downside social capitals" that are not resources but exclusionary forces, such as the notion presented by Portes (1998), Portes and Sensebrenner (1993), and Portes and Landholt (1995). Few would dispute that one of the things that keeps the US cohesive is its police and paramilitary structures that enforce order – witness the problems when there is a reduced police presence. This is not to say it is a non-cohesive society. We saw quite the opposite after the 2001 attacks on the World Trade Center and the Pentagon.

We can see, in the above example, issues of trust, trustworthiness, and norms. Let us take another set of social capital indices. The civic association and civic participation dimensions can be seen through many measures. The voting turnout in a community, or participation in the governance structure, is one example of how one might look at levels of social capital. For example, if the turnout for a band election in a community was universal, we might conclude that a level of inherent association and involvement exists in the community. This could be indicative of high social capital. The test of cohesion would come with the outcome of the election, where we would see whether the governance structure could weld the different competing groups together. It is important to note that intense campaigning in an election and high voter turnout are always indicative of social capital generation, but perhaps not indicative of an actual transposition of capital into a factor of cohesion. Differential outcomes generate different rates of social capital and affect rates of redemption. Figure 1.2 illustrates this point. There are three subgroups, each competing to be elected to run the community government (Band Council).

Figure 1.2   Competing electoral groups

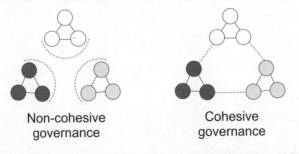

Non-cohesive
governance

Cohesive
governance

The groups have strong intra-group ties of trust (the elected will serve the group) and shared aspirations (norms). However, there can be two results to the election. On the left side ("Non-cohesive governance"), we see the groups remaining hostile; on the right side ("Cohesive governance"), the postelection results lead to a development of ties between the groups. In the first case, the results of an election mean that two of the groups will be shut out. In the case of our imaginary First Nations community, let us say that jobs and housing will go to the supporters of the elected group. This means that there is social capital within the small group, but this is not the case between the groups. Our model predicts that we will have a less cohesive community in the first case. In fact, we would expect that the lack of trust between competing groups that is indicated in the left side of Figure 1.2 will eventually lead to an erosion of participation in elections. The potential loss of jobs and incomes arising from one's participation in elections may lead people to fear involvement or perhaps to feel cynical about the process. We might therefore see lower rates of participation over time, which would indicate a decline in social capital.

Just as we see a process of building social capital, we can see that certain processes depreciate social capital. An example would be migration. Migration means that the composition of a community changes. This has obvious effects on the bonds and interactions between people in the community. If the levels of migration are high, either measured as net migration or in terms of the rate of "churn,"[3] the probability of forming associations, clubs, parent-teacher groups, sports clubs, and so on is diminished. Any community civic life would be negatively affected. Migration is therefore a potential measure of depreciating social capital. The work of Norris and co-workers described in Chapter 5 of this volume indicates how important this can be.

This example brings home another point. The resource "social capital" is generated and held for redemption at multiple levels in society. Wall et al. (1998) notes that social capital can be measured at three levels of analysis: individual, family, and community/region. In the election example presented above, individuals in family/clan groups interact to create social capital. The individuals can redeem this social capital just as the family/clan can redeem obligations and reciprocally developed capital with other clans. The community can also redeem social capital by calling on citizens to be active around some program or action, but, as we will see below, the community may likely benefit more directly as the institutionalization of the obligation takes place in the form of cohesion.

There are many possible approaches to the measurement of social capital. One condition necessary to this process is avoidance of a tautological construct where one operationalizes the concept using its functions. Enright (2000,

2) points to the problem where one "operationally define[s] social capital as the benefits that accrue to the people from the relationships of trust, etc. ... defining social capital by what it does eliminates our ability to test what it does!" To avoid this, he has proposed that we measure social capital along three dimensions: availability, investment, and utilization, where availability refers to the amount of social capital available, investment refers to whether people create social capital through their behaviours, and utilization refers to the extent to which people call on or redeem the accrued social capital. Here availability refers to the amount of existing social capital that can be drawn upon. Investment refers to whether people help others in their network of friends, family, and community, and consequently build up a stock of social capital. Lastly, utilization refers to whether and to what extent people draw upon the available social capital. Grootaert (1999) and many in the World Bank Research Group on Social Capital do just that. At times they define social capital as the collective action that occurs (its outcome). They look at memberships in government and in social, political, and religious organizations, contributions to credit groups, and redemption of support from credit groups as indicators of social capital.

Social capital is affected by, and measured through, seemingly tangential relationships in a community. For example, income is an indicator of the level of social capital. We argue that increased polarization and dispersion of income have a detrimental effect on community cohesion as it undermines social capital. This in turn impacts population outcomes. Income inequality at an individual level of analysis has been looked at in relation to health with fascinating results. For example, studies are mixed on the effect of inequality on mortality. Ichiro et al. (1997) indicate that only when variables related to cohesion intervene can we see income inequality influencing mortality. Socioeconomic status has been found to be associated with a range of "major cause of death" categories (as listed the International Compendium of Diagnosis and Disease [ICD]), as well as other minor and major health outcomes (Fiscella and Franks 1997; Link and Phelan 1995, 81).

Within our framework, Enright (2001) addresses how best to operationalize social capital and how to measure this version of the concept. He settles on the redemption process, trying to ensure that social capital is seen as a resource separate from the sites where it is produced and therefore not confounded with the concept of social cohesion. This confounding of social capital with social cohesion is a major problem in previous studies, and we take it up later in the chapter. In addition to prescribing that the redemption of social capital be at the forefront of its operationalization, Enright (2001) proposes a set of questions that surveys could employ to actually get baseline data on social capital.[4]

The last point we wish to make about social capital relates to how social capital operates or functions to be productive. We can identify two major dimensions on which social capital operates to enhance productivity. The first is the purely economic. Narayan and Pritchett (1997) note that social capital works across many dimensions for affecting economic outcomes:

- It enhances public sector efficacy (as in Putnam's study [1993] of the newly developed Italian governments).
- It helps diffuse innovation through interconnectedness.
- It increases the number of high-risk/high-gain endeavours by spreading the risk. In a community, this may mean that a family can pursue an entrepreneurial idea without fear of abject poverty if it fails, or a group can start a co-op manufacturing or distribution centre.
- It encourages formation of cooperative action around problems that have a "common property" element. For example, the burning and clearcutting of rain forest on village land can be restricted and planned, thereby reducing destructive activity.
- It improves information knowledge (i.e., reduces information imperfections that can cause inaccurate decisions) and therefore encourages actions based on predictability.

The second is the social sphere itself. Enhancement of life experience, reduction in anxiety, reduction in social competition and conflict – all these are potential outcomes on the social side of communities with high social capital. Human capital and physical capital are integral aspects of our model.

Human Capital
Human capital theory posits that when investments are made in human resources, there is a return in terms of increased productivity both individually and collectively. This may be reflected, for example, in the gross income or product of a community. Becker (1964) saw this process in similar terms to the physical capital embodied in machines. Embodied capital enhanced the productive capacity of machines. The investment of education and training was also embodied in human beings, facilitating increased productivity, new ways to act, and enhanced contribution.

Much of the investigation of human capital by economists centres on the question "Is the investment in human resources cost-effective?" or, in simple terms, "Is it worthwhile economically?" We sidestep that particular debate and concentrate on the core of the theory, that there is both a social (collective) return and an individual income return to education and training (Gunderson and Riddel 1988). There is considerable empirical verification for this theoretical proposition (Ashenfelter 1978; Dooley 1986; Hanson 1970). Numerous Canadian studies of First Nations income patterns verify that there is an individual return for each year of education for Aboriginal Canadians (Chapter 9 of this volume; Bernier 1997; George and Kuhn 1994). There are also collective returns to human capital that accrue from this individual growth. Taxes, potential charity donations, and the increase in the skills available to fill jobs in the community are examples of such collective returns.

Human capital is seen as influencing social capital in our model, and having a more direct effect on population outcomes through cohesion. Think of the youth of a community as forming two groups. Youth Group 1 (Y_1) represents school attendees, while Youth Group 2 (Y_2) represents dropouts. Y_1 will form more bonds of mutual obligation and trust. They see the mutual advantage of their skills and have an institutional setting for the redemption of those obligations, as well as norms and values that they share around acquisition of increased education (human capital). Y_2 will share fewer institutional links and will therefore develop fewer bonds of obligation. They may share norms developed outside the school, but by and large these norms would be negative; as they are redeemed, therefore, they will have a depreciating effect on community social capital. For example, school dropouts may engage in petty theft, vandalism, or other deviant behaviours (Gabor 1999; Alder 1992).

Human capital enables community-level growth through interdependence. Those with productive skills interact, and in that interaction they also build social capital. It stands to reason that higher levels of human capital create the possibility of more and better productivity, which will generate more and higher-quality social capital.

The link to population outcomes through this indirect path is also relatively deductive from the model itself. As we noted above, increased social capital is already linked to the rise of institutionalized governance of intra-group difference for the growth of cohesion. The independent effect of human capital comes from its influence on the increased community capacity to develop and successfully run organizations and institutions. We have noted elsewhere (see Maxim, White, and Beavon, Chapter 9 in this volume) that levels of education are an indication of an increased capacity to carry out individual and community tasks, as this increased level of human capital assumes that there is a greater productive potential to call on. In the Davis Inlet case, which we attach as an illustration (Appendix 1.1), we see that the presence of a school has little effect because the school is not utilized. The children do not stay in school and the parents do not promote it because it seems to have little positive effect, given the poor living conditions and lack of work.

Human capital can play differing roles in the creation of population outcomes. Increased levels of human capital in a community that has *diminished* levels of social capital can lead to what appear to be negative population outcomes. Studies indicate some contradictory relationships between human capital and migration, fertility, and social capital (Massey and Besem 1992). We can hypothesize, for example, that the youth in Y_1 above may, if there are no opportunities in the First Nations community, choose to leave. This migration would be a net drain on the community, leaving it with fewer human resources and an even lower average level of human capital on which to draw. This would create a reciprocal decline in institutions and discourage investment in the community from outside and even from within.

We might also hypothesize that a community with little productive capital might have higher rates of social dysfunction and suicide. In our example, those with higher education, Y_1, might be very discouraged by the lack of opportunity facing them and have higher rates of suicide than trained youth with opportunity. Chandler and Lalonde (1999) indicate that there are relationships between cohesion and suicide rates. This has certainly been the case in attempts to lower fertility rates in developing countries. Higher educational attainment for women was key to lowering fertility (Balakrishnan 1993). Human capital, therefore, relies on being combined with some forms of physical capital to become productive. The absence of investment in physical capital may actually have a detrimental effect on the social capital of a community and therefore on its cohesion and population outcomes.

Data also indicate that as human capital increases, social patterns or norms change. This is also part of the production of social capital. We hypothesize that when the data are available, we will find that as education increases, the age of first sexual experience (as measured by first pregnancy) increases (see Balakrishnan 1993). Research indicates that this has an impact on social relations in terms of fertility patterns as well as on cancer rates, particularly cervical cancers associated with sexually transmitted diseases. In this way, human capital has more direct population effects.

We are aware that the level of education in First Nations communities, while improving, still lags behind the national average (DIAND 1997; Four Directions Consulting Group 1997; Hull 2000). Labour force participation rates also lag behind national averages, with lows of less than 47% on reserves (Four Directions Consulting Group 1997, 92; Statistics Canada 1991). These are indications that the issues around human capital are critical in understanding population outcomes in these communities.

Natural or Physical Capital
This form of capital includes both financial resources (e.g., capital for investment, collective income pooled in credit groups, buildings, and/or machines) and natural resources (e.g., land). A community can have an array of physical

resources to call on, but, as in any marginal economy, it depends on the proper combination of fixed and variable capital to create productive circumstances. When the community of Davis Inlet was forced to move by the Newfoundland government in 1948, the new community did not have the same configuration of resources. For example, there were fish in the new location, but no caribou. The skills – the human capital – did not match the physical resources. The same was true when the community was moved from the mainland in 1967. The outcomes were devastating to the community. The level of illness, the suicides, and the breakdowns of social capital in the form of norms and values, which lead to decline in cohesiveness, were evident.

As noted above, physical capital is necessary to enable human capital to enhance the community where it resides. Human capital is held by individuals and resides in the community only as long as the individual stays there. Unless the community creates the structures to release human capital, it remains held by the individuals and therefore does not contribute to the development of the community. We can see that the redemption of human capital, that is, its becoming social, is like a chemical reaction, where the proper balance of elements must be present. The human capital held by the individual members of Y_1 in our previous example becomes a social good only as the skills are employed. This demands the financial and other physical capital resources of the community to be both present and in motion.

Physical capital also includes the collectivized income of the community. Income is an important and influential social form of capital only as it is represented in credit associations and credit unions. These become lower forms or localized forms of investment capital. The World Bank studies of Indonesia (Grootaert 1999) and Tanzania (Narayan and Pritchett 1997) have illustrated this point. Access to funds through borrowing of pooled incomes provides the stability for growth of localized small-scale production. Personal income has community effects, but it is not, in the true sense of the concept, a form of capital for the model.[5] The physical capital variable can, according to our model, have an effect on cohesion. The community with few collective physical resources and low income will not create as many social spaces. These spaces are related to cohesion. For example, the investment socially and individually in a ball field for baseball or lacrosse and the establishment of groundskeeping, referees, and even a central uniform pool constitutes an institution that allows the cohesion of a community to grow. We will discuss this below, but it is clear even at this point how physical resources play a role through the direct path to cohesion as well as through the complex modelled path via social capital.

The relationship between physical capital levels and population outcomes has been the subject of broad-based research. We know that unemployment (a condition that can be directly related to a lack of investment) can be correlated with morbidity levels and mortality, just as income differences have been argued to have a relationship to mortality (Wilkinson 1998, 77).

First Nations communities have differing resources and access to resources. These resources can include natural capital such as a forest open to logging, fisheries that can be worked, animal stocks, and even hydro power. Legal access to resources and commercial capital to exploit the resources, including manufacturing, constitutes this variable. Our data sets under development will produce a picture of these differences and permit us to measure differences and the population outcomes associated with these differences. It is already documented that physical resources are scarce and that access to equity and debt capital is very restricted in First Nations communities (Royal Commission on Aboriginal Peoples 1996). Our model indicates that physical and natural resources play a role in population outcomes both directly and through community cohesion. It is to the cohesion variable that we turn next.

Social Cohesion: The Intervening Variable
In recent years, the concept of social cohesion has been gaining importance in debates surrounding national policy and research, both in Canada and Europe (Social Cohesion Network 1998, 2). Social cohesion as an analytical concept potentially allows measurement of a society's ability to "manage the stresses and strains of modern life" (Social Cohesion Network 1998, 23). Social cohesion itself is a complex concept composed of several intricately related issues. It is defined as "the ongoing process of developing a community of shared values (Breton et al. 1980, 12; Policy Research Committee 1996; Robinson and Wilkinson 1995), shared challenges (Breton et al. 1980, 331; Policy Research Committee 1996, 44), and equal opportunity (Amin and Tomaney 1995; Ford et al. 1996; Oreja 1987, 7), based on a sense of trust (Kawachi et al. 1998; Policy Research Committee 1996, 47), hope (Social Cohesion Network 1998, 3, 17), and reciprocity (Breton et al. 1980, 4) among all Canadians" (Social Cohesion Network 1998, 24). The basic definition used by Canada's Social Cohesion Network[6] is a good starting point, but we feel that it tends to be used as an all-inclusive, catch-all descriptive category rather than an analytical variable capable of explaining population outcomes.

The concept became more widely investigated after Putnam's work (1993) on the growing fracturing and reduced integration in Western society. Social cohesion has been employed as a concept in many fields, including political science (Jenson 1998), epidemiology (Lomas 1998), and sociology (Kaufman 1999). Much of the "cohesion" literature rests on the resurrection of Toquevillian liberalism, which argues that voluntary involvement in social movements creates political stability by building cooperation in a population (Toqueville

1995). Some interpretations centre on the institutions of late modern capital-ism and attribute the creation of social order to them. From this perspective, "a cohesive society is one in which accommodation of socio-economic con-flicts is well managed ... [and] will be at risk only if differences are mobilized as grounds for conflicting claims and management of mobilized claims is fumbled" (Toqueville 1995, 4; see also Jenson 1998).

In our use of the concept of cohesion, we take this a step further and ask two sets of questions. First, what is the societal effect of social cohesion? Does it affect population outcomes, the health and well-being of communi-ties? The second set of questions relates to how social cohesion is to be measured. Measurement of social cohesion is predicated on the assumption that social cohesion is an outcome of investments into social capital, the social union, and cultural and social projects (Social Cohesion Network 1999). The model presented here takes these investments into account as it exam-ines the influence of social, human, and physical capital on the intervening variable of social cohesion and its effects on population outcomes. In this model, the level of social cohesion that is created in a society also determines the degree to which investments in the various forms of capital are exploited by the population.

The operationalization and measurement of social cohesion will involve creating a composite index that assesses how the *institutions* of the commu-nity have integrated the differences in that community along such dimen-sions as the sense of well-being in a community, be it economic, social, or cultural; the polarization in a community; the income inequality in a commu-nity; the generated cultural life and consumption and exchange of cultural products; the governance structures and the civic life (voting, volunteering, etc.); the conflict management and resolution mechanisms; the shared insti-tutionalized perspectives on approaches to crime; the institutionalized recon-ciliation of the multiple identities of its members (Indian status, for example); attachment and reattachment mechanisms for those leaving and coming into the community, that is, the institutionalized connectedness to community (migration); and identification with the symbols of the community.

These dimensions of social cohesion are restricted to the *institutionalized* processes because the categories overlap with those of social capital. A key feature of this model is the differentiation between social capital and social cohesion. This enables us to make breakthroughs on the question of mea-surement of the modelled relationships at the community level.

Differentiating between Social Cohesion and Social Capital
Social capital and social cohesion are often collapsed theoretically, creating problems of conceptual circularity. Recent work has contributed to both

empirically and theoretically distinguishing these concepts (Kaufman 1999). We find, however, that there is an ongoing confusion. We propose that these are at least somewhat unique concepts and that the conceptual separation is key to discovery of how they can be modelled to generate a predictive and descriptive theory of community and a descriptive and explanatory understanding of First Nations population outcomes.

We propose the following differentiation as a basic conceptual separation. We see social cohesion as the *outcome* of the accommodation of socio-economic and political differences through institutions. It is the *identity* created through institutional unity of difference. It is observed and hence measured through the institutions that manage the diversity that is created by a community with social capital, physical capital, and human capital. For example, a First Nations community with the necessary business training and access to commercial capital and the proximately located transportation might develop lacrosse stick makers, uniform makers, and wholesaling outlets. The development of a business association to regulate, lobby, and coordinate small enterprise would be indicative of social cohesion. That association would be the outcome of a growing trust and obligation among the entrepreneurs or family groups that established these enterprises. Another example might be the growth of a fishing cooperative in a community. The skills (human capital) around fishing combine with the fish stocks to generate fishers that develop a trust, a set of operating norms, and mutual obligations in the course of their endeavours. This social capital can combine with the educational abilities learned in school (accounting, for example) and the knowledge of the outside markets to push this fishery past subsistence and communalism to the formation of a marketing co-op. The co-op is an outcome of the growth of the social capital, which comes about through the combination of the resources and the relationships that can develop because of the mix. The co-op builds cohesion within the community. We hypothesize that it will enhance the population outcomes.

Just as Enright (2001) has developed a distinction between processes that produce social capital and the commodity itself, which has to be redeemed, we distinguish between the institutions that create cohesion and the components that go into creating that institution.

In this framework, simply put, institutions would be, by their existence and functionality, a measure of cohesion in the community. For example, if we think of the two-parent family as an institution, the proportion of single-parent families and foster care families would be indicative of a lower cohesion in the community. This is not to say that single-parent homes are dysfunctional, but rather that large proportions of broken families are indicative of a problem in the community. Sports teams, leagues, and associations are also institutions. A greater proportion of the numbers of these institutions in a given population would indicate higher levels of cohesion. This is not Putnam's *Bowling Alone* (2000). We simply argue that the fact that people want to join, do join, or remain members build these institutions and indicates that there is a unity or cohesion.

Institutions are different from networks or even non-regulating organizations. This difference is crucial to the differentiation between social capital and social cohesion. An institution is a complex of norms and behaviours that persists over time by serving collectively valued purposes (Uphoff 1993). It may arise originally to play the role of an organization (for example, simple coordination of resource allocation), but it has a special place in that it cements some activity of the collective. Institutions create the frame of the social corpus, like a skeleton. The organization may operate as part of an institution or may evolve into an institution as the social capital generated in process of interaction grows. Institutions are the production sites of social capital. For example, in Belize a group of Garfuna fishermen formed a small fish-marketing co-op in Dangriga. Their purpose was to share labour so that some could fish while others took the fish in quantity to market. The fishers organization became an institution as the fishers up and down the coast began to flock to it and it became a marketing board to stabilize prices, set limits, regulate offshore (Taiwanese) fishing, and set income redistribution mechanisms.

Social capital is therefore distinct. It can be thought of as representative of those elements that contribute to the construction of institutions that represent social cohesion. They are generated in association, through relationships, and they are held only in association but can be redeemed by either individuals or groups. Trust, for example, is created in the interaction of individuals and groups, but it can be experienced individually. Institutions can interact in ways that generate intergroup trust, which also generates social capital. Trust between family members can lead to the creation of clan political activity. We can say that the clan has generated social capital. Political activity may create institutions of governance that cohere a community or ones that create division and suspicion. If the clans compete for resources and these resources are manipulated through governance structures to the detriment of certain clan groups, then the institution is not one that accommodates but one that divides. If the governance structures manage difference – that is, if they accommodate – then there is cohesion in the community.

Conclusion

This chapter presents a conceptual model that is not complete. It has yet to be verified through evidence and leaves many questions unanswered. We contend, however, that it is a powerful model that extends the basic paradigm in terms of explaining population outcomes and the process by which communities generate capacity and well-being. The model provides a relatively clear road forward for both empirical investigation and theoretical development. For a long time, we have tried to unpack social problems by examining individuals. In this model, we also grapple with how groups interact and how communities may be central in understanding significant variation in population outcomes. We have attached a very brief appendix that looks at two communities that have been the subject of public controversy. They may provide some anecdotal context for thinking about the basic concepts we have developed here.

Appendix 1.1
Two Examples: Davis Inlet and the Port Harrison Relocation

These examples give us the opportunity to illustrate how one would approach the assessment of particular communities using the framework of the model. They are unusual cases, but if we are to look at how a community reacts to changes in physical and social environment, the situations are inevitably unusual. The two illustrations are Davis Inlet and Port Harrison. Both are remote settings and both illustrations involve the actual movement of a people, as a community, that results in a change in the mix of our three forms of capital, and subsequent differences in that community along such dimensions as the following: the sense of well-being in a community, be it economic, social, or cultural; the polarization in a community; the income inequality in a community; the generated cultural life, and consumption and exchange of cultural products; the governance structures and the civic life (voting, volunteering, etc.); the conflict management and resolution mechanisms; the shared institutionalized perspectives on approaches to crime; the institutionalized reconciliation of the multiple identities of its members (Indian status, for example); attachment and reattachment mechanisms for those leaving and coming into the community, that is, the institutionalized connectedness to community (migration); and identification with the symbols of the community.

These dimensions of social cohesion are restricted to the *institutionalized* processes because, as the observer can see, the categories overlap with the those of social capital. A key feature of our model is the differentiation between social capital and social cohesion, as discussed previously.

Davis Inlet

The Innu[7] are a nomadic hunting people who have lived in the Quebec-Labrador peninsula for thousands of years. Of the 10,000 Innu, most live in Quebec, while the others live in Labrador in two small communities: Sheshatshit, near Goose Bay, and the island of Davis Inlet, off the north coast of Labrador.

Davis Inlet is an example of the breakdown of social capital and community cohesion and provides an example of how the elements in our model interrelate. The following story is intended as a window on the model.

The community of Davis Inlet has undergone two distinct processes of disintegration of its accumulated cohesion through the dramatic removal of institutional structure and capital resources. The first was at the behest of the government of Newfoundland during the pre-Confederation period. In 1948 the Newfoundland government, without asking or entering into any negotiations, loaded the Innu of Davis Inlet onto a boat and took them 400 kilometres north, to the Inuit town of Nutak. The government wanted to close the government depot at Davis Inlet and had decided that it would be "useful" for the Innu to become fishers. The Innu were hunters, not fishers, and there was no game at Nutak. There were no trees from which the Innu could cut poles to pitch their tents, because Nutak is above the treeline. This meant that the skills they had were of no use in the new setting. One year later, the Innu walked 400 kilometres back to Davis Inlet.

The current community has 530 members and these people were also uprooted from their Davis Inlet home. The 530 Innu who now live on the isolated island were forced to relocate there from the mainland by the Canadian government in 1967. The Innu themselves call Davis Inlet *Utshimasits,* or "place of the boss." Where once they were independent hunters who roamed the Quebec-Labrador peninsula for caribou, the Mushuau Innu, "people of the barrens," have for two generations lived in Davis Inlet (on the island) and watched their traditional way of life be destroyed. Only a kilometre of water separates them from their traditional hunting grounds on the mainland, but during the winter freeze or spring thaw, the crossing is too dangerous for either snowmobile or boat.

If we examine some of the social and health population outcome patterns of Davis Inlet, we see that the tiny community has been plagued by alcoholism, gas sniffing, physical and sexual abuse, and suicide. The pinnacle may have come in 1992, when five brothers and sisters, along with an infant cousin, died in a house fire while their parents were out drinking. At the time, it is estimated that 75% of the 168 adults of Davis Inlet were alcoholic.

When the Innu were moved to Davis Inlet, the Canadian government had promised them houses, running water, and sewers. After many years, the infrastructure projects were still incomplete (Oosthoek and Nethercott 1995). There are very few full-time Innu jobs in Davis Inlet, most of them service jobs with government agencies. In an average year, twenty Innu children enter kindergarten, yet only two students are left in a class by grade 11 and none ever enter grade 12. Innu parents complain that the province-run school has little relevance for the children and teaches curriculum that does not help the Innu learn about their own culture.

After the deaths of the children in the fire, the community was sparked into forming new and functional organizations. Political organizations were formed that culminated in demands for control over capital development, environmental protection from corporate mining developments, self-policing, and courts. In December 1993, the Innu evicted a circuit court judge from their community, complaining that "white justice" did their people more harm than good. For this, the chief of the Innu in Davis Inlet, Katie Rich, was sent to jail (Valpy 1995). The Innu wished to end the military testing on their land and deal with the breaking of laws in their own councils. When the Newfoundland government threatened to send in the RCMP and restore the court, the Innu formed a blockade on the airstrip. In February 1995, the Innu travelled to Voisey's Bay, seventy-five miles north of Davis Inlet, to stop a mining company from drilling on the site (Gray 1999).

From the perspective of our model, the Innu community was trying to re-establish cohesion through the building of institutions that could manage the community's diversity. Re-establishing one's norms of reciprocity, rebuilding of social capital, and attempts to marshall control over physical capital are all aimed at altering the population outcomes. During the rebuilding phase (1993 through 1997), the rate of alcoholism fell to under 35%. The new community associations had some effect.

Under an agreement with the federal government, the Innu left Davis Inlet sometime in 2003 and moved fifteen kilometres to a traditional hunting ground on the mainland, at Sango Bay. Ottawa was expected to pay the estimated $85 million it cost to complete the move, including infrastructure, and Newfoundland provided the site. The Innu name for Sango Bay is *Nutuaiashish,* or "place of good, clean water." Sango Bay has a good water supply, a waterfall with the potential for generating electricity, a good site for an airstrip, a harbour, and abundant fishing; it is also close to traditional hunting grounds.

We predict that the social cohesion of the community should rise dramatically in the first few years after relocation, even given the disruption involved in the movement. There is an infusion of all forms of capital. The proximity of physical resources such as animals, fish, and timber will combine with the financial capital infrastructure that is promised from the state to create the conditions for the rebuilding of cohesive institutions. This should hopefully potentiate the proposed revitalized schooling systems. The political movement that galvanized the community generated the social capital through associationalism and norm reconstruction. We should see drops in suicides and other negative population outcomes.

We will follow the community to assess our hypotheses concerning the relationship between improved population health and increasing social cohesion.

Port Harrison (Inukjuak)

In 1951 Port Harrison was an Inuit community that most described as "thriving." There were major establishments in the village, such as a nursing station, police station, school, Catholic church, and Hudson's Bay Company (HBC) outpost. The community was a mix of cultures, with the white southerners and semi-nomadic Inuit sharing the social space in what was considered, at that point of history, relative harmony. The capital at the disposal of the Inuit community was reasonable. Physical resources included good fish stocks and animals for food and furs. Basic subsistence production was supplemented with furs and stone carvings sold to the HBC for sugar, salt, tobacco, and manufactured goods.

The school was well attended depending on the season, and the Inuit youth had levels of education that were higher than those of other Northern communities. Government involvement in the community was limited, as there were no welfare recipients and little administration of Inuit communities beyond the church and HBC decision makers. The Inuit had their own systems of traditional leadership.

In 1952 the fox fur market collapsed and the result was a decline in the trade price paid by the HBC to the Inuit. This shortfall created problems for the purchase of goods at the company store, and after a short period this necessitated the involvement of the Canadian government in the delivery of assistance. That same year, the government decided to take a more active involvement in the administration of the North of Canada. This was prompted by two things: the increased US military presence due to the escalating Cold War and the increasing financial dependency of the Northern population due to the economic problems in the fur markets.

One of the first acts of the state was to relocate families from Port Harrison to Resolute Bay and Grise Fiord. There were problems. Despite promises of infrastructure at these locations, none was forthcoming and there were no school facilities. Game was not plentiful and fishing was very difficult because of the perpetual freezing near shore. Snow was not suitable for ice houses, so the Inuit had to live in canvas tents. These were culturally foreign and less suited to their lifestyle. Thus, we see that the skills that the community members had (their human capital) were not transferrable, and the physical and natural capital were lacking or mismatched. The result was a decline in the cohesiveness of the community. The community at Resolute Bay began to engage in excessive alcohol consumption. The proximity of the military base led to a ready source of alcohol and degradation of family through interaction with armed forces members. The rates of illness went up, particularly tuberculosis, as did the rates of suicide. Stillbirths were far above both the national and Northern Canadian averages. Fertility rates declined. The social capital of the community had dropped, as did the other forms of capital, which led to severe problems in the cohesiveness of the community and the resultant decline in population well-being.

Had the government permitted it, the population would have opted to return to Harrison. Unfortunately, the option was denied. It would be the 1960s before the Inuit would return to their old homes, and at that point much of their old way of life had died out. This whole process indicates how the interaction of forms of capital has an effect on the population outcomes of a community. The advantage of our model is that it provides a framework within which one may track all these factors in such communities.

Notes

1 We will also be doing an audit of a sample of First Nations communities where we create a grid and database of all organizations active in each community through interviews with key community actors.
2 In 1996, Statistics Canada collected data from 751 populated geographical units that qualified as First Nations communities as defined for this study. Census enumeration was not completed in another 77 communities, representing somewhere in the vicinity of 44,000 residents in First Nations communities. Maxim and White (2001) have determined that the communities that did not participate in the census are not unique in their characteristics, and can therefore be assumed not to present a potential major bias to the analysis.
3 "Churn" is the rate of people leaving and entering a community. Measures of overall population do not necessarily capture the actual changes in the persons who are resident in the community. A seemingly stable population may actually be a community where one-third of the people changed in a year. This churn in population would destabilize the production of social capital.
4 In his work, Enright uses the Aboriginal Peoples Survey to test the relationship between eight measures of social capital and two measures of community health. He examines the relationship between community health and three other measures, all of which are similar to those used by Putnam to operationalize social capital in *Bowling Alone*.
5 Personal income is more related to patterns of cohesion in terms of its polarization and dispersion. Income fluctuations do have effects on the consumption levels of the communities, and therefore have indirect effects on tax-based resources, the success of consumer goods businesses, and the charity-level investment for cohesion-building projects such as playgrounds and parks.
6 The Social Cohesion Network is a working group largely in government that was established to examine issues around cohesion, sustainable growth, and human development in Canada.
7 "Innu" means "human being" in the local Aboriginal language, and should not be confused with Inuit, an Aboriginal people who live further north.

References
Aday, L. 1997. Vulnerable populations: A community-oriented perspective. *Family and Community Health* 19(4): 644-56.
Alder, C. 1992. Violence, gender and social change. *International Social Science Journal* 44: 267-76.
Amin, A., and J. Tomaney. 1995. *Behind the Myth of the European Union: Prospects for Cohesion*. New York: Routledge.
Ashenfelter, O. 1978. Estimating the effect of training on earnings. *R.E. Stats* 63 (February): 47-57.

Avison, W., L. Davies, K. Speechely, and E. Grabb. 1999. *Unemployment and the Mental Health of Families*. Technical Report, NRHDP Project No. 6606-5020-63. London: Centre for Health and Well-Being, University of Western Ontario.

Balakrishnan, T.R. 1993. *Family and Childbearing in Canada*. Toronto: University of Toronto Press.

Beavon, D., and M.J. Norris. 2000. *Migration Patterns of First Nations Peoples in Canada: Data from the 1996 Census*. Talk delivered to the Sociology Department, University of Western Ontario, London, 27 April 2000.

Becker, G. 1964. *Human Capital*. New York: National Bureau of Economic Research.

Bendahmane, D. 1994. The quiet revolution: Child survival comes of age. *Grassroots Development* 18(2): 2-12.

Benediktsson, H. 2000. Contract research conducted for First Nations Cohesion Project. Unpublished report. University of Western Ontario, London.

Bernier, R. 1997. *The Dimensions of Wage Inequality among Aboriginal Peoples*. Research Paper Series No. 109. Ottawa: Analytical Studies Branch, Statistics Canada.

Bourdieu, P. 1990. *Reproduction in Education, Society, and Culture*. London: Sage.

Brenner, M.H. 1979. Mortality and the national economy: A review and the experience of England and Wales. *Lancet* 2: 568-73.

Breton, R., J.G. Reitz, and V.F. Valentine. 1980. *Cultural Boundaries and the Cohesion of Canada*. Montreal: Institute for Research on Public Policy.

Callahan, S. 1996. The capital that counts. *Commonwealth* 123(20): 7-8.

Catalano, R. 1991. The health effects of economic insecurity. *American Journal of Public Health* 81(9): 1148-52.

Chandler, M.J., and Christopher Lalonde. 1999. *Cultural Continuity as a Hedge against Suicide in Canada's First Nations*. Working paper, Department of Psychology, University of British Columbia.

Clatworthy, S.J., J. Hull, and N. Laughren. 1995. Patterns of employment, unemployment and poverty. In *People to People, Nation to Nation*, the Royal Commission on Aboriginal Peoples. Ottawa: Minister of Supply and Services Canada.

Coleman, J. 1988. Social capital in the creation of human capital. *American Journal of Sociology* 94 (Supplement).

–. 1990. *Foundations of Social Theory*. Cambridge, MA: Belknap Press.

DIAND (Department of Indian Affairs and Northern Development). 1997. *Basic Departmental Data*. Ottawa: Department of Indian Affairs and Northern Development.

Dooley, M. 1986. The overeducated Canadian? Changes in the relationships between earnings, education and age. *Canadian Journal of Economics* 19 (February): 142-59.

Enright, D. 2000. Social capital: Its contribution to social cohesion. Paper presented to the First Nations Cohesion Project, 3 May 2000, University of Western Ontario, London.

–. 2001. The Conceptualization and Operationalization of Social Capital. MA thesis, Department of Sociology, University of Western Ontario.

Fiscella, K., and P. Franks. 1997. Poverty or income inequality as predictors of mortality: A longitudinal cohort study. *British Medical Journal* 314: 1724-28.

Ford, G., G. Kinnoch, and A. McCarthy, eds. 1996. *Changing States: A Labour Agenda for Europe*. London: UK: Mandarin Paperbacks.

Four Directions Consulting Group. 1997. *Implications of First Nations Demography: Final Report*. Ottawa: Department of Indian Affairs and Northern Development.

Gabor, T. 1999. Trends in youth crime. *Canadian Journal of Criminology* 41: 385-92.

George, P., P. Kuhn, and A. Sweetman. 1996. Patterns of employment, unemployment and poverty: A comparative analysis of several aspects of the employment experience of Aboriginal and non-Aboriginal Canadians using 1991 PUMF. In *People to People, Nation to Nation*, the Royal Commission on Aboriginal Peoples. Ottawa: Minister of Supply and Services Canada.

Granovetter, M. 1985. Economic action and social structure: The problem of embeddedness. *American Journal of Sociology* 91(3): 481-510.

Gray, J. 1999. Innu fear the impact of Voisey's Bay. *Globe and Mail,* 1 April, A8.

Grootaert, C. 1998. Social capital: The missing link. In *Social Capital for Development: The Initiative on Defining, Monitoring and Measuring Social Capital,* World Bank Social Development Network Social Capital Working Paper Series. Washington, DC: World Bank.

–. 1999. *Social Capital, Household Welfare and Poverty in Indonesia: Local Level Institutions Study.* Service Development Department revised working paper. Washington, DC: World Bank.

Gunderson, M., and W.C. Riddel. 1988. *Labour Market Economics: Theory, Evidence and Policy in Canada.* 2nd ed. Toronto: McGraw-Hill Ryerson.

Hanson, W.L. 1970. *Education, Income and Human Capital.* New York: National Bureau of Economic Research.

Health Canada. 1997. *Basic Departmental Data.* Ottawa: Medical Services Branch, Health Canada.

–. Forthcoming. *Cervical Cancer Screening and Prevention Study 1998.* Ottawa: Health Information Data Base, FNIHP, Medical Services Branch, Health Canada.

Hull, J. 2000. *Post-Secondary Educational Attainment among Registered Indians in Canada.* Ottawa: Indian and Northern Affairs Canada.

Ichiro, B., P. Kennedy, K. Lochner, and D. Prothrow-Smith. 1997. Social capital, income inequality and mortality. *American Journal of Public Health* 87(1): 481-89.

Jenson, J. 1998. Mapping social cohesion. In *Policy Research: Creating Linkages.* Ottawa: Policy Research Initiative Conference.

Kaplan, G.E., E. Pauk, J.W. Lynch, R. Cohen, and J. Balfour. 1996. Income inequality and mortality in the United States. *British Medical Journal* 312: 999-1003.

Kaufman, H. 1999. Associationalism. *American Journal of Sociology* 106(1): 1304-5.

Kawachi, I., and B.P. Kennedy. 1997. Socio-economic determinants of health: Health and social cohesion: Why care about income inequality? *British Medical Journal* 314: 1037-46.

Kawachi, I., B.P. Kennedy, and K. Lochner. 1998. Long live community: Social capital as public health. Social Capital Database, <http://www.worldbank.org/poverty/scapital/biblio/j-l.htm>.

Kennedy, B., I. Kawachi, and D. Prothrow-Smith. 1996. Income distribution and mortality: Cross-sectional ecological study of the Robin Hood Index in the United States. *British Medical Journal* 312: 1004-7.

Knack, S., and P. Keefer. 1997. Does social capital have an economic payoff? *Quarterly Journal of Economics* 112(4): 1251-88.

Krishna, A., and E. Shrader. 1999. Social capital assessment tool. Paper presented at the Conference on Social Capital and Poverty Reduction, 22-24 June 1999, Washington, DC.

Lilliard, Lee, and L.J. Waite. 1993. A joint model of marital childbearing and marital disruption. *Demography* 30(4): 653-81.

Link, B.G., and L. Phelan. 1995. Social conditions as fundamental causes of disease. *Journal of Health and Social Behavior,* Special Edition, Extra Issue, 80-94.

Lomas, J. 1998. Social capital and health: Implications for the public health and epidemiology. *Social Science and Medicine* 47: 181-88.

Massey, Douglas, and L. Besem. 1992. Determinants of savings, remittances, and spending patterns among US migrants in four Mexican communities. *Sociological Inquiry* 62: 185-207.

Maxim, Paul, and Jerry White. 2001. *Assessing the Data Effects of Non-Participation in the Census by Aboriginal Communities.* Working paper, First Nations Cohesion Project. London: University of Western Ontario.

Maxim, Paul, Jerry White, and Dan Beavon. 2001. *Toward an Index of Community Capacity: Predicting Community Potential for Successful Program Transfer.* Discussion Paper 01-3, Population Studies Centre. London: University of Western Ontario.

Narayan, D. 1997. *Designing Community Based Development.* Environmental Department Paper No. 7. Washington, DC: World Bank.

–. 1999. *Bonds and Bridges.* Social Capital and Poverty Research Group Working Paper No. 1896. Washington, DC: World Bank.

Narayan, D., and L. Pritchett. 1997. *Cents and Sociability: Household Income and Social Capital in Rural Tanzania.* Research Working Paper 1796. Washington, DC: World Bank.

Oosthoek, S., and D. Nethercott. 1995. The spirits of Davis Inlet. *Hamilton Spectator,* 14 February, A10.

Oreja, M. 1987. *Social Cohesion and the Dangers Facing It.* Brussels: Secretary General of the Council of Europe.

O'Sullivan, Erin. 2001. Aboriginal Language Use and Socio-Economic Status. MA thesis, Department of Sociology, University of Western Ontario.

Parent, P. 1995. *Comparaison du nombre et des caractéristiques des autochtones selon le Recensement de 1991 et selon l'Enquête auprès des peuples autochtones de 1991.* Interim Version, Employment Equity Data Program, 27 September 1995.

Policy Research Committee. 1996. Canada 20005 [sic] Growth, human development and social cohesion. Draft interim report. Internal working draft.

Portes, A. 1998. Social capital: Its origins and applications in modern sociology. *Annual Review of Sociology* 24: 1-24.

Portes, A., and P. Landholt. 1995. The downside of social capital. *American Prospect* (May/June): 18-21.

Portes, A., and J. Sensebrenner. 1993. Embeddedness and immigration: Notes on the determinants of economic action. *American Journal of Sociology* 9: 1320-50.

Putnam, R.D. 1993. *Making Democracy Work: Civic Traditions in Modern Italy.* Princeton, NJ: Princeton University Press.

–. 2000. *Bowling Alone: The Collapse and Revival of American Community.* New York: Simon and Schuster.

Robinson, D., and D. Wilkinson. 1995. Sense of community in a small mining town: Validating a neighbourhood cohesion scale. *American Journal of Community Psychology* 23: 137-48.

Royal Commission on Aboriginal Peoples (RCAP). 1996. *People to People, Nation to Nation.* Available on CD-ROM: *For seven generations: An information legacy of the Royal Commission on Aboriginal Peoples.* Ottawa: Minister of Supply and Services Canada.

Sandefur, R.L., and E. Lauman. 1998. A paradigm for social capital. *Rationality and Society* 10(4): 481-501.

Social Cohesion Network. 1998. Sustaining growth, human development and social cohesion in a global world. Ottawa: PRI.

–. 1999. May 17th workshop: What is social cohesion and why does it matter? <http://policyresearch.schoolnet.ca/networks/cohsoc/socialco-e.htm> (Fall 2000).

Solicitor General of Canada. 1997. *Basic Departmental Data.* Ottawa: Solicitor General of Canada.

Statistics Canada. 1991. *Aboriginal Peoples Survey.* Report. Ottawa: Minister of Supply and Services Canada.

Teachman, J., K. Paasch, and K. Carver. 1997. Social capital and the generation of human capital. *Social Forces* 75(4): 21-32.

Toqueville, A.D. 1995. *The old regime and the revolution.* Garden City, NY: Doubleday.

Uphoff, N. 1993. Grassroots organizations and NGOs in rural development: Opportunities with diminishing stand and expanding markets. *World Development* 21(4): 607-22.

Valpy, M. 1995. Where is CNN? *Globe and Mail,* 27 April, A4.

Veenstra, Gerry. 2001. Social capital and health. *ISUMA* 2(1): 72-81.

Wall, E., G. Ferrazzi, and F. Schryer. 1998. Getting the goods on social capital. *Rural Sociology* 63(2): 300-22.

Wilkinson, R.G. 1996. *Unhealthy Societies: The Afflictions of Inequality.* London: Routledge.

–. 1997. Comment: Income, inequality and social cohesion. *American Journal of Public Health* 87: 1504-6.

–. 1998. What health tells us about society. *IDS Bulletin* 29(1): 77-84.

Wolfson, M., G. Kaplan, J. Lynch, N. Ross, and E. Backlund. 1992. The relation between income inequality and mortality: An empirical demonstration. *British Medical Journal* 319: 953-55.

World Bank Social Development Network. 1998. *Social Capital for Development: The Initiative on Defining, Monitoring and Measuring Social Capital.* Social Capital Working Paper No. 1. Washington, DC: World Bank.

The Limits of Our Knowledge and the Need to Refine Understandings

Jerry P. White

In October 2001, federal government policy analysts wanted to provide the Ministers' Reference Group on Aboriginal Policy with one number: the current total Aboriginal population in Canada. While this seems like a very straightforward and simple question, it is not, and understanding this complex issue has deep policy and program implications. Over two years later, the issue is still being debated. This is an important issue, as pointed out in Chapter 2, because population projections play a central role "in preparing for future health needs, housing requirements, social security, educational planning and a variety of other public services." The impact of modest differences between projections and actual population growth can be great. Demographers and other sociologists have been developing their technical expertise in the fields of population projections and the assessment of those changes for half a century. This book is in part the exploration of this issue with regards to Aboriginal peoples.

In Part 2 of this book, we approach a set of questions that are central to the planning and programmatic implementation of any strategy aimed at improving the Aboriginal condition in Canada. We look first at the limitations of the research done in the past. With Don Kerr, Eric Guimond, and Mary Jane Norris, we examine the most recent Aboriginal population projections released through the Royal Commission on Aboriginal Peoples (RCAP) in 1996. The authors conclude that, despite the fact that the RCAP based its projections out to the year 2016 on the 1991 Census and Aboriginal Peoples Survey (APS), as soon as the 1996 Census data were released it was clear "that the RCAP projections have completely missed the mark." The authors found that the projection for Aboriginal peoples understated growth by 58%, and the growth of the Status Indian population, which the commission was most confident of, was off by 73%. Kerr and co-authors report that error levels were 730% for Non-Status Indians and 278% for the Métis. In this part, we look at why this kind of problem arose. We open up the assumptions that underlie the research on population projections, such as the one-step/one-sex reproduction process where Aboriginal births are a function of fertility rates multiplied by the number of women in their reproductive years. Scientists and researchers are asked to drop simple assumptions like this and adopt more sophisticated and integrated approaches.

In Chapter 3, Stewart Clatworthy puts a complex question in front of us. How do the changes in the legal structures, the defining acts that set out federal/Aboriginal relations, impact populations and their growth? Clatworthy has been developing his expertise on this issue for a decade. Through his unique understanding and sophisticated probability models, he takes us step by step through the implications of the changes made to the Indian Act through Bill C-31 in 1985. He examines both the short-term impact from 1985 to 1999 and the longer-term impacts out to the end of this century. He finds that the changing definition of who is and who is not entitled to registration as a First Nations member with status has a dramatic effect on the populations both on and off reserves, in and out of communities. He also notes that the policies, as we go out into the future, will in some ways have reverse effects. The next fifty years will see "significant incremental growth ... most of the incremental growth ... is expected to occur on reserve." As we move out past that point, however, there will be changes, and Clatworthy explains that "within four generations, only one of every six children born to First Nations populations is expected to qualify for registration." Astonishing as it may seem, by the time we reach the end of the century, there will hardly be any children who will qualify for Registered Indian status.

What are the implications of these findings? Clatworthy points out that loss of entitlement to Indian registration among growing numbers of descendants is likely to result in very pronounced changes in the population's age structure, as well as causing pronounced changes in the political and social structure of First Nations communities. The policy implications are staggering. I would argue that, when the generation that is registered as of 2099 dies, there may be no Registered Indians left in Canada. Such an outcome is based on the assumption that the current status inheritance provisions of the Indian Act remain the same. In many corners of Canada, policy makers, legislators, academics, and Aboriginal peoples are debating the relative merits of more integration versus less integration, reserves versus no reserves, special rights versus equal rights. We are saying as scientists that these questions are somewhat moot and are being answered with the passage of time. There needs to be careful consideration of what is actually taking place as we ponder how we, as academics, legislators, policy analysts, and Aboriginal leaders, will intervene in the history that is unfolding.

Clatworthy tells us that the chosen marriage patterns will eventually lead to an ever shrinking Status population and that band membership rules will create classes of First Nations citizens. He takes us through how the First Nations define themselves and the effect those decisions will have on who will constitute their nation. Clatworthy also indicates that, as Indian registration interacts with First Nations membership rules, we will see the formation of classes among First Nations citizens with unequal rights and entitlements. This relates directly to the model presented in Part 1 of this book. The changing rights and entitlements, as well as the changing age distribution, will impact the production of social capital and directly impact social cohesion in First Nations communities. Differential access to housing, educational programs, and even health services for related family members will contribute to a breakdown of these institutions and a disintegration of institutional coherence.

We are being asked to contemplate who is a member or citizen of a First Nation? Who is a Non-Status Indian? Who is an Inuit? And who is a Métis? These questions have demographic implications, but they are also sociological issues on the terrain of ethnicity and identity. Kerr and co-authors first raise this question when they say that "ethnicity is typically understood as a fundamental ascribed characteristic of all persons ... is fixed at birth, remains the same over one's lifetime, and is subsequently transferred to one's offspring." As a sociologist, I would say that we teach this as a basic assumption. However, we also recognize that processes of assimilation and integration are breaking down some ethnic identities, while processes of nationalism and ethnocentrism are reinforcing and re-creating others.

In Chapter 4, Eric Guimond takes us right into this issue. As a scientist, he finds a perplexing problem. The normal explanations of population change such as migration, fertility, and mortality cannot account for the shifts in Aboriginal population that we observed in the 1990s. Guimond concludes that there is an important process, which he calls "ethnic drift," taking place, where non-Aboriginal and Aboriginal peoples are shifting and changing their declared identities. His painstaking analysis leads to a convincing case that leaves us with several key issues to look at in the future. How and why does the identification of the ethnicity of a set of persons shift over time? How can we predict these types of self-redefinition, and what are their implications? At its heart, this chapter takes us through the choices made by individuals concerning how they define themselves and the implications that this has on Aboriginal policy. In effect, policy makers need to understand that there is a relationship between how people define themselves and their rights and entitlements. As policies or laws are changed to confer rights on groups, individuals will change their identity to take advantage of the perceived benefits.

Similarly, if new programs are constituted for specific groups (for example, Métis or urban Aboriginals), then we can expect more people to change their ethnic affiliation or identity in order to qualify. This is a most important point for policy makers and legislators to understand. In other words, actions have consequences and research is needed to understand such phenomena.

This is far from trivial, as we know from the turbulent affairs of the world through the transition years of the twenty-first century. The ethnic cleansing, ethnic intolerance, ethnocentrism, and narrow nationalism that has disrupted hundreds of millions of lives around the world are testaments to the importance human beings place on who they are and whom they identify with.

In Chapter 5, Mary Jane Norris, Martin Cooke, and Stewart Clatworthy make some important discoveries in their examination of the migration between reserves and cities. They find that there is net migration to reserves. This has many policy implications, given that the provinces and the federal government have been engaged in heated debate over this issue for the last three decades. The provinces have argued that there has been a steady stream of First Nations people coming to the cities, and when they do, the responsibility for services puts pressure on the provincial budget. The finding that there is actually a net migration to reserves strengthens the argument by the federal government that there is no dramatic outflow and therefore the costs of services are being picked up in large part by the senior level of government.

The migration research also gives us a picture of who migrates. Registered Indian women are more migratory than their male counterparts, and those who've moved tend to be in the young adult age group. We find that women tend to stay in urban areas, whereas males move back. Norris and co-authors conclude that in terms of the high growth rates of Registered Indians, the net effect of migration (in-migrants minus out-migrants) is far less significant than the contribution of natural increase (births minus deaths) and Bill C-31 reinstatements. They find that the reserves are more stable than the cities.

All these findings tell us more about what programs might be targeted toward urban First Nations people, and for organizations, such as the National Association of Friendship Centres, there is a wealth of information about who their long-term clients are and what might be the proper allocation of the scarce resources available.

Part 2 of this book leaves many questions unanswered, but it points to a sounder and more carefully constructed foundation on which to build our policies for the future. It develops and extends our scientific understanding of how to build those foundations, and finally it leaves us with some key questions to explore as we proceed further in this volume.

2
Perils and Pitfalls of Aboriginal Demography: Lessons Learned from the RCAP Projections

Don Kerr, Eric Guimond, and Mary Jane Norris

Population projections are used for all sorts of planning purposes. Demographic forecasts have considerable utility in preparing for future health care needs, housing requirements, social security, educational planning, and a variety of other public services. Population projections are probably the application of demographic knowledge most frequently requested by government and non-academic organizations. For this reason, demographers have been repeatedly contracted by government departments to generate Aboriginal population projections (Perreault et al. 1985; Loh 1990; Nault et al. 1993; Nault and Jenkins 1993; Clatworthy 1994; Loh 1995; Norris et al. 1995; Loh et al. 1998).

Among the most widely publicized sets of projections of Aboriginal populations to date were those contracted by the Royal Commission on Aboriginal Peoples (RCAP).[1] Summarized in the first volume of the Royal Commission's final report to Parliament, these projections received high profile with the initial press release of the commission's work (Dussault and Erasmus 1996). Basing these projections on 1991 Aboriginal people survey data, considerable energy went into dealing with many of the shortcomings that have characterized demographic data on Aboriginal populations in the past. The purpose of this chapter is to take a second look at this set of projections and to provide a general overview of some of the insights gained and difficulties encountered in projecting the future growth of Canada's Aboriginal populations.

This chapter begins with an introduction to some of the definitional issues and data sources currently involved in working with demographic data on the Aboriginal populations in Canada. This is followed by an overview of the methodology used in the Royal Commission projections, along with a brief presentation of the projection results. Comparisons are made between the projected and observed population counts for 1996. There are significant differences between what the Royal Commission projected and the actual census count just five years later. These comparisons lead to a two-part discussion.

In the first part, we highlight some of the methodological difficulties that are encountered, given our current knowledge, in efforts to project Aboriginal populations. In the conclusion, we discuss the relevance and implications of these findings with respect to policy development.

Defining Aboriginal Populations

According to the Constitution Act, 1982 (Royal Commission on Aboriginal Peoples 1996, vol. 1), there are three major groups of Aboriginal people in Canada: the North American Indians, the Métis, and the Inuit. In addition, Canada's Indian Act, which has gone through many iterations since it was first established in 1876 (Savard and Proulx 1982), draws a further distinction between North American Indians who hold legal Indian status and those who do not. While the Constitution Act recognizes three Aboriginal groups, it does not actually define what constitutes their populations. In contrast, the Indian Act provides a specific but partial definition of Aboriginal populations by setting the legal criteria for a person to be recognized as a Status Indian. Nonetheless, both the Canadian constitution and the Indian Act have considerable impact on the classification of Aboriginal peoples by government administrators and social scientists, past and present (Goldman 1993).

The Indian Register, maintained by the federal Department of Indian Affairs and Northern Development (DIAND), has been a major source of information on Status Indians in Canada. Births and deaths occurring in this population are documented in this register. Information on the size, age structure, and geographic distribution of Status Indians is available, as well as information useful in the calculation of birth and death rates. However, because the Indian Register exists only for Status Indians, it is necessary to look elsewhere for information on the Non-Status Indians, the Métis, and the Inuit. Until the early 1980s, the Department of Demography at the Université de Montréal maintained a population register for the Inuit of Northern Quebec (Choinière and Robitaille 1982). This Inuit register came to a close in the early 1980s with the signing of the James Bay agreement between Quebec's provincial government, the Cree, and the Inuit (1974). As no other population register exists, the Census of Canada and the related 1991 post-censal Aboriginal Peoples Survey (APS) have been relied upon as the only other major sources of information on Aboriginal peoples.[2]

In shifting the emphasis from the Status Indians to all Aboriginals as defined in terms of how individuals report their ancestry in the census, a series of difficulties surface relating primarily to definition and measurement. Given the diverse origins of Canada's population and the long history of intermarriage, which has been particularly true among Aboriginal peoples (Dickason 1992, 162-69), the measurement of ancestry or cultural origins is not an easy task. Efforts to establish time series data on Aboriginal populations will always be hindered by the "fluid or situation character" of such concepts as ancestry or cultural origins (Boxhill 1984; Lieberson 1985). Persons of Aboriginal ancestry may deny their origins, others may have a passionate commitment to them, while still others may be somewhat passive, indifferent, or simply unaware.

In 1991 Statistics Canada introduced the large-scale Aboriginal Peoples Survey, designed to gather additional information on Aboriginal peoples in Canada. A large proportion of persons who reported an Aboriginal ancestry in the 1991 Census were sampled, and asked whether they actually "identify" with their reported ancestry.[3] This "Aboriginal identity" population has been understood to more accurately capture the essence of what has been denoted as a "core Aboriginal population" (Siggner et al. 2001). Beyond mere reporting of Aboriginal ancestry, the concept of identity was meant to act as an "indicator of an individual's feelings, allegiance or association" with an Aboriginal culture (Goldman 1995, 11). This narrower definition of the Aboriginal population applied to only about 60% of all persons with North American Indian ancestry, 67% of persons with Métis ancestry, and 82% of persons with Inuit ancestry. It was in this context that the Royal Commission on Aboriginal Peoples was asked to report on the social and economic conditions of Aboriginal Canadians, and to substantiate recommendations on the basis of carefully documented demographic trends.

Projections of the Royal Commission on Aboriginal Peoples
In this section, we briefly present how the population projections were arrived at by the Royal Commission on Aboriginal Peoples. We touch on the methods used, the issues confronted, and the results of the Royal Commission's work.

Methodology
The cohort component method was used for the Royal Commission 1991-2016 projections of Aboriginal populations. The cohort component approach is by far the most preferred technique for generating population projections and forecasts (Preston et al. 2000). Without providing the technical details associated with this method, the basic ideas that underlie it are relatively straightforward. Beginning with a base population classified by age and sex, assumptions about future trends of the components of demographic growth are used to project the base population into the future.

The RCAP population projection model considered four components to the demographic growth of Aboriginal groups, for which explicit assumptions about future trends were developed. These components were fertility, mortality, migration, and the 1985 Indian Act legislation concerning reinstatements and status inheritance rules.

The first three components are standard demographic items of any population projection model. The fourth element relates specifically to the North American Indians who hold legal Indian status. The model used recognized that Indian Act legislation also impacts the evolution of Non-Status Indians through gains (reinstatements) or losses (inheritance rules) of legal status. The implications of these types of changes are explored in depth in Chapter 3.

Base Population

The base population for the Royal Commission projections was selected from the 1991 Aboriginal Peoples Survey. After extensive consultations with representatives from Aboriginal organizations such as the Assembly of First Nations, the Council of Aboriginal Peoples,[4] the Inuit Tapirisat of Canada, and with representatives from numerous research and government organizations, the decision was made to disregard the 1991 Census information on Aboriginal ancestry. Alternatively, the more restrictive definition of Aboriginal population based on "Aboriginal identity" was selected, because it better portrayed the population that the Royal Commission was mandated to represent.

Table 2.1 includes the Royal Commission's base population subdivided into four distinct groups: (1) Status North American Indians, (2) Non-Status North American Indians, (3) Métis, and (4) Inuit. Using data from the Aboriginal Peoples Survey, adjustments were introduced in light of two problems. First, a limited number of reserves, primarily for political reasons, refused to participate in either the post-censal survey and/or the 1991 Census. Second, beyond this issue of nonparticipating reserves, additional persons were missed, both on and off reserve, as part of the more general problem of census undercoverage.[5] The base populations in Table 2.1 were adjusted for both of these problems and also arrayed by age and sex.[6] The base population was also generated separately by province/territory, on and off reserve, and rural and urban areas.

With this base population, a wide range of potential projection scenarios was possible for the 1991-2016 period. As one example, after deriving current fertility, mortality, and migration rates, projections could be generated by simply setting such rates as constant into the future. While it is reasonable to assume that this might apply for the first few years of a projection, however, typically most projections rely on more realistic assumptions about future change. For instance, the assumption that runs through most attempts at population projection is that mechanisms that have operated in the past will continue to operate into the future. If recent years have witnessed major gains in terms of reducing mortality, then a continuation or extrapolation of

Table 2.1 Base population by Aboriginal group, 1991

Aboriginal population	Aboriginal identity population			Percent increase due to		
	1991 APS[a] estimate (unadjusted)	Adjusted for incomplete enumeration	Adjusted for incomplete enumeration and undercoverage	Adjustment for incomplete enumeration	Adjustment for undercoverage[a]	All adjustments, incomplete enumeration and undercoverage
North American Indians						
Status[b]	353,055	406,755	438,030	15.2	8.9	24.1
Non-Status[b]	107,625	109,050	112,640	1.3	3.3	4.7
Métis[b]	135,260	136,070	139,395	0.6	2.5	3.1
Inuit[b]	36,215	36,250	37,825	0.1	4.3	4.4
Total Aboriginal[c]	625,700	681,940	720,650	9.0	6.2	15.2

a Aboriginal Peoples Survey (1991).

b Aboriginal group counts do contain some minor double-counting of those giving more than one identity response. For example, those giving a Métis and North American Indian identity and status responses are counted as both Métis and North American Indian.

c "Total Aboriginal" does not double-count multiple Aboriginal identity responses. Therefore, the individual group counts above do not add up to this total.

Source: Norris et al. 1995.

this trend is advisable in projecting the future. In the context of Aboriginal population projections, a large part of the challenge rested on locating a time series of reasonable quality to guide projections on the underlying components of demographic change (see also Statistics Canada 1994).

Mortality, Fertility, and Migration

For Status Indians and the Inuit of Northern Quebec, mortality and fertility rates were available directly from the two previously discussed population registers. With adjustments for data quality problems and late reporting, these population registers have been used in the past to develop time series of reasonable quality (Nault et al. 1993; Robitaille and Choinière 1987). With regard to the other Aboriginal groups, census information and techniques of indirect estimation have been used periodically (Piché and George 1973; Romaniuc 1981; Ram 1991). As we noted, this has various limitations relating to definitional and measurement issues. Overall, a review of the varied data sources available provided some guidance to the Royal Commission in the development of its projections.

Table 2.2 portrays fertility (total fertility rates) and mortality (life expectancy at birth) for the aforementioned base populations as estimated in 1991 and projected for the year 2016. For comparative purposes, summary indicators were also obtained for Canada as a whole, as derived from Vital Statistics. Briefly, the 1991 estimates indicated important differences across Aboriginal groups. For example, both Inuit fertility and mortality were consistently higher than those of Status Indians,[7] which in turn exceed those of the Métis and Non-Status Indians. Total fertility rates (TFRs) for 1991 using indirect estimation techniques yielded the following ranking: Inuit, 3.4 children; Registered Indians, 2.9; Métis, 2.5; and Non-Status Indians, 2.1. With regard to mortality, the relative ranking of Aboriginal groups was much the same, although the disadvantages that characterize the Inuit appear particularly striking: the life expectancy at birth of Inuit males is estimated at only 57.6 years. On the basis of recent trends, both mortality and fertility were projected to decline into the future, while the relative rankings of these Aboriginal groups was largely maintained.

With regard to migration, the census has long been considered the most comprehensive source of information, as the one-year and five-year mobility questions provide detailed information on both interprovincial and intraprovincial movements (rural/urban, on-reserve/off-reserve). The patterns observed over the 1986-91 intercensal period were expected to continue over the full projection period. Migration was projected both in terms of interprovincial migration and intraprovincial migration (rural/urban, on-reserve/off-reserve). In terms of international migration, the negligible net

Table 2.2 Estimates for 1991 and projections for 2016 of demographic components, by Aboriginal identity group

		1991	2016			
			Projection 1 Current trends without migration	Projection 2 Current trends with migration	Projection 3 High growth	Projection 4 Low growth
Aboriginal group						
Registered Indians						
Total fertility rate (births per woman)		2.9	2.2	2.2	2.9	2.2
Life expectancy at birth (in years)	Male	66.9	72.9	72.9	72.9	66.9
	Female	74.0	80.1	80.1	80.1	74.0
Internal Migration			0	Current trend	Current trend	Current trend
Non-Status Indians						
Total fertility rate (births per woman)		2.1	1.6	1.5	2.1	1.6
Life expectancy at birth (in years)	Male	71.4	76.2	76.2	76.2	71.4
	Female	77.9	82.3	82.3	82.3	77.9
Internal migration			0	Current trend	Current trend	Current trend
Métis						
Total fertility rate (births per woman)		2.5	1.8	1.8	2.5	1.8
Life expectancy at birth (in years)	Male	70.4	75.5	75.5	75.5	70.4
	Female	76.9	81.3	81.3	81.3	76.9
Internal migration			0	Current trend	Current trend	Current trend

▲

▲ Table 2.2

		1991	2016			
			Projection 1 Current trends without migration	Projection 2 Current trends with migration	Projection 3 High growth	Projection 4 Low growth
Aboriginal group						
Inuit						
Total fertility rate (births per woman)		3.4	2.5	2.5	3.4	2.5
Life expectancy at birth (in years)	Male	57.6	63.6	63.6	63.6	57.6
	Female	68.8	76.3	76.3	76.3	68.8
Internal migration			0	Current trend	Current trend	Current trend
Canada						
Total fertility rate (births per woman)		1.7				
Life expectancy at birth (in years)	Male	74.6				
	Female	81.0				

Source: Norris et al. 1995.

inflow of Aboriginal peoples indicated that it was reasonable to drop such migration from the projection model (Clatworthy 1996).

After a thorough review of relevant time series, four separate projection scenarios were chosen to provide a range of growth, including two medium-growth scenarios (one with migration and one without migration), one high-growth scenario, and one using low-growth assumptions. The scenario utilizing medium growth with migration assumptions was considered the most plausible projection, as it represented most closely the continuation of recent trends. With regard to the underlying components of demographic change, both fertility and mortality were projected to decline moderately over the 1991-2016 period. In so doing, the most pronounced change was projected to occur early in the period, based on curvilinear extrapolation of past rates.

Legislative Reform as Non-Conventional Growth Factor

With most population forecasts, projections fail to the extent that future trends in fertility, mortality, and migration are off the mark. Uncertainty about future trends in these fundamental demographic components is what makes the production of long-term projections such a difficult enterprise. In the case of the Royal Commission projections, additional complications surface due to a legislative component not normally encountered in standard population projections.

Reinstatements

The federal government has repeatedly introduced revisions and reforms to the Indian Act (Savard and Proulx 1982), which can have a direct impact on the size and growth of the Status Indian population. The last legislative changes in this regard were made in 1985. These amendments to the Indian Act, also referred to as Bill C-31, provided for the restoration of Indian status to individuals, most notably women and their children, who had lost status under provisions of previous legislation. Prior to 1985, a Status Indian woman who married a Non-Status man lost her Indian status, whereas a Status Indian man who out-married not only retained his status but also transferred eligibility to his wife. With regard to children, only the offspring of Status Indian men could inherit Indian status.

With its introduction, Bill C-31 had an immediate impact on the size and composition of the Status Indian population. For example, over the 1985-94 period, a little more than 96,000 persons were formally reinstated as Status Indians (DIAND 2001). As a particularly important yet unconventional component of demographic growth for the Status Indians, this impact of Bill C-31 was added to the basic population projection model used for the Royal Commission projections. An additional 47,300 reinstatements were forecast over the projection period, an assumption introduced across all four projection scenarios. The annual number of reinstatements was assumed to gradually decline. This assumption stems from the idea that the potential pool of Bill C-31 applicants would gradually become depleted. In addition, it was forecast that a disproportionate number of reinstatements would involve Indian women and/or their offspring.

In the projection model, the "reinstated population" was sourced from two Non-Status populations: (1) the population with North American Indian identity and (2) the population with North American Indian origins but who do not currently identify with their Aboriginal origins. In the case of the latter population, the assumption is implicitly made that after reinstatement individuals identify with their North American Indian origins.

Inheritance Rules and Assumptions
A motivating factor behind Bill C-31 was the need to eliminate discriminatory status inheritance rules defined by the Indian Act, whereas the reinstatements were meant to correct for the past. Bill C-31 redefined the inheritance rules so that the status of children is no longer defined on a patrilineal basis, acknowledging two specific parenting combinations[8] and hence two separate ways by which one could acquire status under the revised Indian Act: under either Section 6(1) or Section 6(2). By definition, children born to parents both of whom were Status Indians acquired entitlement under Section 6(1). Children born to parent combinations involving a parent registered under Section 6(1) and a non-registered parent (male or female) acquired entitlement under Section 6(2). Accordingly, offspring from parental combinations involving a non-registered parent and a parent registered under Section 6(2) were not entitled to Indian status.

In thinking through the long-term implications of this legislation, it was realized that RCAP projections of the Status Indian population that failed to consider the impact of descent rules were likely to overstate population growth for Registered Indians and understate the Non-Status population base over time.

In the preparation of the Royal Commission projections, relatively little information was available on the propensity of Status Indians to marry Non-Status individuals. Upon consultation with the Department of Indian Affairs and Northern Development, evidence from the Indian Register suggested that in 1991 the percentage of births to Status Indians who retained status according to the new rules was about 90% (Clatworthy 1994). On the basis of simulations, this percentage was projected to decline toward the end of the projection period, such that about 75% of all births to Status Indians would retain status by 2016. On this basis, it was projected that about 10% of births

to Status Indian women in 1991 be allocated to the Non-Status Indian population, a proportion projected to increase to about 25% by 2016. In the absence
of carefully documented out-marriage rates and a formal modelling of the impact of out-marriage on the status of newborns, this was considered an improvement over merely allocating all births to the Status Indian population.[9]

Projection Results

While population projections can provide us with a sense of the future size,
growth, and age/sex structure of Aboriginal groups, their eventual success
rests on the degree to which underlying assumptions on future fertility, mortality, and migration prove to be correct. In the context of the Royal Commission projections, an additional non-conventional legal component of growth
also has an impact and adds an additional element of uncertainty. In reaction
to such uncertainty, most attempts to project population growth either implicitly or explicitly underline the difficulties involved through the development of alternative scenarios. While appreciating the logic behind such an
approach, for the sake of simplicity our primary emphasis in summarizing the
Royal Commission projection results will be on the most expected scenario
of medium growth with migration.

The medium-growth scenario was described as involving "the continuation
of current trends" and combines fertility decline with declining mortality and
internal migration (Table 2.3, projection 2). This scenario was highlighted in
the Royal Commission's final report to Parliament and generally judged to be
the most plausible. As in all four scenarios, the impact of Bill C-31 was included, both in terms of reinstatements and the allocation of births in light of
the revised status inheritance rules. Table 2.3 also summarizes the projection
results of the three other scenarios, for the total Aboriginal population of
Canada as well as for Status Indians, Non-Status Indians, Métis, and Inuit.

To summarize the results from the medium-growth scenario, overall population with Aboriginal identity was projected to increase from an estimated
720,600 in 1991 to over a million (1,093,400) by 2016. This implies an increase of 52% over a period of twenty-five years. To put this into context, the
Canadian population overall has been projected to increase by about 30%
over the same period (medium-growth scenario; George et al. 2001). In light
of what was known at that point of the demographics of Aboriginal peoples
in Canada, the growth rate of its population was expected to outpace that of
the Canadian population in general. The growth differential observed between these two populations was the result of Aboriginal women having
more children than other Canadian women.

Between 1991 and 2016, the medium-growth scenario projected considerable growth across all Aboriginal groups. Among North American Indians,

Table 2.3 Projected annual growth rate by Aboriginal total and group, 1991-2016

	Population projection				Five-year average annual %			
	Projection 1 Current, zero migration	Projection 2 Current with migration	Projection 3 High growth	Projection 4 Low growth	Projection 1 Current, zero migration	Projection 2 Current with migration	Projection 3 High growth	Projection 4 Low growth
Total Aboriginal[a]								
1991	720.6	720.6	720.6	720.6	–	–	–	–
1996	811.4	811.4	818.4	810.9	2.5	2.5	2.7	2.5
2001	890.6	890.5	914.4	887.9	2.0	1.9	2.3	1.9
2006	959.6	959.1	1,006.7	952.4	1.5	1.5	2.0	1.5
2011	1,028.7	1,027.5	1,104.6	1,014.5	1.4	1.4	1.9	1.3
2016	1,095.9	1,093.4	1,207.1	1,071.3	1.3	1.3	1.9	1.1
Registered Indians								
1991	438.0	438.0	438.0	438.0	–	–	–	–
1996	505.7	505.7	509.9	505.3	3.1	3.1	3.3	3.1
2001	561.5	561.3	575.8	559.5	2.2	2.2	2.6	2.1
2006	601.7	601.1	629.0	596.5	1.4	1.4	1.8	1.3
2011	636.8	635.5	679.0	626.7	1.2	1.1	1.6	1.0
2016	667.7	665.6	727.0	650.6	1.0	0.9	1.4	0.8

Non-Status Indians

1991	112.6	112.6	112.6	112.6	–	–	–	–
1996	118.3	118.3	119.4	118.3	1.0	1.0	1.2	1.0
2001	126.0	126.1	130.0	125.8	1.3	1.3	1.8	1.3
2006	139.6	139.7	148.4	139.0	2.2	2.2	2.8	2.1
2011	157.7	157.7	173.5	156.4	2.6	2.6	3.4	2.5
2016	178.6	178.4	204.1	176.0	2.7	2.6	3.5	2.5

Métis

1991	139.4	139.4	139.4	139.4	–	–	–	–
1996	152.8	152.8	154.1	152.8	1.9	1.9	2.1	1.9
2001	165.0	165.0	169.2	164.6	1.6	1.6	2.0	1.5
2006	176.7	176.7	185.1	175.8	1.4	1.4	1.9	1.4
2011	188.6	188.6	202.1	186.7	1.3	1.3	1.8	1.2
2016	199.5	199.4	219.1	196.2	1.2	1.2	1.7	1.0

Inuit

1991	37.8	37.8	37.8	37.8	–	–	–	–
1996	42.5	42.5	43.0	42.5	2.5	2.5	2.7	2.4
2001	46.6	46.6	48.1	46.4	1.9	1.9	2.4	1.9
2006	50.7	50.7	53.7	50.2	1.7	1.7	2.3	1.6
2011	55.3	55.3	60.4	54.3	1.8	1.8	2.5	1.7
2016	60.3	60.3	68.1	58.6	1.8	1.8	2.6	1.6

a The total Aboriginal population has been adjusted for multiple identities to avoid double-counting. The sum for the individual Aboriginal groups, which include multiples, is therefore greater than the total Aboriginal count.

Source: Norris et al. 1995.

the status population was projected to increase from 438,000 to 665,600 (+52%), whereas the Non-Status population was projected to grow from 112,600 to 178,400 (+58%). The Métis population was projected to jump from 139,400 to 199,400 (+43%), whereas the Inuit population was projected to increase from 37,800 to 60,300 (+60%).[10]

While the total Aboriginal population in Canada was projected to grow rapidly, the projected pace of growth was expected to decline noticeably throughout the projection period. With the medium-growth scenario, the growth rate would decline from 2.5% annually between 1991 and 1996 to 1.3% between 2011 and 2016. Corresponding rates under the low-growth scenario were 2.5% to 1.1%, while even under the high-growth scenario, population growth was expected to slow down from 2.7% to 1.9%. In comparing growth rates across Aboriginal groups, this slowdown was true of only three of the four Aboriginal groups. Growth rates of the Non-Status Indian population were projected to increase rather than decline, from an average of 1.0% for 1991-96 to 2.6% by 2011-16.[11]

The projected growth of both the Métis and Inuit populations is based solely on natural increase since identity is assumed to be inherited, with the declining rates of population growth a result of reduced fertility. In the case of Status Indians, while a declining rate of natural increase was fundamental in defining a declining overall growth, Bill C-31 reinstatements represent an important component of the projected growth by limiting this decline. With the Non-Status population, Bill C-31 was expected to have both a positive and a negative impact. On the one hand, Bill C-31 reinstatements offset population growth, as the Non-Status group was assumed to be the primary source population for reinstatements. On the other hand, Bill C-31 status inheritance rules have a positive impact on the growth of Non-Status Indians, particularly toward the latter part of the projection period. On the assumptions that as many as 25% of all births to the status population would not qualify for status toward the latter part of the projection period, *and* again that identity is inherited, the growth rate for the Non-Status population was projected to increase, irrespective of reduced natural increase. Overall, the impact of Bill C-31 through out-marriage and descent rules was projected to accelerate throughout the projection period, yielding a growing population not entitled to status.

And Then Came the 1996 Census of Canada

Prior to 1996, census data on Aboriginal persons were obtained through a question on ancestry. The 1996 Census of Canada was the first census to include a question that asked persons directly for their Aboriginal identity. Did they consider themselves to be North American Indian, Métis, or Inuit? As

Table 2.4 Royal Commission on Aboriginal Peoples (RCAP) population projections
for 1996 and adjusted 1996 Census of Canada Aboriginal populations

| Aboriginal group | 1991 APS[a] base population (1) | 1996 RCAP projections | | | 1996 Census of Canada (5) | Relative difference between RCAP and census figures (5/3)–1 |
		Low-growth scenario (2)	Medium-growth scenario with migration (3)	High-growth scenario (4)		
Total Aboriginal	720.6	810.9	811.4	818.4	864.0	6.5%
Status Indians	438.0	505.3	505.7	509.9	554.9	9.7%
Non-Status Indians	112.6	118.2	118.3	119.4	76.7	–35.2%
Métis	139.4	152.7	152.8	154.1	190.1	24.4%
Inuit	37.8	42.2	42.5	43.0	42.4	–0.2%

a Aboriginal Peoples Survey.

the wording is very similar to the identity question in the 1991 Aboriginal peoples post-censal survey, one can reproduce the exact 1991 RCAP definition of Aboriginal populations by merging the 1996 identity concept with the census concepts of ancestry and Indian legal status (see Appendix 2.1).

Table 2.4 includes both the Royal Commission projections for 1996 and the 1996 Census-based figures by Aboriginal group. In theory, with a consistent definition of Aboriginal populations, one could expect figures coming out of the 1996 Census to fall reasonably close to the RCAP projections for that same year, to the extent that the RCAP 1991 base population and the 1991-96 assumptions are accurate.[12]

The 1996 figures presented in Table 2.4 have been adjusted for census coverage error in a manner consistent with the 1991 population characteristics. To provide a range in the projections, the RCAP medium-growth scenario (with migration) is supplemented by both the low- and high-growth projections. With the expectation that 1996 Census-based figures fall within the resultant range of projections, Table 2.4 indicates a rather poor performance over a short period of five years. At the very least, this suggests the need for caution in working with the Royal Commission projections, given the apparent imprecision in projecting population size (see Appendix 2.2).

In terms of the total Aboriginal population, the adjusted 1996 Census figure (864,000) is much higher than anticipated by the RCAP projections (810,900 to 818,400). Relative to the medium-growth scenario, the census count is

6.5% higher than the projected count. This difference is extremely large in light of the duration of the time frame (1991-96). Even for the Status Indian population, a population defined with clear objective criteria (i.e., the Indian Act), the 1996 Census figure (554,900) is surprisingly much higher than the projected figure (505,300 to 509,900). As the current set of projections included Bill C-31 reinstatements, it is not clear why the projections would have understated the Status Indian population growth. With the Non-Status Indian population, the opposite occurs, as the 1996 Census figure (76,700) is significantly lower than projected (118,200 to 119,400). In fact, according to APS and 1996 Census figures, this population decreased tremendously between 1991 and 1996 (-35.2%). Among the Métis, the 1996 Census population is much higher than projected (with 190,100 persons relative to a projected range of 152,700 to 154,100). Even with a doubling or tripling of projected fertility, the Métis projections would have fallen short. It is only among the Inuit that the projections are reasonable, the 1996 Census figure (42,400) falling within the projected range (42,200 to 43,000).

In terms of projected growth (Table 2.5), which is another way of assessing the validity of projections (assumptions are made on the projected growth through its components, not the population size itself), it is apparent that the RCAP projections have completely missed the mark in attempting to project the demographic growth of Aboriginal groups. Overall, the projected growth of Aboriginal groups for the 1991-96 period is understated by approximately 58%. The observed growth of the Status Indian population, for which it was thought that all components were well understood, is 73% larger than expected. This error term reaches levels totally unacceptable by any standard for the Non-Status Indians (729.8%) and Métis (278%)!

Table 2.5   RCAP-projected and 1996 Census-based population growth of Aboriginal populations

Aboriginal group	1996 RCAP projections			1996 Census of Canada (4)	Relative difference between RCAP and census figures (4/2)–1
	Low-growth scenario (1)	Medium-growth scenario with migration (2)	High-growth scenario (3)		
Total Aboriginal	90.3	90.8	97.8	143.4	57.9%
Status Indians	67.3	67.7	71.9	116.9	72.7%
Non-Status Indians	5.6	5.7	6.8	–35.9	–729.8%
Métis	13.3	13.4	14.7	50.7	278.4%
Inuit	4.6	4.7	5.2	4.6	–2.1%

In light of what was known at that point of the demographics of Aboriginal peoples in Canada, nobody could have predicted such growth of the Status Indians, Non-Status Indians, and Métis. For the Métis, the observed growth exceeds by far what is theoretically possible for a population that is subject only to the natural movement of births and deaths (Guimond 1999). Factors beyond the components of growth considered in the Royal Commission projections played a crucial role in generating the impressive demographic growth of Aboriginal populations between 1991 and 1996.

Discussion

On the surface, the generation of projections of Aboriginal groups appears straightforward. As Aboriginal affiliation, and more generally ethnicity, is typically understood as a fundamental ascribed characteristic of all persons, it is generally assumed that a person's ethnicity is fixed at birth, remains the same over one's lifetime, and is subsequently transferred to one's offspring. If one adopts this simplistic view of ethnicity, then population projections require only data on past fertility, mortality, and migration with realistic scenarios as to future trends. In projecting this future, a convergence toward rates as observed nationally is often considered reasonable, assuming a diffusion of cultural practices and living standards across ethnic boundaries.

Unfortunately, as the analysis in this chapter suggests, the development of Aboriginal population projections is much more complex. In the context of the discussed population projections, we identify three complicating factors: (1) reinstatements, (2) inheritance rules, and (3) shifts in self-reporting of ethnicity. Only the first two factors were alluded to, although not sufficiently elaborated upon, in the Royal Commission projections.

Reinstatements

The Bill C-31 reinstatement assumptions over the 1991-96 period are critical in accounting for the observed deviation between the RCAP-projected and census-adjusted population counts for 1996. These assumptions were developed without any knowledge about the identity of reinstated persons prior to their actual reinstatement. As noted earlier, in the projection model, reinstatements to the Status Indian population were sourced from a combination of both identity and ancestry of North American Indian populations: 25% of reinstatements were assumed to come from the Non-Status Indian identity population, and the remaining 75% from the Non-Status and non-Aboriginal identity population with North American Indian ancestry.

These "sourcing" assumptions, while having no effect whatsoever on the projected size of the Status Indian population, were extremely critical in projecting the size of the Non-Status Indian population. During the preparation of the RCAP projections, it was estimated that sourcing all reinstatements (100%) from the Non-Status Indians would have resulted in a projected decline of this population (approximately 95,000 persons in 1996), a scenario deemed unreasonable. In retrospect, the sole-sourcing assumption would have reduced the deviation between the 1996 Census figure and the projected figure for the Non-Status Indian population. However, within the limitations of the projection model, it would have at the same time widened the census/projection discrepancy for the overall Aboriginal population.

Inheritance Rules

The demographic impact on the Status Indians of inheritance rules as defined by Bill C-31 has raised broader issues relevant to all Aboriginal groups. In examining the impact of status inheritance rules, the importance of future marriage patterns was acknowledged in the RCAP projections as having an impact on the number of births that would be entitled to status. Yet just as intermarriage is relevant to the future size and characteristics of the Status Indian group, it is also relevant to the Non-Status Indian, the Inuit, and the Métis, or, for that matter, any population defined in terms of ethnic self-identification.

In the projections prepared for the Royal Commission,[13] the use of the classic formulation of the cohort component method implicitly meant relying on the basic "one-step/one-sex reproduction process" assumption: future Aboriginal births are a function of assumed fertility rates multiplied by the number of Aboriginal women in their reproductive years. Yet in the case of populations defined in terms of ethnicity, the situation is complicated greatly by the possibility of out-marriage. A first and valiant attempt was made with the RCAP projections to model the effect of intermarriage, but it still basically relied on the classic approach. Robitaille and Guimond (2001) have illustrated the limits of the "one-step reproduction process" assumption of the classic demographic analytical approach. They conclude that the reproduction process of Aboriginal groups, and more generally of any ethnic group, involves not one but three steps: (1) marriage patterns with regard to ethnic affiliation of spouses; (2) fertility patterns of same-group couples versus mixed couples, allowing the fertility of exogamous males to be taken into account; and (3) ethnic identification patterns of children, especially those from mixed couples.

The Research and Analysis Directorate of Indian and Northern Affairs Canada has recently begun to address some of these methodological challenges, in explicitly incorporating the interplay among out-marriage, fertility, and inheritance within projection models (Clatworthy forthcoming; Norris et al. 2001). Similarly, in light of many of these same issues in the United States, the

National Research Council Panel on the Demographic and Economic Impacts of Immigration produced population projections by race and ethnicity that incorporate current levels of intermarriage and variations in ethnic identification across generations (Smith and Edmonston 1997). We may conclude that intermarriage and ethnic identification can rival, if not surpass, other fundamental components, such as fertility, in generating population projections by ethnic group. This is shown to be particularly true over the longer term.

Failure to consider such factors certainly throws into question the validity of many long-term forecasts, but they also do so over the shorter term, as we see in our discussion here. While a more careful modelling of intermarriage, fertility, and the intergenerational transmission of ethnicity would likely lead to improved estimates, a substantial proportion of the discrepancies as documented in this chapter remains: preliminary estimates indicate that differences between the projected and observed numbers of Aboriginal children born during the 1991-96 period represent only 30% of the overall discrepancies.

Shifts in Self-Reporting of Ethnicity

In a recent critique of ethnic population projections, Hirschman (forthcoming) highlights what he considers the most fundamental shortcoming of most published works: the assumption – rarely stated explicitly – of ascriptively defined populations. As argued, the measurement and reporting of ethnic identity involves increasingly permeable and fuzzy boundaries, particularly in multicultural societies such as the United States and Canada. Instead of ethnicity being a purely ascriptive characteristic assigned at birth for a growing number of persons, a significant level of choice is exercised in defining their ethnicity. Consequently, it becomes extremely difficult to make assumptions about ethnic identities and boundaries. Building on a growing body of research, it is argued that many census and survey respondents select an ethnic identity for largely idiosyncratic reasons (Alba 1990; Waters 1990; Farley 1991; Perlmann 1997).

Recent analyses of census data that have explicitly controlled for various factors affecting comparability across censuses over time have demonstrated how natural increase, migration, and data quality cannot account for the spectacular growth observed among Aboriginal groups between 1986 and 1996 (Guimond 1999). Changes in self-reporting of ethnic affiliation, or ethnic mobility, have occurred from the non-Aboriginal group to Aboriginal groups, and from one Aboriginal group to another. Over the 1991-96 period, census respondents appeared more likely to report a Métis identity but less likely to report a North American Indian identity if they were not registered under the Indian Act. In the case of the Métis, this ethnic mobility could explain as much as 70% of the total growth between 1991 and 1996 (Guimond forthcoming). With so little information available about this phenomenon of ethnic mobility before the preparation of the RCAP projections, no demographer could have predicted such a demographic outcome of the Aboriginal populations during that period.

Conclusion

Irrespective of their shortcomings, one relatively safe conclusion to come out of the Royal Commission population projections is that, overall, the Aboriginal population of Canada will grow at a rapid but declining pace for the next two decades. Even though mortality remains relatively high, fertility also remains well above replacement level, such that a high rate of natural increase is expected to continue to characterize this population for some time to come. As demonstrated in the discussed set of projections, even with a rapid decline in fertility and mortality, considerable growth is still anticipated. This growth is expected to easily outpace the national growth rate, although our ability to quantify it with a reasonable level of precision, especially for the specific Aboriginal groups, appears to be seriously hindered by several factors.

Beyond the usual difficulties involved in projecting future fertility behaviour and mortality conditions, additional complications relate to future marriage patterns and the manner in which descendants of mixed marriages identify with their Aboriginal origin, not to mention the immediate and future impact of the current Indian Act. Yet, after considering all such factors, perhaps the most serious difficulty relates to the permeability and fuzziness of ethnic boundaries. Population projections that assume that ethnicity is inherited and permanent are becoming increasingly obsolete. This is already the case with Aboriginal groups in Canada. A new generation of projection models will have to be developed before attempting to generate new Aboriginal population projections. Why? Because population projections are used for all sorts of policy and program planning purposes: health, education, housing, social security, and so on. Demographers produce population projections to answer the question of how many. The policy and program analysts rely on these projections to answer the question of how much. If present demographic models cannot accurately say how many, how can policy analysts effectively determine program costs?

Appendix 2.1
How to Use the 1996 Census of Canada Concepts to Generate the Definition of Aboriginal Groups in the 1991 Census-Based Population Projections of the Royal Commission on Aboriginal Peoples (RCAP)

Aboriginal group as defined for RCAP projections	1996 Census of Canada concepts		
	Aboriginal identity	Ancestry	Indian legal status
Status Indians	North American Indian or non-Aboriginal	Aboriginal or non-Aboriginal	Status
Non-Status Indians	North American Indian	Aboriginal	Non-Status
Métis	Métis	Aboriginal	Non-Status
Inuit	Inuit	Aboriginal	Non-Status

Appendix 2.2
Factors Affecting the Historical Comparability of Census Data

To the degree that census coverage shifts over time, demographic growth as implied in population figures is potentially biased. Adjustments to the 1996 Census figures are necessary in order to make them comparable with the 1991 population figures. As for the 1991 figures, two separate adjustments are introduced. Population counts of Indian reserves require an adjustment for partial enumeration, while the 1996 Census coverage studies allow for undercount adjustments in a manner consistent with 1991. As a result, an estimated 44,000 persons are added to the 1996 Status Indian count living on Indian reserves, while the Aboriginal identity population is raised by an additional 61,000 persons, given the general problem of census undercount.

Content or reporting error exists to an unknown degree in census data. While it is generally assumed by methodologists working with the census that content error is very low, if not negligible (Statistics Canada 1999), it is noted that if only a very small proportion of Canadians misinterpret questions relating to Aboriginal identity, the resultant error might have a disproportionate impact on specific Aboriginal population counts. This observation relates to the fact that Aboriginal Canadians make up a relatively small proportion of Canada's overall population (2.9% in 1996), whereas millions of Canadians are required to respond to the Aboriginal item in the census. As Statistics Canada has yet to publish a systematic study on the possibility of content error in its Aboriginal data, it is reasonable to assume a comparatively low level over time.

Notes
1 For a general overview, see Norris et al. 1995.
2 Unlike in the United States, Canadian Vital Statistics do not compile information on births and deaths by race, nor is information collected on the ancestry or ethnicity of persons involved.
3 Also included were persons of non-Aboriginal ancestry who had declared themselves as Status Indians.

4   Formerly the Native Council of Canada.
5   In generating national population estimates, Statistics Canada routinely produces inde-
    pendent estimates of both of these forms of census coverage error. Since the post-
    censal survey's sampling frame was the 1991 Census, adjustments were obviously
    necessary for both forms of coverage error.
6   With minor adjustments due to sampling error.
7   The terms "Status Indian" and "Registered Indian" are used interchangeably through-
    out this book.
8   See explanation of Section 6 of Bill C-31 in Chapter 3.
9   Clatworthy has corrected these shortcomings in Chapter 3. Implicitly, individuals born
    to Status Indian women but who do not qualify for status due to the Bill C-31 inherit-
    ance rules were assumed to identify as North American Indian. Similarly, children born
    to Métis or Inuit women are assumed to identify as Métis or Inuit.
10 Inuit fertility is the highest of all groups, as we discussed earlier.
11 In terms of the total Aboriginal population, the high-growth scenario projected a popu-
    lation of 1,207,100 persons by 2016, 114,000 more than the medium-growth scenario.
    The high-growth scenario maintained fertility rates at 1991 levels, whereas the medium-
    growth scenario projected a steady decline in fertility toward the replacement level of
    2.1 children per woman. The low-growth scenario maintained mortality rates at 1991
    levels, while the medium-growth scenario projected a steady decline toward levels as
    observed overall in Canada. By 2016, the low-growth scenario projected the total
    Aboriginal population at 22,000 less than the medium-growth scenario. This indicates
    that mortality has less effect than fertility on the overall population growth of Aborigi-
    nal peoples.
12 Beyond the need for consistency in definition, additional factors such as census
    undercoverage, questionnaire format, and quality of data have also been raised as
    affecting the comparability of census and survey data (Pryor 1984; Goldman and Signner
    1995; Guimond 1999; Norris 2000). These are important issues but our assessment is
    that the effect would be comparatively low. For example, census coverage shift re-
    quires that 44,000 be added, and content error is very low if not negligible (Statistics
    Canada 1999).
13 And any other projection of Aboriginal groups done in the past.

References
Alba, R. 1990. *Ethnic Identity: The Transformation of White America.* New Haven,
    CT: Yale University Press.
Boxhill, W. 1984. *Limitations of the Use of Ethnic Origin Data to Quantify Visible
    Minorities in Canada.* Working paper, Housing, Family and Social Statistics Divi-
    sion, Statistics Canada. Ottawa: Minister of Supply and Services Canada.
Choinière, R., and N. Robitaille. 1982. Description et utilisation du registre de popu-
    lation des Inuit du Nouveau-Québec. *Cahiers québécois de démographie* 11(1):
    69-99.
Clatworthy, S.J. 1994. *Revised Projections Scenarios Concerning the Population Im-
    plications of Section 6 of the Indian Act.* Winnipeg: Four Directions Consulting
    Group.
–. 1996. *The Migration and Mobility Patterns of Canada's Aboriginal Population.*
    Prepared for the Royal Commission on Aboriginal Peoples. Ottawa: Canada
    Mortgage and Housing Corporation, and the Royal Commission on Aboriginal
    Peoples.
–. Forthcoming. *Re-assessing the Population Impacts of Bill C-31.* Report prepared for
    Research and Analysis Directorate, Indian and Northern Affairs Canada. Winnipeg:
    Four Directions Consulting Group.

DIAND (Department of Indian Affairs and Northern Development). 2001. *Basic Departmental Data 1994*. Information Quality and Research Directorate, Information Management Branch, Corporate Services.
Dickason, O.P. 1992. *Canada's First Nations: A History of Founding Peoples from Earliest Times*. Toronto: Oxford University Press.
Dussault, R., and G. Erasmus. 1996. Address on release of the Royal Commission on Aboriginal Peoples, 21 November 1996, Ottawa: Museum of Civilization.
Farley, R. 1991. The new census question about ancestry: What did it tell us? *Demography* 28: 411-30.
George, M.V., S. Loh, R. Verma, and E.Y. Shin. 2001. *Population Projections for Canada, Provinces and Territories, 2000-2026*. Ottawa: Statistics Canada.
Goldman, G. 1993. The Aboriginal population and the census: 120 years of information 1871-1991. In *Proceedings of the 22nd General Population Conference for the Scientific Study of Population*. Montreal: IUSSP.
Goldman, G., and A. Siggner. 1995. Statistical concepts of Aboriginal people and factors affecting the counts in the census and the Aboriginal Peoples Survey. In *Towards the 21st Century: Emerging Socio-Demographic Trends and Policy Issues in Canada*. Ottawa: Federation of Canadian Demographers.
Guimond, E. 1999. Ethnic mobility and the demographic growth of Canada's Aboriginal Populations from 1986 to 1996. In *Report on the Demographic Situation in Canada, 1998-1999*. Catalogue no. 91-208-XPE. Ottawa: Statistics Canada.
–. Forthcoming. L'explosion démographique des populations autochtones du Canada de 1986 à 1996. PhD diss., Department of Demography, Université de Montréal.
Hirschman, C. Forthcoming. The meaning of race and ethnic population projections. In *American Diversity: A Demographic Challenge for the Twenty-First Century*, edited by S. Tolnay and N. Denton. Albany, NY: SUNY Press.
Loh, S. 1990. *Population Projections of Registered Indians, 1986-2011*. Report prepared by Population Projections Section, Demography Division, Statistics Canada, for Indian and Northern Affairs Canada.
–. 1995. *Projections of Canada's Population with Aboriginal Ancestry, 1991-2016*. Report prepared by Population Projections Section, Demography Division, for Employment Equity Data Program, Housing, Family and Social Statistics Division, Statistics Canada.
Loh, S., et al. 1998. *Population Projections of Registered Indians, 1996-2021*. Report prepared by Population Projections Section, Demography Division, Statistics Canada, for Indian and Northern Affairs Canada.
Nault, F., and E. Jenkins. 1993. *Projections of Population with Aboriginal Ancestry, Canada, Provinces/Regions and Territories, 1991-2016*. Catalogue no. 91-539-XPE. Ottawa: Statistics Canada.
Nault, F., J. Chen, M.V. George, and M.J. Norris. 1993. *Population Projections of Registered Indians, 1991-2016*. Report prepared by Population Projections Section, Demography Division, Statistics Canada, for Indian and Northern Affairs Canada.
Norris, M. J. 2000. Aboriginal peoples in Canada: Demographic and linguistic perspectives. In *Visions of the Heart: Canadian Aboriginal Issues*, edited by D. Long and O.P. Dickason. Toronto: Harcourt Brace.
Norris, M.J., D. Kerr, and F. Nault. 1995. *Summary Report on Projections of the Population with Aboriginal Identity, Canada, 1991-2016*. Prepared by Population Projections Section, Demography Division, Statistics Canada, for the Royal Commission on Aboriginal Peoples and Canada Mortgage and Housing Corporation.
Norris, M.J., S. Clatworthy, and E. Guimond. 2001. Demography, legislation and ethnic mobility: considerations and implications for projections of Canada's Aboriginal populations. Paper presented at the annual meeting of the Population Association of America, Washington, DC.

Perlmann, J. 1997. *Reflecting on the Changing Face of America: Multiracials, Racial Classification, and American Intermarriage.* Jerome Levy Economics Institute Public Policy Brief No. 35. Annandale on Hudson, NY: Bard College.

Perreault, J., L. Paquette, and M.V. George. 1985. *Population Projections of Registered Indians, 1982-1996.* Report prepared by Population Projections Section, Demography Division, Statistics Canada, for Indian and Northern Affairs Canada.

Piché, V., and M.V. George. 1973. *Estimates of Vital Rates for the Canadian Indians, 1960-1970.* Ottawa: Statistics Canada.

Preston, S., P. Heuveline, and M. Guillot. 2000. *Demography: Measuring and Modeling Population Processes.* Oxford: Blackwell Publishers.

Pryor, E. 1984. *Profile of Native Women: 1981 Census of Canada.* Ottawa: Minister of Supply and Services.

Ram, B. 1991. Assimilation and fertility of Native Indians, some new evidence. Paper presented at the annual meeting of the Canadian Population Society, June 1991, Kingston, ON.

Robitaille, N., and R. Choinière. 1987. *An Overview of Demographic and Socioeconomic Conditions of the Inuit in Canada.* Ottawa: Indian and Northern Affairs Canada.

Robitaille, N., and E. Guimond. 2001. The reproduction of Aboriginal groups: Exogamy, fertility and ethnic mobility. Communication presented at the Conference of the International Union for the Scientific Study of Population (IUSSP), Salvador de Bahia, Brazil, 2001.

Romaniuc, A. 1981. Increase in natural fertility during the early stages of modernization: Canadian Indians case study. *Demography* 182: 157-72.

Royal Commission on Aboriginal Peoples (RCAP). 1996. *People to People, Nation to Nation.* Available on CD-ROM: *For seven generations: An information legacy of the Royal Commission on Aboriginal Peoples.* Ottawa: Minister of Supply and Services Canada.

Savard, R., and J.R. Proulx. 1982. Derrière l'épopée, les autochtones. Montreal: L'Hexagone.

Siggner, A.J., et al. 2001. Understanding Aboriginal definitions: Implications for counts and socio-economic characteristics. Communication presented at the Annual Meeting of the Canadian Population Society, Université Laval, Quebec.

Smith, J., and B. Edmonston. 1997. *The New Americans: Economic, Demographic and Fiscal Effects of Immigration.* Washington, DC: National Academy Press.

Statistics Canada. 1994. *Population Projections for Canada, Provinces and Territories, 1993-2016.* Catalogue no. 91-520 Occasional. Ottawa: Minister of Industry, Science and Technology.

Statistics Canada. 1999. *Coverage: 1996 Census Technical Reports.* Catalogue no. 21-21. Ottawa: Statistics Canada.

Waters, M. 1990. *Ethnic Options: Choosing Identities in America.* Berkeley: University of California Press.

3

Impacts of the 1985 Amendments to the Indian Act on First Nations Populations

Stewart Clatworthy

The 1985 amendments to the Indian Act (widely known as Bill C-31) introduced a number of important changes affecting First Nations communities and populations. This chapter describes the nature of the new provisions contained in Bill C-31 and assesses the short- and long-term implications of these provisions for First Nations populations.[1] Specifically, I address four questions, including:

- What changes were introduced by Bill C-31 and how do these changes differ from the prior Indian Act?
- What effects has Bill C-31 had on the size and composition of First Nations populations since its enactment?
- How is Bill C-31 likely to affect the future size and composition of First Nations populations?
- How might these changes impact on First Nations and other governments responsible for providing or administering services to First Nations populations and communities?

Understanding the Nature of Bill C-31's Amendments

As noted by Jamieson (1978) and Smith (1991), Canada's Indian Act has a long history of tracing "Indian-ness" through the male line.[2] Section 12 of the 1951/56 Indian Act, the predecessor of Bill C-31, excluded or authorized the removal from the Indian Register of (1) women who married non-Indian men, (2) the descendants of these marriages, (3) illegitimate children of Indian women and non-Indian men,[3] and (4) people whose mother and father's mother were both non-Indian (the "double mother" clause).

Section 11 of that same Indian Act, on the other hand, provided the ability for Indian men, subject to the "double mother" clause, to transmit entitlement to Indian registration to all their children, regardless of the child's mother and without the considerations of marriage. In addition, Section 11 provided for the non-Indian wives of Indian men to acquire Indian registration. Not surprisingly, the rules embodied in Sections 11 and 12 of the 1951/56 Indian Act were subject to political and legal challenges based on the grounds of gender discrimination.

Bill C-31 introduced three main provisions. First was the reinstatement of Registered Indian status to individuals who had been removed from the Indian Register by the rules of prior versions of the Indian Act, and the first-time registration of their children. Second were new gender-neutral rules governing entitlement to Indian registration for all children born to a Registered Indian parent on or after 17 April 1985. Third was the opportunity for individual First Nations to establish their own rules governing First Nations (band) membership.

By addressing the inequalities of the past (through reinstatements) and eliminating the discriminatory clauses, Bill C-31 attempted to bring the Indian Act into conformity with the gender equality provisions of the Canadian Charter and Rights and Freedoms.

Entitlement to Registration under Bill C-31
Bill C-31 completely changed the rules governing entitlement to Indian registration. Under the new rules, entitlement to Indian registration became a birthright that cannot be gained or lost through marriage or other events. One qualifies according to the registration characteristics of one's parent(s).[4]

However, as Figure 3.1 illustrates, the inheritance rules in Section 6 imply that parenting patterns will greatly influence the future population entitled to Indian registration. Parenting between Indians and non-Indians (out-marriage) over two successive generations results in loss of entitlement to Indian registration among the offspring of the second generation.[5]

Application of the Section 6 Rules: A Detailed Analysis of How Bill C-31 Works
In order to understand the application of the new rules, it is important to distinguish among three population groups. For simplicity we refer to these groups as:

- the pre-Bill C-31 population, including all those who were on (or entitled to be on) the Indian Register as of 16 April 1985
- the Bill C-31 population, including all those who were born on or before 16 April 1985 and were not on (or not entitled to be on) the Indian Register at that time, but have (re)acquired registration under Bill C-31
- the post-Bill C-31 population, including all those who were born after 16 April 1985.

Figure 3.1   Section 6 entitlement to Indian status of children born to various parenting combinations

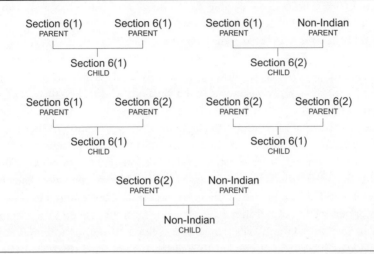

Bill C-31 does not apply the rules of Section 6 to these populations equally. To illustrate this, a detailed description of the subclauses of Section 6 would be required. At this time, I will give the reader an overview. Section 6(1) contains six subsections, 6(1)(a) to 6(1)(f).[6] The pertinent subsections of Section 6(1) and the populations entitled to registration under these subsections are as follows:

- Section 6(1)(a) applies to all persons actually registered (or entitled to be registered) as of 16 April 1985, including those who were entitled to registration from birth and those (women) who acquired registration through marriage to an Indian male under the provisions of the 1951/56 Indian Act.
- Section 6(1)(c) applies to those persons who became entitled to registration under Bill C-31 because they were removed from the Indian Register as a result of their (or their mother's) marriage to a non-Indian prior to 17 April 1985.
- Section 6(1)(d) applies to men (and their wives and children) who became entitled to registration under Bill C-31 because they had been removed from the Indian Register through "voluntary" enfranchisement.
- Section 6(1)(e) applies to all persons (men and women) who became entitled to registration under Bill C-31 because they had been removed from the Indian Register for residing outside of Canada for more than five years prior to 1951, or for joining a profession or obtaining a university degree prior to 1920.

- Section 6(1)(f) applies to persons both of whose parents are (or would be) entitled to registration under Bill C-31, including persons born prior to 17 April 1985 who became eligible for registration as a result of the changes introduced by Bill C-31, as well as persons born on or after 17 April 1985 who have two Registered Indian parents.

Under the provisions of Bill C-31, all members of the pre-Bill C-31 population were assigned registration under Section 6(1)(a). For those not entitled to be on the Indian Register as of 16 April 1985, the inheritance rules of Section 6 are applied retroactively. Retroactive application of the rules to the Bill C-31 population results in a variety of outcomes, including individuals who are entitled to registration under Sections 6(1)(c) to 6(1)(f) if they had been previously removed from the Indian Register or have (had) two parents entitled to registration under Section 6; persons entitled to registration under Section 6(2) if they have (had) one parent entitled to registration under Section 6(1) and one parent not entitled to registration; and some individuals who are not entitled to register, if they have (had) one parent entitled to registration under Section 6(2) and one parent who is not entitled to registration.[7]

Entitlement to Indian registration for those individuals born on or after 17 April 1985 is determined according to the new inheritance rules. All individuals comprising this post-Bill C-31 population can be registered under one of two subsections: Section 6(1)(f) if both parents are registered or Section 6(2) if one parent is registered under Section 6(1) and the other parent is not registered. Obviously these changes have a cascade of impacts on the First Nations peoples.

Population Impacts of Bill C-31 to 31 December 1999
The nature of the changes introduced by Bill C-31 leads to the potential for incremental population growth in the Registered Indian population through reinstatements and registrations; children born to Bill C-31 and pre-Bill C-31 registrants after 16 April 1985 who would not have qualified under the rules of the previous Indian Act; Indian women who have not been removed from the Indian Register since 17 April 1985 as a result of their marriage to non-Indian men; and Indian children who have not been removed from the Register as a result of the marriage of their mother to a non-Indian since 17 April 1985. It is interesting that under Bill C-31 a non-Indian woman can no longer acquire Indian registration through marriage to an Indian man. This has the possibility of reducing population growth, and it also marks a further increase in equality for First Nations women.

Figure 3.2   Annual applicants for registration under Bill C-31, 1990-99

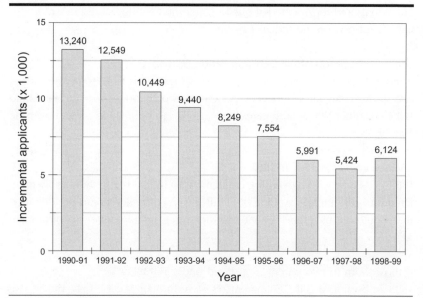

Bill C-31 Reinstatements and Registrations

Figure 3.2 illustrates the annual patterns of applicants for registration under Bill C-31. As of 31 December 1999, applications relating to 218,802 individuals had been filed with Indian and Northern Affairs Canada (INAC) (up from 139,800, an increase of about 79,000 over those that had been received nine years earlier).[8] Annual trend data for the 1990-99 period reveal a significant reduction in the number of new applicants over the period. For the last three years, the number of new applicants averaged about 5,850 annually, considerably less than one-half the number received annually at the outset of the decade. Further declines in the numbers of new applicants are expected in the future.

According to data compiled from the Reinstatement of Status Information System (RSIS) file maintained by INAC, roughly 114,700 individuals were registered under the provisions of Bill C-31 to 31 December 1999.[9] Over the decade there was a general slowdown in the number of new Bill C-31 registrations. Registrations over the course of the last three-year period (1997-99) averaged about 2,350 annually, less than one-half the number reported annually at the outset of the decade. As in the case of new applicants, the number of new registrations under Bill C-31 is expected to continue to decline in the future.

As of 31 December 1999, surviving Bill C-31 registrants numbered 106,781 individuals and represented about 16.3% of the total Registered Indian population reported on the Indian Register.

Other Components of Bill C-31 Population Growth

Although reinstatements and registrations under Bill C-31 form the largest and most readily identifiable component of population growth attributable to Bill C-31, other Bill C-31 changes have also led to population growth over the 1985-99 period.

Children Born after 16 April 1985

Bill C-31's new rules governing entitlement to Indian registration apply to all children born after 16 April 1985. Four groups of children can be identified that would not have been entitled to Indian registration under the old Indian Act:

- those born to two parents registered under Bill C-31
- those born to a Bill C-31 parent registered under Section 6(1) and whose other parent is not registered
- those born to a pre-Bill C-31 female and a non-Indian male
- those born to a pre-Bill C-31 female and a male registered under Bill C-31.

To assist in identifying the numbers of these children, a custom data file linking all children born between 17 April 1985 and 31 December 1999 to their parents has been constructed from the Indian Register. These data allow one to construct the "parenting" patterns of males and females within the Bill C-31 and pre-Bill C-31 population.[10] These patterns are summarized in Table 3.1 (data on children born to the specific parenting combinations noted above are in italics).

As of 31 December 1999, an estimated 59,798 children had been born who qualify for Indian registration due to the new rules of Bill C-31. Most of these children (about 77%) resulted from parenting between pre-Bill C-31 women and males who would not have been entitled to registration under the new or old rules. About 23% of these children resulted solely from parenting by individuals registered under Bill C-31.

Table 3.1 also reveals a large number of children born to women registered under Section 6(1) for whom information concerning fathers has not been provided to the Indian Register. Nationally, nearly 37,500 children, born since Bill C-31, have unstated fathers (over 16% all of children). These children qualify for registration under Bill C-31 and would have qualified under the previous Indian Act (provided that the father could not be proven to be non-Indian).

Table 3.1   Children born after 16 April 1985, showing Section 6 and Bill C-31 registry status of mother and father, to 31 December 1999

Father's registry status	Pre-Bill C-31 Sec. 6(1)	Bill C-31 Sec. 6(1)	Sec. 6(2)	Not registered	Total
		Mother's registry status			
Pre-Bill C-31					
Sec. 6(1)	103,977	2,900	5,281	21,197	133,355
Bill C-31					
Sec. 6(1)	*2,712*	*499*	*473*	*2,552*	6,236
Sec. 6(2)	*5,205*	*738*	*1,111*	0[a]	7,054
Not registered	*37,963*	*6,223*	0[a]	0[a]	44,186
Not stated	35,173	*2,322*	0[a]	0[a]	37,495
Total	185,030	12,682	6,865	23,749	228,326

Note: Excludes 372 children with unknown paternal and maternal detail.
a Unknown, as children would not qualify for registration.
Source: Indian Register, 31 December 1999 (adjusted for late birth reporting). (The Indian Register is subject to error due to the late reporting of births and other events. The procedure used in this study to adjust for late-reported births is described in a recent report by Clatworthy [2000b]).

Under Bill C-31, the registration entitlement of children with unstated fathers is based solely on their mothers' registry status. The 37,500 children with unstated fathers qualify for registration under Section 6(2), as their mothers are registered under Section 6(1). In the future, out-marriage by these children will result in offspring who are not entitled to registration. Bill C-31's changes in relation to unstated fathers have not had an incremental impact on the population entitled to Indian registration to this point in time. However, when children with unstated fathers become parents themselves, failure to identify fathers will result in a growing number of children who will not qualify for registration under the new rules, but who would have qualified under the previous rules. As such, Bill C-31's changes concerning the treatment of children with unstated fathers have quite significant implications for the future population entitled to Indian registration.

Retention of Women Who Married Non-Indians after 16 April 1985

As Bill C-31 no longer allows for the removal of women from the Indian Register for marriage to non-Indians, some portion of the population growth reported during the period derives from the retention (on the Register) of pre-Bill C-31 women who "marry out." As data concerning the actual marriage patterns of Registered Indians were not available for the time period, precise estimates of the number of women involved cannot be obtained. This number can be approximated by applying estimates of the total fertility rate of Registered Indian females to the number of children born to pre-Bill C-31 females and non-registered males.[11] Based on this procedure, 13,557 Indian women are estimated to have been retained on the Indian Register as a result of the new rules of Bill C-31.

Retention of Children Whose Mothers Married Non-Indians

The change from the previous Indian Act also resulted in Indian children remaining on the Register even where their mothers married non-Indians. This has also led to incremental growth in the Registered Indian population. For the same reasons noted above, the actual number is not available. Data contained in the RSIS file do allow one to estimate the ratio of children to women who were removed from the Register as a consequence of the woman's marriage to a non-Indian. As of 31 December 1999, this ratio was 0.137 (or 137 children for every 1,000 women). By applying this ratio to the estimated number of pre-Bill C-31 women retained (i.e., 13,557) during the period, the number of children retained is estimated to be 1,937.

Women Not Added through Marriage to Indian Males after 16 April 1985

The total fertility rate (TFR) procedure described above may also be used to provide a rough estimate of the number of non-Indian women who did not gain Indian registration through marriage to Indian men during the period. Application of the TFR to the number of children born after 16 April 1985 to pre-Bill C-31 males and non-registered females results in an estimate of 7,571 women who have not gained registration as a result of changes introduced by Bill C-31.

Summary of Bill C-31 Population Impacts to 31 December 1999

The individual components of population change associated with Bill C-31 can be aggregated to provide an estimate of the total incremental growth that has resulted from Bill C-31 during the period from 17 April 1985 to 31 December 1999. The total incremental growth of the national Registered Indian population during the period is estimated to be about 174,500 individuals, or 35% over that estimated under the rules of the previous Indian Act. Regional-level estimates reveal that Bill C-31 has contributed to significant incremental growth in the Registered Indian populations of all provinces/regions. Bill C-31–induced growth has been especially pronounced in the Yukon (73%), Northwest Territories (42%), Ontario (40%), and British Columbia (39%).

Based on the analyses undertaken for this chapter, the additional population growth associated with Bill C-31 has resulted in an incremental increase of about 79% to those residing off reserve and about 15% to the Registered Indian population residing on reserve.

Demographic Characteristics of the Bill C-31
and Pre-Bill C-31 Populations

As noted previously, the rules governing entitlement to Indian registration were not applied in the same fashion to the Bill C-31 and pre-Bill C-31 populations. As a consequence, these two components of the Registered Indian population exhibit differences with respect to gender composition and age structure. There are also differences in terms of registry status, but we do not pursue that issue in this chapter.

Gender Composition

The changes introduced by Bill C-31 were partially motivated by the desire to remove gender inequalities embedded in the old Indian Act and to restore registration to those who had lost their registration, mainly women, as a consequence of those inequalities. As a result, females form a larger segment of the Bill C-31 population registered under Section 6(1).[12] At the national level, nearly 72% of the Bill C-31 population registered under Section 6(1) is female, compared with about 50% of the pre-Bill C-31 population. Among the Bill C-31 population, females outnumber males by a wide margin, both on and off reserve.

Age Structure

Quite substantial age differentials also exist between the Bill C-31 and pre-Bill C-31 populations (Figure 3.3). In the on-reserve context, the average age of the Bill C-31 population registered under Section 6(1) in 1999 was roughly 43.5 years, about 15 years older than its pre-Bill C-31 counterpart. Among reserve residents registered under Section 6(2), the Bill C-31 population was about 24 years older, on average, than the pre-Bill C-31 population. Age differentials between the Bill C-31 and pre-Bill C-31 population were even larger among off-reserve residents.

The large age differentials identified in Figure 3.3 result from several factors. Many of the individuals reinstated under Bill C-31 had been removed from the Register as a result of clauses of the Indian Act that applied in earlier time periods (i.e., prior to 1985, 1951, or 1920). Second, the rules of Section 6 of Bill C-31 were applied only to descendants of the pre-Bill C-31 population born after 16 April 1985. As such, all of the pre-Bill C-31 population registered under Section 6(2) have been born since 1985. Third, some descendants of the Bill C-31 population (see Figure 3.1) do not qualify for registration under Bill C-31's rules. As a result, children (younger cohorts) tend to form a much smaller segment of the Bill C-31 population compared with the pre-Bill C-31 population.[13]

Figure 3.3 Average age of Registered Indian population, by location of residence, Bill C-31 status and Section 6 registry group, 1999

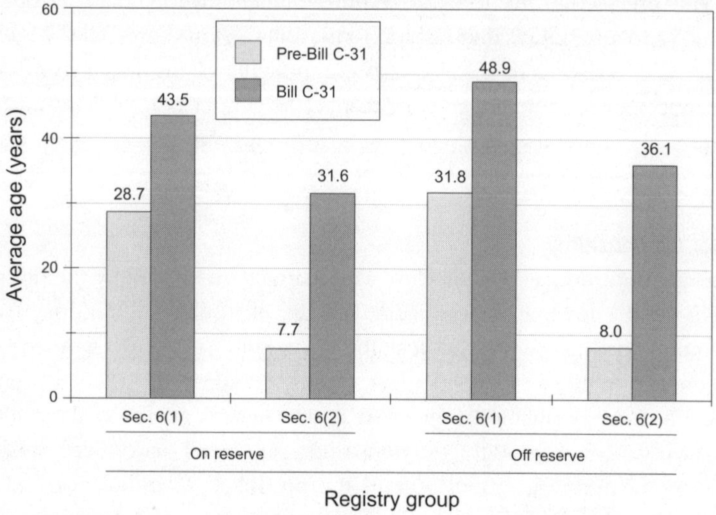

Source: Indian Register, 31 December 1999 (adjusted for late reporting).

The much older age structure of the Bill C-31 population suggests that Bill C-31 has likely resulted in a shift of the age structure of the Registered Indian population toward older age cohorts. This finding also implies that in the future, population growth associated with the existing Bill C-31 population is likely to decline rapidly, as the majority of this population has already passed the prime ages for childbearing. This will impact public policy directly.

Projecting the Longer-Term Population Impacts of Bill C-31

The preceding analysis demonstrates that the changes introduced by Bill C-31 have led to substantial short-term growth in the Registered Indian population, especially off reserve. The rules governing entitlement imply that future descendants may lose entitlement to registration through the process of out-marriage. Two successive generations of out-marriage will result in the loss of entitlement to Indian registration for the offspring of the second generation.

A projection methodology initially developed by Clatworthy and Smith (1992) and subsequently refined by Clatworthy (1993, 1999b, 2000a) has been used to explore the future impacts of Bill C-31's rules on the population entitled to Indian registration. The method uses a cohort-survival model adapted to incorporate not only fertility, mortality (survival), and migration but also the rules governing entitlement to Indian registration (i.e., Section 6 of Bill C-31) and parenting patterns. To accommodate additional issues of interest to this study, several refinements have been incorporated into the projection model.[14] These changes create the opportunity to isolate the contribution of Bill C-31 registrants to future changes in the population, and to explore the population effects of altering the rules governing entitlement to registration. The next step in this chapter is to apply the model to specific scenarios, to examine the effect of continuation of the status quo under Bill C-31, while also providing comparisons based on the "old Act" rules (i.e., as though Bill C-31 had not occurred).

Components of the Projection Model

Although standard population projections are typically designed to incorporate only five factors (the age and gender structure, female fertility, mortality, and migration), legislation governing Indian registration requires that several additional factors also be explicitly incorporated into the projection model. These additional factors include:

- the Section 6 registry status of the baseline population
- the fertility characteristics of not only females but also males
- future additions to the population through Bill C-31 registrations
- the parenting patterns of males and females (rates of out-marriage).

Projection Results: Continuation of the Current Rules (Bill C-31 Status Quo)

In the scenario where the current rules of Bill C-31 continue, the total population of survivors and descendants is projected to increase throughout the 100-year projection period from the current level of about 698,000 to about 2.1 million after four generations (see Figure 3.4). The population entitled to Indian registration would grow for about two generations (fifty years), reaching a peak of about 1.1 million. Thereafter, accelerating declines would reduce the population entitled to registration to about 768,500 after four generations. The number of survivors and descendants who do not qualify for registration is expected to increase from the current level of about 21,700 to nearly 400,000 within two generations. After three generations (year 2074), individuals who are not entitled to registration are projected to form the majority of the population.

Figure 3.5 illustrates the projected population entitled to Indian registration according to Bill C-31 and pre-Bill C-31 ancestry. Individuals who trace their ancestry entirely through the pre-Bill C-31 population are expected to increase from the current level of about 540,800 individuals to about 864,800 individuals over the next two generations. Over the course of the following two generations, this segment of the Registered Indian population is expected to decline to about 547,400 individuals. By way of contrast, the Bill C-31 population (and descendants who trace their ancestry entirely through this population)

Figure 3.4   Population of survivors and descendants, by entitlement to Indian registration under the current rules of Bill C-31, 1999-2099 (projected)

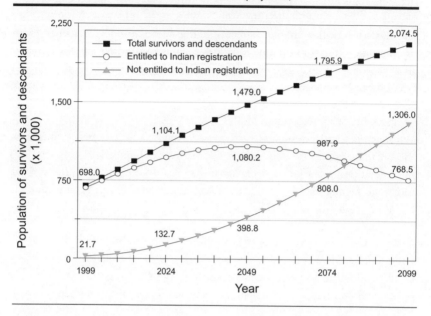

Figure 3.5   Population entitled to Indian registration, by Bill C-31 and pre-Bill C-31 ancestry group, 1999-2099 (projected)

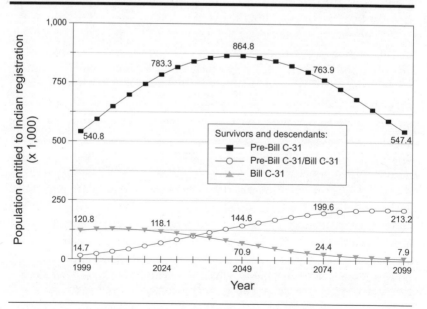

are expected to increase only slightly for about ten years. After that time, this component of the Registered Indian population is expected to decline at a gradual rate and include only 7,900 individuals after four generations.

The population resulting from intermarriage between pre-Bill C-31 and Bill C-31 registrants is projected to grow throughout most of the 100-year period from about 14,700 currently to about 213,200 after four generations. At that time, descendants with mixed Bill C-31 and pre-Bill C-31 ancestry would account for about 28% of the total population entitled to registration.

Entitlement to Indian Registration On and Off Reserve

Figure 3.6 displays the projected population entitled to Indian registration on and off reserve. The population on reserve is expected to increase for about 2.5 generations (sixty-five years), reaching a peak of about 811,000 individuals. Population declines after that point in time would reduce the on-reserve population entitled to registration to about 683,600 after four generations. In contrast to the situation on reserve, the off-reserve population entitled to registration is projected to increase for only twenty years, reaching a peak of about 317,000 individuals. After four generations, the off-reserve population entitled to registration is expected to be reduced to about 84,900 individuals.

Figure 3.6 Population entitled to Indian registration, by location of residence, 1999-2099 (projected)

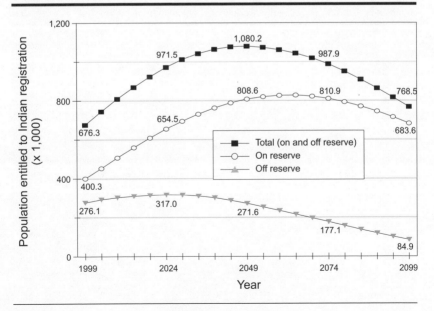

Although the population entitled to Indian registration is projected to increase for about two generations, Registered Indians are expected to form a declining share of the total population of survivors and descendants, both on and off reserve. On reserve, the share of survivors and descendants entitled to registration is expected to decline to about 83.5% after two generations. Within four generations, on-reserve descendants entitled to registration are projected to form a minority. More rapid declines in the share of survivors and descendants entitled to registration is projected to occur among the off-reserve population. Within two generations, individuals entitled to registration are expected to form only 53% of the surviving and descendant population. Within four generations, those entitled to registration are expected to form only 12% of all descendants.

Entitlement to Registration among Descendant Children

The declining share of the population entitled to Indian registration is projected to be much more pronounced among children. As illustrated in Figure 3.7, within two generations less than one-half of all children born to an Indian parent are expected to qualify for Indian registration. Children who qualify for registration on reserve are projected to form a minority within 2.5 generations. In the off-reserve context, this is projected to occur within twenty years. The projection's trends suggest that sometime around the end of the

Figure 3.7 Share of all children born during the prior five-year period with entitlement to Indian registration, by location of residence, 1999-2099 (projected)

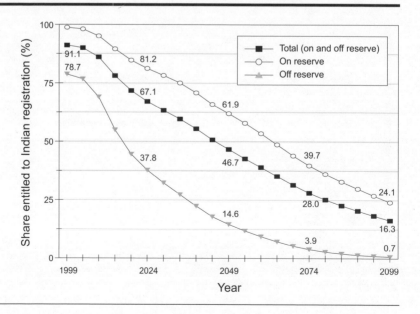

sixth generation, no further children would be born with entitlement to Indian registration.

Unstated paternity may be responsible for the loss of entitlement among a significant portion of descendant children. Children with unstated fathers and who are not entitled to Indian registration are currently estimated to number 13,000. Over the course of the next two generations, this number is expected to increase to about 127,800 if current rates of unstated paternity remain unchanged. Further increases after that point are expected to raise the number of non-entitled descendants with unstated fathers to more than 167,000.

Incremental Population Impacts of Bill C-31

As noted above, as of 31 December 1999, Bill C-31 had resulted in incremental growth in the Registered Indian population of about 174,500 individuals. As illustrated in Figure 3.8, the projected population entitled to registration under Bill C-31 is expected to remain substantially larger than that projected under the rules of the "old Act." The incremental contribution of Bill C-31's changes to growth in the Registered Indian population is expected to continue increasing for about two more generations, resulting in a Registered Indian population that is roughly 327,700 individuals larger than that projected under the old Act. Although further incremental growth is projected in both the on- and off-reserve contexts, most of the growth is

Figure 3.8   Incremental population entitled to Indian registration under Bill C-31 (versus the old Indian Act), by location of residence, 1999-2099 (projected)

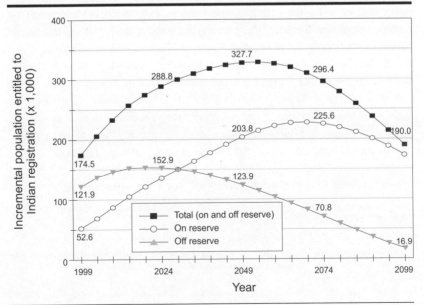

expected to occur on reserve. In the on-reserve context, the changes introduced by Bill C-31 are expected to result in an incremental population of 225,600 individuals entitled to registration within three generations.

Although the size of the growth increment associated with Bill C-31 is expected to decline after two generations (three generations on reserve), the projected trend suggests that in relation to the old Act, Bill C-31 could result in a larger population (than the old Act population) entitled to Indian registration for roughly six generations.

First Nations Membership

Under the previous Indian Act, the concepts of Indian registration and First Nations membership were equivalent. In other words, all Registered Indians were also First Nations members. Because Bill C-31 created the opportunity for individual First Nations to adopt their own rules governing membership eligibility, the population entitled to Indian registration may now differ from that eligible for First Nations membership. The distinction would appear to have quite important implications for the social and political structure of First Nations populations and communities.

First Nations membership implies political rights under the Indian Act. A "band member" is someone who, if eighteen years of age or older, is entitled to vote in elections or run for council. In many First Nations, membership may also be a defining criterion for access to a wide range of programs and services (such as housing and social assistance) administered by the First Nation. Being a Registered Indian, on the other hand, conveys another set of rights and benefits, for example, the right to exemption from taxation on reserve, eligibility for health services administered under the Non-Insured Health Benefits program of Health Canada, and access to postsecondary education assistance. I examine the impact of these "self-defined" rules as they affect our population numbers and the social sturcture in First Nations communities.

First Nations membership codes, in conjunction with Bill C-31's rules concerning Indian registration, have the potential to produce "classes" of citizens in First Nations communities, with quite different rights and entitlements. Inequalities among classes of citizens are likely to become embedded in the social and political life of First Nations and may serve to heighten tensions and conflicts within First Nations communities (see Clatworthy and Smith 1992).

Type of First Nations Membership Rules

A detailed review of all membership rules adopted by First Nations as of May 1992 indicates that there are four main types of membership rules. These include:

- *Indian Act rules,* where a person's eligibility for membership is determined on the basis of the rules governing entitlement to Indian registration, as set forth in Section 6 of Bill C-31
- *Unlimited one-parent rules,* where a person's eligibility for membership requires that at least one of the person's parents be a member
- *Blood quantum rules,* where a person's eligibility for membership is determined on the basis of the "amount of Indian blood" that the person possesses in relation to a minimum standard (most typically 50%)[15]
- *Two-parent rules,* where a person's eligibility for membership requires that both of the person's parents be members.

Table 3.2 identifies the distribution of First Nations by type of membership rule in May 1992. At that time, membership in the majority of First Nations was governed by the rules for determining Indian registration. These rules were identified to apply in 360 First Nations that did not adopt their own membership rules and 49 additional First Nations that adopted membership rules that were structurally equivalent to the rules of Section 6 of the Indian Act.[16] Collectively, these First Nations accounted for about 69% of all First Nations and contained about 70% of the national Registered Indian population.

The remaining 187 First Nations adopted membership rules that differed from those of the Indian Act. Membership in 90 First Nations was governed by unlimited one-parent rules. These First Nations accounted for about 15% of all First Nations and about 13% of the national population. Sixty-seven First Nations representing about 9% of the national population were identified as having two-parent membership rules. The remaining 30 First Nations, with about 8% of the national Registered Indian population, adopted various forms of blood quantum rules for determining membership eligibility.

Table 3.2 also reveals considerable variations among provinces/regions with respect to the types of rules governing band membership. Although Indian Act rules apply to the majority of First Nations in all provinces/regions, significant minorities of First Nations in all provinces/regions except Quebec have elected to use alternative rules. Membership rules that differ from those of the Indian Act are especially common among First Nations in Saskatchewan and Alberta.

Each type of membership rule contains provisions based on descent (i.e., the characteristics of one's parents). As such, the effects of the rules on the future population eligible for membership will be greatly influenced by marriage patterns. Depending upon the type of membership rule used, out-marriage (i.e., parenting between Indians and non-Indians or between members and non-members) will produce descendants who differ with respect to

Table 3.2 Distribution of First Nations membership rules by type and province/region, 1992

Province/ region	Type of membership rule				
	Indian Act or equivalent	Unlimited one-parent	Two-parent	Blood quantum	Total
Atlantic region	21 (67.7%)	4 (12.9%)	6 (19.4%)	0 (0.0%)	31 (100.0%)
Quebec	36 (90.0%)	4 (10.0%)	0 (0.0%)	0 (0.0%)	40 (100.0%)
Ontario	82 (65.1%)	19 (15.1%)	11 (8.7%)	14 (11.1%)	126 (100.0%)
Manitoba	50 (83.3%)	8 (13.3%)	0 (0.0%)	2 (3.3%)	60 (100.0%)
Saskatchewan	38 (55.9%)	5 (7.4%)	24 (35.3%)	1 (1.5%)	68 (100.0%)
Alberta	23 (54.8%)	10 (23.8%)	3 (7.1%)	6 (14.3%)	42 (100.0%)
British Columbia	135 (69.2%)	34 (17.4%)	23 (11.8%)	3 (1.5%)	195 (100.0%)
Northern Canada	24 (70.6%)	6 (17.6%)	0 (0.0%)	4 (11.8%)	34 (100.0%)
Canada	**409 (68.6%)**	**90 (15.1%)**	**67 (11.2%)**	**30 (5.0%)**	**596 (100.0%)**

membership eligibility and registration entitlement. Collectively, the various rules have the potential to produce four different classes of citizens:

- Registered Indian members – those who are eligible for band membership and are also entitled to Indian registration
- Registered Indian non-members – those who are entitled to Indian registration but do not meet the requirements for band membership
- Non-registered members – those who meet the requirements of band membership but who do not qualify for Indian registration
- Non-registered non-members – those who meet neither the requirements for band membership nor those for Indian registration.

The specific citizen groups (and the relative size of the groups) that emerge in individual First Nations depends largely on two factors: the type of membership rule followed and the rate of out-marriage. The possible impacts of the various types of rules on First Nations populations are very policy-relevant and deserve some elaboration. We can see that the effects of the different rules are of concern to both the Canadian government and First Nations leadership.

Indian Act or Equivalent Membership Rules

First Nations that follow the rules of the Indian Act for determining membership can be expected to contain two classes of citizens: those who are entitled to both Indian registration and membership and those who are entitled to neither registration nor membership. The population projections presented earlier in this chapter serve to illustrate what might be expected to occur with respect to the population composition in these First Nations. First Nations with rates of out-marriage similar to the national average are expected to face a future in which an ever-increasing segment of their population fails to meet the requirements for Indian registration and membership. Within two generations, those lacking entitlement to registration and membership are projected to form about one-quarter of the total population. Within four generations, the non-entitled population is expected to form a majority. The rate of growth of the non-entitled segment of First Nations populations that follow the Indian Act rules will be greatly affected by out-marriage rates. In general, each 10 percentage point increase (decrease) in the rate of out-marriage has the effect of reducing (extending) by about one decade the length of time required for the non-entitled population to form a majority.

Unlimited One-Parent Membership Rules

Under this type of membership rule, descendants are eligible for membership

Figure 3.9   Effects of out-marriage on membership and Indian registration in bands with an unlimited one-parent membership rule

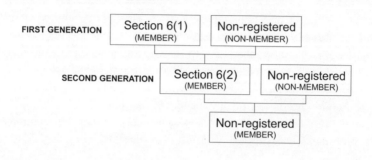

even if only one parent is a member, regardless of the registration status of the descendant. As illustrated in Figure 3.9, out-marriage within the context of this type of membership rule can result in two groups of descendants: a group eligible for both membership and Indian registration, and a group eligible for membership but not Indian registration.

The nature of the population changes that are expected to occur in First Nations that follow unlimited one-parent membership rules can be illustrated with the results of a custom membership projection constructed recently for the Little Black River First Nation (Clatworthy 2001a).[17] The 1999 rates of out-marriage estimated for Little Black River (about 35% on reserve and 70% off reserve) are about 10 percentage points higher than the national averages.

Figure 3.10 illustrates the projected structure of the member population of the Black River First Nation according to entitlement to Indian registration. Members of the Little Black River First Nation who are also entitled to Indian registration are projected to form a declining segment of the total population throughout the period. The projection results suggest that Registered Indians would form a minority of members within 3 generations and would be reduced to less than 30% of all members after 4 generations. Based on the projected trend over 4 generations, the Registered Indian component of the Little Black River member population is expected to be reduced to zero within about 5.5 generations. This is not a unique case and the implications are staggering in terms of the flow of resources from the state, for example.

Blood Quantum Membership Rules
As noted above, thirty First Nations adopted membership rules that establish eligibility for membership on the basis of the amount of Indian blood that a person possesses. Most (twenty-one) of these First Nations set the minimum blood quantum for membership at 50%. Within the context of out-marriage,

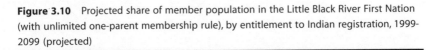

Figure 3.10   Projected share of member population in the Little Black River First Nation (with unlimited one-parent membership rule), by entitlement to Indian registration, 1999-2099 (projected)

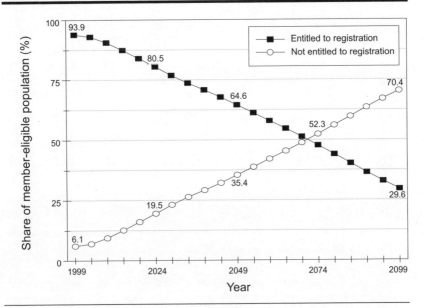

this type of blood quantum membership rule has the potential to create three classes of descendants: those who are entitled to both Indian registration and membership, those who are entitled to Indian registration but who are not eligible for membership, and those who are entitled to neither registration nor membership. A 50% minimum blood quantum rule is more restrictive in terms of the population admitted into membership than the rules of the Indian Act. Therefore, some portion of the Registered Indian population will not meet the minimum blood quantum for membership.

The results of a recent membership projection model developed for the Cumberland House First Nation can be used to illustrate the nature of population changes that can occur in First Nations that use 50% blood quantum rules. The 1999 rate of out-marriage of the population of Cumberland House is estimated to be about 52%, roughly 1.5 times higher than the national average.

Figure 3.11 illustrates the projected distribution of the population of survivors and descendants of Cumberland House by eligibility for Indian registration and membership. It suggests that the share of the Cumberland House population that is eligible for both Indian registration and membership will decline throughout the period and form a minority of all survivors and descendants within about 2.5 generations (about sixty years). Within about three

Figure 3.11   Projected share of survivors and descendants in the Cumberland House First Nation (blood quantum membership rule), by eligibility for band membership and entitlement to Indian registration, 1999-2099 (projected)

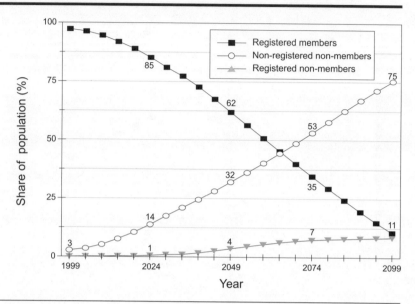

generations, the population eligible for neither membership nor Indian registration is projected to become a growing majority. After four generations, this group would account for about 75% of the total population. The projections also suggest that a growing segment of the Registered Indian population will not meet the blood quantum requirements for membership. Within about two generations this population is projected to form about 4% of the total population and about 10% of the population entitled to registration. After four generations, this group would form about 11% of the total population and nearly one-half of the population eligible for Indian registration.

Two-Parent Membership Rules

Two-parent membership rules form the most restrictive rules identified. Under this type of rule, descendants are eligible for membership only if both parents are members. One out-marriage by a member extinguishes eligibility for membership for all future descendants of that member, regardless of the descendant's entitlement to Indian registration.

Like blood quantum membership rules, two-parent rules create three classes of descendants: those entitled to both registration and membership, those entitled to registration but not eligible for membership, and those eligible for neither registration nor membership. The highly restrictive nature of

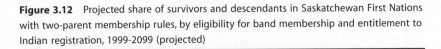

Figure 3.12   Projected share of survivors and descendants in Saskatchewan First Nations with two-parent membership rules, by eligibility for band membership and entitlement to Indian registration, 1999-2099 (projected)

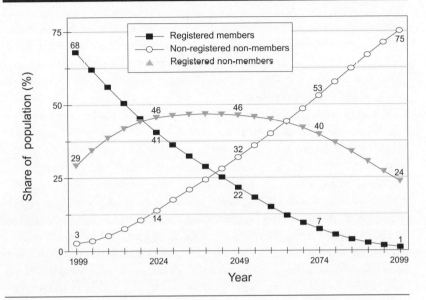

two-parent rules implies that even when low rates of out-marriage prevail, a large portion of the future population of the First Nation will not qualify for membership.

All of the sixty-seven First Nations that adopted this type of membership rule are expected to experience quite rapid changes to the registration and membership structure of their populations. The extent and nature of these population changes can be illustrated with the results of a membership projection constructed for a group of First Nations in Saskatchewan that have adopted this type of membership code. First Nations comprising this group (which includes Lucky Man, Yellowquill, Kahkewistahaw, Standing Buffalo, Fishing Lake, Canoe Lake, Flying Dust, English River, Big C, and Turnor Lake) are similar in that they have 1999 out-marriage rates that are about 1.5 times the national average.

Figure 3.12 displays the projected distribution of survivors and descendants of this group of First Nations according to membership and registration eligibility. It indicates that the share of the population eligible for both registration and membership is expected to decline very rapidly. This population subgroup is projected to form a minority of all survivors and descendants within fifteen years and be reduced to nearly zero over the course of four generations.

The projection suggests that within one generation, the majority of the population entitled to Indian registration will not be eligible for membership. This population subgroup (registered non-members) would form the largest segment of the total population during the second and third generation. Very rapid growth is also projected in the share of the population that is eligible for neither registration nor membership. Within about three generations, this subgroup is expected to form a majority of the population of survivors and descendants.

Implications and Conclusions

This chapter has explored the nature of the main changes introduced by the 1985 amendments to the Indian Act (Bill C-31) and some of the short- and longer-term impacts of these changes on First Nations populations. In the short term (1985-1999), the changes introduced by Bill C-31 have had quite substantial impacts in terms of increasing population growth. The increase to the national population of Registered Indians is estimated at 35%. A significant majority of this short-term growth has occurred as a result of reinstatements and registrations. Much of this growth has accrued to the off-reserve population and has served to increase the size of the off-reserve population by nearly 80%. In general, the short-term population impacts of Bill C-31 on First Nations reserves have been modest and have resulted in incremental growth of about 15%.

As new reinstatements and registrations have declined markedly and are expected to continue to decline, this factor will constitute a small and declining component of future population growth. Nevertheless, in relation to the previous Indian Act, Bill C-31 is expected to continue to result in significant levels of incremental population growth for about two more generations (about fifty years). The main source of incremental growth during this period will not be new reinstatements or registrations but rather the changes introduced by Bill C-31 to the rules governing entitlement to Indian registration (i.e., Section 6). In contrast to the growth resulting from reinstatements and registrations, which largely occurred off reserve, most of the incremental growth associated with the new rules governing entitlement to registration is expected to occur on reserve over the next two generations.

Although Bill C-31's registration rules are projected to result in a larger population entitled to Indian registration for about five more generations, these rules are expected to deny registration to a growing segment of descendants. Within two generations, most of the children born to First Nations populations are not expected to qualify for registration under the new rules. Within four generations, only one of every six children born to First Nations populations is expected to qualify for registration. Unlike the rules of the old

Act, which guaranteed registration to nearly all of the descendants of Registered Indian males, Bill C-31's rules have the potential to result in the extinction of the Registered Indian population.

The loss of entitlement to Indian registration among growing numbers of descendants is likely to result in very pronounced changes in the demographic composition of the Registered Indian population, including a pronounced shift in the population's age structure to older age cohorts. Demographic changes will also be accompanied by pronounced changes in the political and social structure of First Nations communities, as the new rules governing entitlement to Indian registration interact with First Nations membership rules to form classes of First Nations citizens with unequal rights and entitlements.

Those First Nations that follow the rules of the Indian Act for determining membership will face a future with two classes of descendants: a group entitled to the rights and benefits of both Indian registration and First Nations membership and a second group that lacks these rights and entitlements. Given prevailing levels of out-marriage, this latter group is expected to form a majority of descendants within about three generations.

First Nations that have adopted one-parent membership rules will confront a future where all descendants are eligible for membership, but where a growing segment of the member population lacks entitlement to the Indian registration. Within about three generations, these "non-Indian" descendants are expected to form the majority of their membership.

First Nations that follow two-parent membership rules will experience a future in which a growing share of descendants (including many Registered Indians) will lack the rights and benefits of membership. At current levels of out-marriage, non-members would form the majority of their Registered Indian populations within one generation. Within two generations, the population entitled to both registration and membership would form a small and dwindling minority. A similar class structure and sequence of events is expected among those First Nations using blood quantum membership rules.

Inequalities associated with these class distinctions would appear to have several quite serious implications for the political and social stability of First Nations and for their economic, social, and political development. There are clearly implications for the cohesion of communities, as outlined in Chapter 1 of this book. These inequalities have the potential not only to produce or enhance internal conflicts within First Nations communities but also to lead to legal challenges and jurisdictional squabbles among governments (First Nations, federal, and provincial) over responsibilities for the provision and funding of services to the various classes of First Nations populations.

Many First Nations are continuing to seek ways to extend or improve their systems of governance or to achieve self-governance. The concepts of citizenship and social inclusion are fundamental to governance. From the perspective of citizenship and social inclusion, the registration rules of Bill C-31 and the various forms of membership rules adopted by First Nations would appear to be highly problematic. Bill C-31's rules concerning Indian registration will in the short term result in the denial of citizenship to many First Nations descendants. In the long term, these rules will lead to the extinction of First Nations (as defined under the Indian Act).

Other types of membership rules are also problematic in that they serve to separate political rights from other rights. These rules are likely to result in political systems where some have power while others do not, or in political systems where all share political power but where only some have access to other rights and benefits. Like the current Indian Act, the First Nations membership codes that have emerged from it also embrace inequality as an underlying principle and would appear to provide an unsatisfactory basis for defining citizenship in self-governing First Nations. Given the state of current affairs, the task of resolving issues of citizenship would appear to represent the most fundamental and demanding challenge to First Nations as they proceed toward self-governance.

Notes

1   Some prior research concerning the impacts of Bill C-31 has been undertaken. The 1990 report published by INAC entitled *Impacts of the 1985 Amendments to the Indian Act (Bill C-31)* provided a national review of selected impacts, including an assessment of short-term population impacts. Wherrett (1990) provides a review of the major changes introduced by Bill C-31, and some analysis of short-term population impacts. At the national level, prior studies of the longer-term population implications of Bill C-31 have been undertaken by Clatworthy and Smith (1992) and Clatworthy (1993). In addition to these national studies, a few studies have explored the short- and longer-term population impacts of Bill C-31 on specific First Nations or groups of First Nations, including Smith 1991; Clatworthy 1991, 1998, 1999a, 2001a, 2001b; and United Anishnaabeg Councils 1999.

2   Jamieson's work (1978) traces the history of the system of inheritance through the male line back to the Indian Act of 1869, two years after Confederation. This system remained in effect up to the time of Bill C-31's enactment.

3   Who could be removed by successful band or individual protest within twelve months of registration.

4   See Sections 6(1) and 6(2).

5   The inheritance rules contained in Section 6 of Bill C-31 are effectively the same as a gender-neutral version of the "double mother" clause – Section 12(1)(a)(iv) – contained in the previous Indian Act.

6   Section 6(1)(b) relates to people registered to newly created bands after 1985 and is not pertinent to our discussion.

7   The retroactive application of Bill C-31's rules to the population not on the Indian Register as of 16 April 1985 is one basis for claims (and litigation) that Bill C-31 continues to discriminate against the descendants of women who were removed from

the Register through marriage to a non-Indian (i.e., out-marriage). Some of these descendants – those registered under Section 6(2) – are able to pass entitlement to their children only if they parent with another Registered Indian. A child born to a Bill C-31 descendant who does not meet the requirements for registration under Bill C-31 will qualify for registration only if the child's other parent is registered under Section 6(1). By way of contrast, a child born to any member of the pre-Bill C-31 population will qualify for registration, regardless of the registration status of the child's other parent.

8 Statistical data concerning registrations under Bill C-31 are contained in two data files maintained by Indian and Northern Affairs Canada (INAC): the Reinstatement of Status Information System (RSIS) and the Indian Register System (IRS). The former system provides not only counts of registrations but also counts of applications and applicants for registration.

9 The actual number of registrations reported in 1999 is 123,964. This number, however, includes 9,220 individuals registered under Section 6(1)(a). These individuals are believed to be entitled to registration under the previous Indian Act and are not considered to be part of the Bill C-31 population.

10 As the Indian Register contains data only for those children who are registered, it is not possible to provide a complete picture of Registered Indian parenting. Specifically, children born to an Indian registered under Section 6(2) and a non-Indian do not qualify for registration and are not on the Register.

11 The total fertility rate (TFR) estimates used in this study are those reported by Nault et al. (1993) for 1990. At the national level, this rate was 2.72. The regional estimates of the Bill C-31 growth components developed for this study apply the regional TFR estimates prepared by Nault et al. National-level estimates of Bill C-31–induced growth are derived from aggregating the regional growth estimates.

12 The Bill C-31 population registered under Section 6(2) consists of the children of those registered under Bill C-31 who are registered under Section 6(1). As such, the gender composition of the Section 6(2) population does not differ greatly between the Bill C-31 and pre-Bill C-31 population.

13 Some portion of the age differential between Bill C-31 and pre-Bill C-31 registrants may also result from differences in mortality. Data concerning the mortality characteristics of the two components of the Registered Indian population are not available at present.

14 These include modifications to the model's birth assignment components that enable the allocation of future births not only to Section 6 registry groups but also to gender and Bill C-31 status groups; the inclusion of separate fertility, survival, and on-/off-reserve migration parameters for females and males; and the inclusion of separate out-marriage rates for females and males and for the Bill C-31 and pre-Bill C-31 populations.

15 The typology developed by Clatworthy and Smith also distinguished membership rules on the basis of additional, discretionary criteria. These criteria, which included residency requirements, acceptance of cultural norms/values of the community, language ability, marital status, and sibling membership status, tended to be restrictive in nature and would likely serve to further limit access to membership.

16 The forty-nine First Nations referred to here adopted what Clatworthy and Smith (1992) referred to as limited one-parent membership rules. Under this type of rule, a person can qualify for membership when two conditions are met: the person has at least one parent who is a member and the person is entitled to Indian registration. Together, these two conditions are the same as the rules governing entitlement to Indian registration.

17 The projection models highlighted in this and succeeding sections have been constructed to incorporate the age, registration, membership, fertility, and migration characteristics of each First Nation population, as well as the First Nation's membership rules.

References

Clatworthy, S. 1991. *Future Population Eligible for Indian Registration and Band Membership: Select Communities of the Meadow Lake Tribal Council.* Meadow Lake, SK: Meadow Lake Tribal Council.

–. 1993. *Revised Projection Scenarios Concerning the Population Implications of Section 6 of the Indian Act.* Ottawa: Indian and Northern Affairs Canada.

–. 1998. *Population and Membership Projection: Mohawks of Kahnawake.* Ottawa: Research and Analysis Directorate, Indian and Northern Affairs Canada.

–. 1999a. *Population Implications of Proposed Revisions to the Blood Tribe Membership Code.* Standoff, AB: Blood Tribe Membership Review Committee, Blood Tribe.

–. 1999b. *Projection of the Registration Status of Descendants of the Registered Indian Population: 1998-2032.* Ottawa: Information Analysis Section, Indian and Northern Affairs Canada.

–. 2000a. *Re-assessing the Population Impacts of Bill C-31.* Ottawa: Research and Analysis Directorate, Indian and Northern Affairs Canada.

–. 2000b. *Paternal Identity and Entitlement to Indian Registration: The Manitoba Context.* Ottawa: Research and Analysis Directorate, Indian and Northern Affairs Canada.

–. 2001a. *First Nations Membership and Indian Registration.* Winnipeg: Manitoba Southern Chiefs Organization.

–. 2001b. Membership and Indian registration: Implications of Bill C-31 for First Nations in Saskatchewan. Paper presented at the Federation of Saskatchewan Indians Membership/Citizenship Symposium, Regina, 2001.

Clatworthy, S., and A.H. Smith. 1992. *Population Implications of the 1985 Amendments to the Indian Act.* Ottawa: Assembly of First Nations.

INAC. 1990. *Impacts of the 1985 Amendments to the Indian Act (Bill C-31).* Ottawa: Research and Analysis Directorate, Indian and Northern Affairs Canada.

Jamieson, K. 1978. *Indian Women and the Law in Canada: Citizens Minus.* Ottawa: Supply and Services Canada.

Nault, F., J. Chen, M.V. George, and M.J. Norris. 1993. *Population Projections of Registered Indians, 1991-2016.* Report prepared by Population Projections Section, Demography Division, Statistics Canada, for Indian and Northern Affairs Canada.

Smith, A.H. 1991. *Bill C-31 Impact Study: Meadow Lake First Nations,* vol. 2. Meadow Lake, SK: Meadow Lake Tribal Council.

United Anishnaabeg Councils. 1999. *Impacts of the Authority to Determine Band Membership.* Ottawa: Research and Analysis Directorate, Indian and Northern Affairs Canada.

Wherret, J. 1990. *Indian Status and Band Membership.* Ottawa: Political and Social Affairs Division, Library of Parliament.

4
Changing Ethnicity:
The Concept of Ethnic Drifters
Eric Guimond

From 1971 to 1996, Aboriginal populations defined on the basis of ancestry more than tripled in size (+252%), increasing from 312,800 to 1,102,000 persons. By comparison, the total increase in the Canadian population as a whole was 30% during the same period. To triple in twenty-five years, a population must experience phenomenal annual growth rates. Among Aboriginal populations, growth rates equal to and in excess of 7% were observed during the periods 1981-86 and 1986-91 (Figure 4.1). These increases greatly exceed the maximum of 5.5% per year that is theoretically possible for a population that is subject only to the natural movement of births and deaths.[1] The growth rates are above 5.5% for populations reporting Aboriginal origin. A population maintaining a growth rate of 5.5% per year doubles every thirteen years. After a hundred years, that population would be more than 200 times larger than at the outset. Clearly, phenomena other than fertility and mortality are at work here. It is important that we determine what they are, as they have repercussions on the people themselves and the policies that are developed concerning Aboriginal Canada.

In this chapter, I first document the extent of the observed growth among the Aboriginal groups. Once growth patterns are established, I identify and evaluate the different components of this growth, moving from the better-known components of fertility and migration to the unexpected component of ethnic mobility. This unexpected component has profound implications in terms of interpretation of demographic and socio-economic trends. Three illustrations of the compositional effect of ethnic mobility are presented. Finally, this chapter concludes with a brief overview of possible explanations for ethnic mobility and the policy implications that emanate from this phenomenon.

The data used for this analysis are from the 1986 and 1996 Censuses of Canada and the 1991 Aboriginal Peoples Survey (APS). The available information enables us to distinguish populations of Aboriginal origin according

Figure 4.1   Average annual growth rates of the population of Aboriginal origin and the total population of Canada, 1971-96

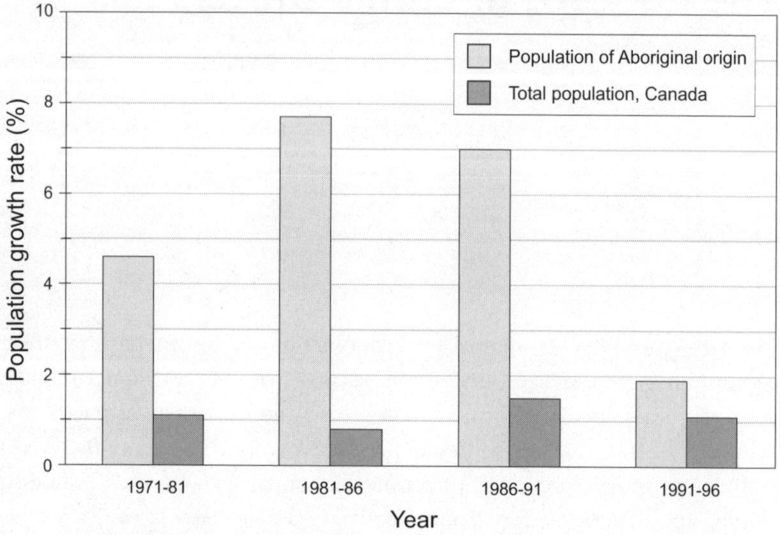

Sources: Statistics Canada, 1971-96 Censuses of Canada.

to Aboriginal identity, a concept first introduced in 1986[2] in order to improve the enumeration of Aboriginal populations (Statistique Canada 1989). The concept of origin refers to the ethnic or cultural group to which one's ancestors belonged, while the concept of identity refers to the respondent's current ethnic identification or sense of belonging. The question on Aboriginal identity in the 1996 Census contains four response choices: Indian, Métis, Inuit, and non-Aboriginal. In this particular study, we focus exclusively on those persons with an Aboriginal origin who self-identify as Indian, Métis, or Inuit, excluding persons with Aboriginal origin but no Aboriginal identity.[3]

Growth of Canada's Aboriginal Populations from 1986 to 1996
From 1986 to 1996, Aboriginal populations grew from 464,500 persons to 718,950 persons, with the bulk of the increase occurring in the first five-year period (Table 4.1).[4] This increase varied considerably depending on the identity reported. The North American Indian population, which accounts for nearly two-thirds of the whole, grew from 329,700 persons to 494,800 persons from 1986 to 1996. More than for any other Aboriginal group, the explosive growth of the Indian population during the first five-year period (7.1%) contrasts with the low growth in the second period (0.9%). Remarkably, the growth rate for this last intercensal period is lower than for the Canadian population (1.2%) as a whole!

Table 4.1 Population size and growth rate of Aboriginal-identity populations, 1986-96

Aboriginal group	1986		1991		1996		Average annual growth rate[a] (%)	
	N	%	N	%	N	%	1986-91	1991-96
Total Aboriginal	464,455	100.0	613,820	100.0	718,950	100.0	6.6	2.3
North American Indian	329,730	71.0	443,285	72.2	494,830	68.8	7.1	0.9
Métis	103,085	22.2	128,700	21.0	178,525	24.8	5.1	6.7
Inuit	30,105	6.5	35,495	5.8	39,705	5.5	3.4	2.3
Multiple Aboriginal	1,540	0.3	6,340	1.0	5,880	0.8	33.4	-1.5

a Adjusted for partially enumerated Aboriginal communities.
Source: Statistics Canada, 1986 and 1996 Censuses of Canada, special tabulations; Statistics Canada, 1991 Aboriginal Peoples Survey, special tabulations.

The number of Métis rose from 103,100 persons in 1986 to 178,500 persons in 1996. At 5.1%, the annual growth rate of the Métis population from 1986 to 1991 was already near the theoretical maximum for natural increase of 5.5% per year, but from 1991 to 1996 it was even higher (6.7%). Among the Inuit, the numbers climbed from 30,100 to 39,700 persons, with faster growth in the first five-year period (3.4%). This was the only Aboriginal group to grow at a rate below the theoretical maximum in both periods.

Components of Population Growth

Natural Increase

The natural increase of a population is the difference between the number of children born and the number of persons who die in a given period. If we assume that Aboriginal populations perpetuate themselves solely through births, then natural increase and the total increase should logically be equal. As Figure 4.2 shows, however, this is far from the case. Surprising differences between the natural increase and the total increase of the Indian and Métis populations are observed for both periods. Only among the Inuit does the total increase approach the natural increase.

Clearly, while the Aboriginal populations have more children, as reflected by the high natural increase, than the Canadian population as a whole, this alone does not explain their exceptional growth. Since the contribution of international migration is virtually nil,[5] other factors must be considered (Clatworthy 1996).

Variation in the Quality of Enumerations

It is a known fact that in each enumeration exercise, some individuals are missed (undercoverage), while others are counted more than once (overcoverage). The difference between these two quantities is called *net undercoverage*. It is not so much the value of undercoverage that causes concern in our ability to measure growth but rather the variation in that value from one census to the next. In the absence of any variation, the enumerated and missed populations increase at the same rate, and undercoverage does not bias the measurement of growth rates. If, on the other hand, net undercoverage varies, then the error on growth rate estimates is proportional, but its sign is opposite to that of the variation. Therefore, an increase in undercoverage results in an underestimation of growth, while a decrease in undercoverage results in an overestimation of growth.

In order for differential undercoverage to be the only explanation for the difference observed between the 7% increase in the Indian population between 1986 and 1991 and the highest rate of natural increase observed at present (3.5%), the quality of enumeration would have to have improved by

Figure 4.2 Average annual natural increase and total growth rates of Aboriginal-identity populations, 1986-91 and 1991-96 (adjusted for partially enumerated Aboriginal communities)

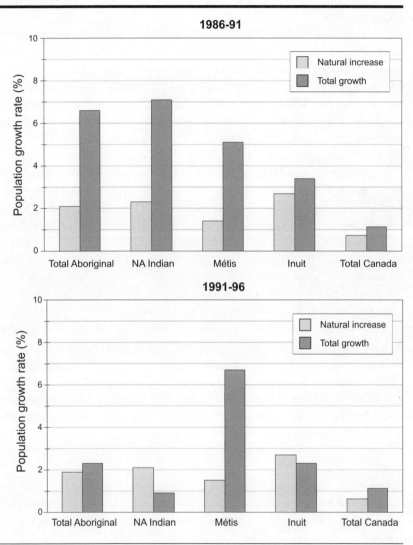

Sources: Statistics Canada, 1986 and 1996 Censuses of Canada, special tabulations; Statistics Canada, 1991 Aboriginal Peoples Survey, special tabulations; Statistics Canada 1999.

more than 15% between 1986 and 1991. According to the information available on the undercoverage of the population residing on fully enumerated Indian reserves, there was no significant change in the quality of the enumeration between 1991 (12.6%)[6] and 1996 (13.4%).[7] On this basis, we can conclude that there is no significant error in the measurement of growth rates due to undercoverage.

Ethnic Mobility

The last avenue to explore leads us beyond the paths traditionally trod by demographers and sociologists, to how persons report their ethnicity in the censuses. In light of the information available, on natural increase, migration, and quality of enumeration, the extraordinary growth of Canada's Aboriginal populations from 1986 to 1996 is due, in variable proportions depending on the period and the Aboriginal group, to changes over time in the ethnic identity that individuals report. This phenomenon is known as ethnic mobility and, from the perspective of a specific group, it includes both entries and exits.

Thus, for the period 1986-91, when the phenomenon appears to have been more prevalent, transfers from a non-Aboriginal group to an Aboriginal group (entries) were more numerous than transfers from an Aboriginal group to a non-Aboriginal group (exits). This phenomenon of ethnic mobility has also been observed in the Aboriginal populations of the United States, Australia, and New Zealand (Guimond et al. 2000; Guimond et al. 2001; Ross 1996; Eschbach 1993; Pool 1991).

It is basically the exceptional nature of the growth of Aboriginal populations from 1986 to 1996 that draws attention to the existence of this phenomenon. However, ethnic mobility has long been a component of the demographic growth and changing composition of Canada's Aboriginal populations. There are numerous signs that it is a contributing factor to population changes:

- Persons of Aboriginal origin who report more than one ethnic origin outnumber those who report a single Aboriginal origin;[8] this is the cumulative result of several generations of ethnic mobility.
- More than a third of persons of Aboriginal origin do not identify with an Aboriginal group.[9]
- The Métis, the second largest Aboriginal group (see Table 4.1), are the product of ethnic mobility. Particular circumstances relating to the mode of colonization led to the emergence of this Aboriginal cultural group made up of descendants of Aboriginals and non-Aboriginals.

There are two types of ethnic mobility (Robitaille and Choinière 1987). The first type, intergenerational ethnic mobility, can occur when a child's ethnic affiliation is first stated. Parents and children do not necessarily have the same ethnic affiliation, especially when parents do not belong to the same ethnic group. The second type, intragenerational ethnic mobility, may result from a change in individuals' ethnic affiliation over time (i.e., between censuses). Only

Figure 4.3 Estimates of the net ethnic mobility rates of Aboriginal-identity populations, 1986-91 and 1991-96 (based on the residual estimates method, excluding children born during the interval)

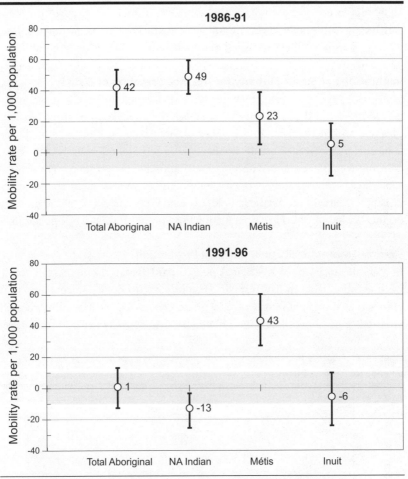

Sources: Statistics Canada, 1986 and 1996 Censuses of Canada, special tabulations; Statistics Canada, 1991 Aboriginal Peoples Survey, special tabulations.

the latter type of ethnic mobility is dealt with in this analysis. Estimates of ethnic mobility are obtained by the method of estimation by residual briefly described in Appendix 4.1.

For the period 1986-91, substantial net intragenerational ethnic mobility is observed for Aboriginal populations overall. According to available information on the other components, the balance of ethnic transfers stood at 103,200 persons, representing an average annual rate of 42 per 1,000 (Figure 4.3). Over the period 1986-96, ethnic mobility resulted in an increase of almost

20%. The population benefiting most from this phenomenon is the North American Indian population (49 per 1,000). For the period 1991-96, the ethnic mobility of Aboriginal populations as a group was negligible, although the Métis registered strong ethnic mobility (43 per 1,000). For the North American Indians, this intercensal period was characterized by negative ethnic mobility (-13 per 1,000), meaning that there were more exits than entries.

Implications of Ethnic Mobility for the Interpretation of Data

Ethnic mobility affects more than just the size of ethnic groups. It also contributes to the social demographic and socio-economic makeup of ethnic groups. This has serious implications for public policy. In this section, I highlight the compositional effects of ethnic mobility with three examples. In the first, I discuss trends in the residential distribution of Aboriginal populations. The second example describes the effect of ethnic mobility on another demographic component, fertility. In the final example, I consider the impact of ethnic mobility on the evolution of educational attainment among Aboriginal populations.

Effect of Ethnic Mobility on Residential Distribution

In 1996 the majority of Aboriginal people participating in the census (68%) were living outside Indian reserves (Figure 4.4), up by 3% since 1986. Most off-reserve Aboriginal people live in urban centres (47%). The proportion of urban Aboriginal people increased by more than 5% between 1986 and 1996.

Figure 4.4 Percentage distribution of Aboriginal-identity populations, by location of residence, 1986 and 1996

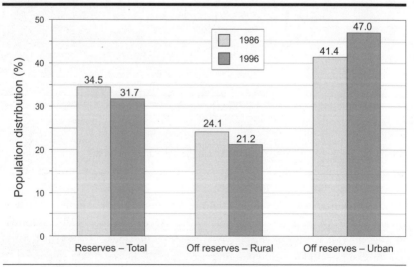

Sources: Statistics Canada, 1986 and 1996 Censuses of Canada, special tabulations.

Migration from Indian reserves is often proposed as an explanation for the variation in the residential distribution of Aboriginal populations, and more specifically for their sizeable increase in Canada's major urban centres. Recent studies (Norris et al. 2001; Clatworthy 1996) clearly show, however, that there is not a massive exodus of Aboriginal populations from Indian reserves to cities. In fact, from 1966 to 1996, Indian reserves posted a net gain due to migration. For the last two intercensal periods, Indian reserves showed a net migration of +9,200 persons (1986-91) and +14,100 persons (1991-96) (Norris et al. 2001). There have therefore been increases in both on-reserve and off-reserve populations.

Some would identify fertility as the single most important component of growth of the off-reserve population. Again, the available information does not support this statement. First, the fertility of Aboriginal populations is lower outside Indian reserves than on reserves. In 1996 the child/woman ratio[10] reached 0.55 in Indian reserves, compared with only 0.41 outside reserves. This fertility differential would have generated a faster growth of the on-reserve population if fertility was the single most important component of growth. Also, during the period 1986-91, Aboriginal populations in rural and urban off-reserve areas increased at the remarkable rate of 6.6% and 9.4% per year, respectively (Figure 4.5). These rates substantially exceed the theoretical maximum for natural increase (5.5%), which again means that growth cannot be explained by fertility alone. Thus, the ethnic mobility previously

Figure 4.5 Average annual growth rate of Aboriginal-identity populations, by location of residence, 1986-96 (adjusted for partially enumerated Aboriginal communities)

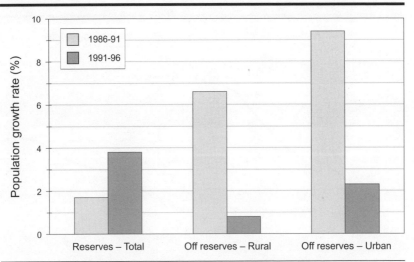

Sources: Statistics Canada, 1986 and 1996 Censuses of Canada, special tabulations; Statistics Canada, 1991 Aboriginal Peoples Survey, special tabulations.

identified and measured at the national scale is taking place outside Indian reserves,[11] mostly in urban centres. In terms of the compositional effect of ethnic mobility, we can therefore conclude the following: between 1986 and 1996, part of the increase in the percentage of Aboriginals living in urban areas was due to changes in self-identification by city dwellers, from non-Aboriginal to Aboriginal.

Effect of Ethnic Mobility on Fertility Trends

With this second example, we compare the fertility by age group of Aboriginal and non-Aboriginal women, as measured by the 1981 and 1991 Censuses of Canada. Numbers reveal that the average number of children ever born per woman has decreased between 1981 and 1991 for practically all ages, for both Aboriginal and non-Aboriginal women (see Figure 4.6). In a "normal" demographic situation, the observed downward trend in fertility could be interpreted as a consequence of the changing reproductive behaviour of women. But this analysis has already shown that Aboriginal groups are not following normal socio-demographic patterns.

Rather than comparing the fertility levels of age groups in 1981 and 1991, let us instead compare the fertility of women belonging to the same cohort. The same census information is used, but it is now classified according to the age of women in 1981 (i.e., a woman aged 45 in 1991 was 35 years old in 1981). Demographers refer to this technique as a cohort analysis. First focusing on

Figure 4.6 Average number of children ever born to women of Aboriginal and non-Aboriginal origin, by age group, 1981 and 1991

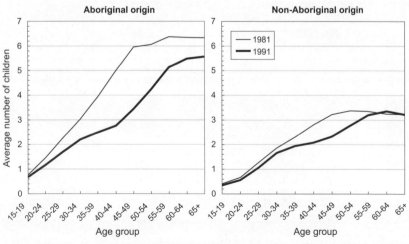

Sources: Statistics Canada, 1981 and 1991 Censuses of Canada, special tabulations.

non-Aboriginal women, we find no noticeable differences between 1981 and 1991 in the fertility of women aged 35 and over (see Figure 4.7). For these women, the family formation stage was completed by 1981.

For Aboriginal women, the situation is strikingly different and unusual. According to census data, the average number of children ever born to Aboriginal women belonging to the cohort aged 30 and over in 1981 decreased between 1981 and 1991 (see Figure 4.7). In other words, these Aboriginal women had "negative" children during that decade! Obviously this is impossible. This can be explained only by ethnic mobility.[12] Between 1981 and 1991, the observed decrease in the fertility of Aboriginal women aged 30 and over is due to women with low fertility "moving into" the Aboriginal population during that period. In other words, by self-reporting as Aboriginal in 1991, contrary to 1981, these low-fertility women have decreased the overall fertility of Aboriginal women.

This has policy implications. If this very rapid increase in population were attributed to fertility, it would mean that there is a need for birth control education. It would spark a major investigation. The recognition that this is due to ethnic redefinition or ethnic drift sets us on a very different policy road. Behaviour is not dramatically changing, and a change in the composition of the group has different implications for the cohesion of communities, as noted in Chapter 1 of this volume.

Figure 4.7 Average number of children ever born to women of Aboriginal and non-Aboriginal origin who were the same age in 1981, by age group, 1981 and 1991

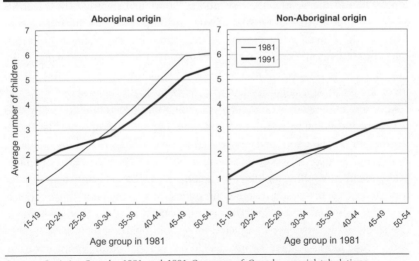

Sources: Statistics Canada, 1981 and 1991 Censuses of Canada, special tabulations.

Table 4.2 Percentage of the Aboriginal-identity and non-Aboriginal populations with a university degree, 1986-96 (adjusted for partially enumerated Aboriginal communities)

Group	% with a university degree 1986	% with a university degree 1996	% increase of population with a university degree, 1986-96
Total population aged 15 and over			
Aboriginal identity	1.4	3.4	275.6
Non-Aboriginal	9.7	13.4	57.0
Cohort of persons aged 35 and over in 1986			
Aboriginal identity	1.9	3.9	97.0
Non-Aboriginal	9.7	13.4	1.3

Sources: Statistics Canada, 1986 and 1996 Censuses of Canada, special tabulations.

Effect of Ethnic Mobility on Educational Attainment

Our third example can be closely related to government policy and programs. It looks at the evolution of educational attainment in Aboriginal groups. More specifically, the analysis focuses on the increase in the number and proportion of university graduates, two indicators often used to evaluate the efficacy of postsecondary educational programs. Between 1986 and 1996, the number of Aboriginals aged 15 and over with a university degree increased by 276%, from 3,900 to 14,500 (see Table 4.2). As a result, the proportion of Aboriginal university graduates moved from 1.4% to 3.4%. In comparison, the number of non-Aboriginal university graduates grew by 57% during that period, and the proportion within the overall adult population is almost four times (13.4%) the level observed among Aboriginal people. These census numbers indicate that more Aboriginals are progressing to the higher echelons of the Canadian educational system, and are successful in doing so. One could therefore conclude that Aboriginals in Canada are benefiting from: (1) the existing postsecondary educational programs and policy; and (2) the involvement of Aboriginal leaders in promoting higher education.

Very few individuals would contest the fact that promoting education and existing educational programs and policy are beneficial to Aboriginals. This is not the only explanation for the improvement in educational attainment among Aboriginal groups, however. Ethnic mobility has also contributed. To illustrate the effect of ethnic mobility, we again adopt a cohort approach. In order to tease out the actual improvement in educational attainment, the analysis is limited to persons aged 35 and over in 1986 (45 and over in 1996), whom we can safely assume to have completed the school phase of their lives. If there is no ethnic mobility, then the increase in the number of university graduates in this cohort, if any, should be marginal.

This is exactly the case for the non-Aboriginal population: between 1986 and 1996, the number of university graduates belonging to the cohort aged 35 and over increased by only 1%.[13] In the case of the Aboriginal population, the growth in the number of university graduates is spectacular: 97%! As an explanation, some might argue that many Aboriginal people go back to school and obtain their degree at a later age than non-Aboriginal people. Census data reveal that, for this particular cohort in 1996, the school attendance rates of Aboriginal people (3.7%) and non-Aboriginal people (2.8%) were similarly low.[14] Therefore, the only explanation left is once again ethnic mobility. Based on this analysis, we can conclude that, generally speaking, persons who "drifted" into the Aboriginal population in 1996 have higher education than those who reported being Aboriginal in both the 1986 and 1996 Censuses.

Jerry White poses a question in his introduction to this volume. He asks the reader to consider the impact of the scientific understandings we bring to the table. In this case, policy on education provides an interesting point for us to consider. If we were to take the superficial findings as our guide to policy, we would say that the phenomenal success in increasing the numbers of more highly educated Aboriginal persons indicates that we simply have to wait or pursue the same path we are on to find overall improvements. If we look at the actual causes of the improvement in the numbers, however, we can see that we still have to pursue policy alternatives that address an ongoing set of problems in educational attainment.

Conclusion

According to census data, Aboriginal populations registered phenomenal growth during the 1986-96 period. This growth has four components: (1) natural increase, (2) migration, (3) variations in the quality of data, and (4) ethnic mobility, both intra- and intergenerational. The latter component is not traditionally within the scope of demographic analysis. However, the extent of ethnic mobility, or ethnic drift, in Aboriginal populations in Canada supports the idea that this component should be considered in the demographic analysis of all ethnic groups. This phenomenon has also been observed among Aboriginal populations of the United States, Australia, and, to a lesser extent, New Zealand. In Canada, ethnic mobility has had a profound impact on the composition of Aboriginal populations. As illustrated in this study, persons who drifted into the Aboriginal populations between 1986 and 1996 came with their own set of demographic and socio-economic characteristics: mostly urban, lower fertility, and higher education.

While there is no definitive answer to explain the observed intragenerational ethnic mobility in Aboriginal populations, several factors may be cited. These factors can be grouped into three types (Guimond forthcoming). First, we have predisposing demographic factors. Mixed ethnocultural ancestries, which are the result of intergenerational ethnic mobility, are possibly the most important demographic factor in relation to intragenerational ethnic mobility. In an ethnically mixed environment such as in the major urban centres of Canada, we see people from different ethnocultural backgrounds meet, marry, and have children. These children, with their mixed ethnocultural background, have the possibility of choosing their ethnic identity, and many will do so according to the situation. In short, intergenerational ethnic mobility, or mixed ancestries, can lead to intragenerational ethnic mobility. Location of residence and age (not documented here) are two other noticeable demographic characteristics related to ethnic mobility (Guimond forthcoming).

Social factors can also be cited as an explanation of ethnic mobility among Aboriginal populations. Socio-political events and their media coverage, spontaneous (e.g., the Oka crisis in the summer of 1990) and organized (e.g., the Royal Commission on Aboriginal Peoples, 1991-96), have all served to heighten the awareness of the public and, most importantly, to restore the image and pride of Aboriginal peoples. The increased public attention and the improved general self-perception of Aboriginals could have influenced individuals to self-report as Aboriginal.

Finally, legal factors could encourage even more ethnic mobility. At present, the Canadian legal framework (i.e., existing laws and court decisions, land claims, and agreements) creates a favourable environment for mixed-ancestry persons to be drifting in and out of Aboriginal groups. The central element with this particular set of factors is the notion of benefits, real or perceived, attached to Aboriginal identity. The demographic implications of the 1985 amendments to the Indian Act for the Status Indian population have been well documented and are explored in Chapter 3 by Stewart Clatworthy (see also Clatworthy 1997). Other legal factors and their relationship to Aboriginal identity have not yet been closely studied by social demographers. One area of research that requires attention and is currently being investigated by the University of Western Ontario's First Nations Cohesion Project involves the social and demographic implications of legal factors (such as the Indian Act) for the Métis (Bivens and White forthcoming).

More analyses of this type will have to be conducted in order to improve our understanding of the phenomenon of ethnic mobility and its consequences. Such analyses are invaluable tools for evaluating *a posteriori* the social and demographic implications of programs, policies, and legislation designed to improve the social and economic conditions of Aboriginal peoples.

Appendix 4.1
Method for Estimating Ethnic Mobility

The estimate of ethnic mobility is obtained by "estimation by residual." The steps in this method are as follows:

1 Calculating the population expected in year t+n (P^x_{t+n}) by taking the population observed in t (P_t) and subtracting an estimate of deaths (D), adding net migration (M) and all other known factors (net undercoverage of the population) (V) for the observation period (t, t+n), assuming that ethnic mobility is nil:
$P^x_{t+n} = P_t - D_{(t, t+n)} + M_{(t, t+n)} + V_{(t, t+n)}$

2 Subtracting the population expected in year t+n (P^x_{t+n}) from the population observed in that year (P^0_{t+n}). The result of this subtraction represents the estimate of net ethnic mobility (ß) during the observation period (t, t+n): $ß_{(t, t+n)} = (P^0_{t+n}) - (P^x_{t+n})$

This method may be applied to a population as a whole or by age group. In the past, it has been used to estimate changes in the ethnic identification of Aboriginal populations in the United States (Eschbach 1993) and ethnic minorities in the former USSR (Anderson and Silver 1983).

In the case of a population for which statistics are imperfect, it is preferable to formulate more than one estimation scenario: a reference scenario and a higher and lower scenario establishing a range of possible variation in ethnic mobility. Furthermore, since the estimate thus obtained suffers from the variable quality of enumerations and estimates of components, it is preferable to limit comments to estimates for which the range of variation falls outside the band of -10 to +10 per 1,000.

Acknowledgment
Parts of this analysis were initially published in the *Report on the Demographic Situation in Canada, 1998-1999* (Statistics Canada, Catalogue no. 91-208-XPE).

Notes
1 Theoretically, the maximum rate of natural increase is 5.5% per year. It is obtained from the highest crude birth rate (60 per 1,000 persons) observable under exceptional conditions – a young population, marrying young and practising no form of contraception – from which is subtracted the lowest crude death rate (5 per 1,000 persons) (Pressat 1979). Such a combination of a high birth rate and a low death rate has probably never been observed. Today, the highest national rates of natural increase in the world are approximately 3.5% per year. A growth rate in excess of 5.5% cannot be explained by natural increase alone: phenomena other than births and deaths are contributing to the increase.

2 The 1986 Census data on Aboriginal identity have never been the subject of an official release, primarily because of reporting errors detected within the population reporting no Aboriginal origin. This analysis focuses solely on the Aboriginal identity of populations with Aboriginal origin, for which data on identity are reliable.

3 In the 1996 Census of Canada, 383,000 persons self-reported an Aboriginal origin but no Aboriginal identity.

4 Some Aboriginal communities refuse to participate in enumeration activities. From one census to the next, the list of these communities varies, giving rise to a serious problem of data comparability. The growth rates shown here are calculated for populations that participated in the censuses. Preliminary studies by Maxim and White (2001) indicate that the nonparticipating communities are not outliers and would not influence the analysis.

5 In practical terms, the contribution of international migration may be considered nil. According to the Census of Canada, between 1981 and 1996, only 13,200 persons of Aboriginal origin entered the country, while the overall population growth reached 610,500 persons.

6 Author's calculations. See Norris et al. 1995.

7 Author's calculations. Statistics Canada, unpublished table of the Reverse Recode Check Survey (1996).

8 In the 1996 Census of Canada, 624,300 persons of Aboriginal origin reported more than one ethnic origin. This was more than half (57%) of all persons of Aboriginal origin.

9 See note 3 above.

10 This is a crude measure of fertility obtained by dividing the number of children under age 5 by the number of women aged 15 to 49.

11 To live on an Indian reserve, it is necessary to have legal Indian status or be recognized or accepted by the resident First Nation. Since the right to settle on a reserve is governed by legal and community considerations, it is therefore unlikely that residents of Indian reserves would change their ethnic identification.

12 Migration, mortality, and quality of data have also been considered as possible explanation. Individually or collectively, these factors cannot account for the unusual decrease in the average number of children ever born to Aboriginal women (Guimond forthcoming).

13 The rise in the percentage of non-Aboriginal people aged 35 or more in 1986 with a university degree is in large part attributable to the death of older, less-educated individuals.

14 Statistics Canada, 1996 Census of Canada, Public Use Microdata File (PUMF).

References

Anderson B.A., and B.D. Silver. 1983. Estimating Russification of ethnic identity among non-Russians in the USSR. *Demography* 20(4): 461-89.

Bivens, R., and J. White. Forthcoming. *Who Are the Métis?* Working paper, First Nations Cohesion Project. London: University of Western Ontario.

Clatworthy, S.J. 1996. *The Migration and Mobility Patterns of Canada's Aboriginal Population.* Prepared for the Royal Commission on Aboriginal Peoples. Ottawa: Canada Mortgage and Housing Corporation, and the Royal Commission on Aboriginal Peoples.

–. 1997. *Implications of First Nations Demography.* Ottawa: Research and Analysis Directorate, Indian and Northern Affairs Canada.

Eschbach, K. 1993. Changing identification among American Indians and Alaska Natives. *Demography* 30(4): 635-52.

Guimond, E. 2000. Ethnic mobility and demographic growth of Canada's Aboriginal population from 1986 to 1996. In *Report on the Demographic Situation in Canada 1998-1999.* Catalogue no. 91-208-XPE. Ottawa: Statistics Canada.

–. Forthcoming. L'explosion démographique des populations autochtones du Canada de 1986 à 1996. PhD diss., Department of Demography, Université de Montréal.

Guimond, E., D. Beavon, M. Cooke, and M.J. Norris. 2001. *Emerging Aboriginal Identities Moving into the New Millennium: The Canadian, American, Australian and New Zealand Experiences.* Poster presented at the Population Association of America (PAA) meeting, May 2001, Washington, DC.

Maxim, Paul, and Jerry White. 2001. *Assessing the Data Effects of Non-Participation in the Census by Aboriginal Communities.* Working paper, First Nations Cohesion Project. London: University of Western Ontario.

Norris, M.J., D. Beavon, E. Guimond, and M. Cooke. 2001. *Registered Indian Mobility and Migration: An Analysis of 1996 Census Data.* Ottawa: Research and Analysis Directorate, Indian and Northern Affairs Canada.

Norris, M.J., D. Kerr, and F. Nault. 1995. *Summary Report on Projections of the Population with Aboriginal Identity, Canada, 1991-2016.* Prepared by Population Projections Section, Demography Division, Statistics Canada, for the Royal Commission on Aboriginal Peoples and Canada Mortgage and Housing Corporation.

Pool, I. 1991. *Te Iwi Maori: A New Zealand Population Past, Present and Projected.* Auckland: Auckland University Press.

Pressat, R. 1979. *Dictionnaire de démographie.* Paris: Presses Universitaires de France.

Robitaille, N., and R. Choinière. 1987. L'accroissement démographique des groupes autochtones du Canada au XXe siècle. *Cahiers Québécois de démographie* 16(1).

Ross, K. 1996. *Population Issues, Indigenous Australians.* Canberra: Australian Bureau of Statistics Occasional Paper 4708.0.

Statistics Canada. 1999. *Report on the Demographic Situation in Canada, 1998-1999.* Catalogue no. 91-208-XPE. Ottawa: Statistics Canada.

Statistique Canada. 1989. *Revue générale du recensement de 1986.* Catalogue 99-137F. Ottawa: Ministère des Approvisionnements et services.

5
Aboriginal Mobility and Migration Patterns and the Policy Implications
Mary Jane Norris, Martin Cooke, and Stewart Clatworthy

Canada's Aboriginal populations and communities are often viewed as being homogeneous in their characteristics. While there are similarities, however, there are also significant differences among Aboriginal populations. Registered Indian, Non-Status Indian, Métis, and Inuit communities vary in their size, geographic distribution, and demographic characteristics, including mobility and migration patterns. Variations in population movement among these four groups reflect not only differences in location and urbanization but also distinctions in legal status among the populations and communities. Formalized membership and residency requirements create different push-and-pull factors that influence migration and mobility. This chapter looks at the origin-destination flows of each of the four Aboriginal groups in Canada. Our analysis covers movement among four geographies: reserves and settlements combined, rural areas off reserve, urban census metropolitan areas (CMAs), and urban non-CMAs. Migration patterns are also explored in different types of Aboriginal communities (reserves, settlements, Métis, and Inuit) to provide some insight into the influence community type has on movement.

   This chapter also considers the role of migration patterns in relation to the considerable growth of Aboriginal populations since the 1960s, especially in urban areas. This growth is often believed to be due to a continuing pattern of migration from Aboriginal communities into large cities, primarily in search of employment. As we demonstrate, however, there are other factors besides migration that affect the size of the urban Aboriginal population. Migration is currently not the major contributor to urban growth. Furthermore, it appears that for now the most important considerations of Aboriginal migration are not redistribution of the population but rather the high rate of movement or "churn" both within and to and from cities. We use data from the 1996 Census of Canada to compare the movement of these four different Aboriginal populations in terms of the direction and size of migration flows and age-specific rates of mobility and migration. We also discuss the reasons for and the potential impacts of these patterns. The chapter is designed to provide another piece of the puzzle that faces policy makers. The significance of population movements has been underestimated in the sociology of Aboriginal peoples and has a direct influence on how we should approach the issues of programs and services to their communities.

Definitions of Populations

While the Canadian Aboriginal population is composed of a large number of distinct cultural and linguistic groups, they are often, for analytical purposes, more broadly based on both ethnic affiliation (ancestry and identity) and legal status measures used in the census. The Constitution Act, 1982 defines the Aboriginal population of Canada as including the North American Indian, Métis, and Inuit people of Canada. A further distinction is made by the Indian Act, which establishes the criteria for a person to be recognized as a Registered Indian. This therefore defines four major groups: Registered Indian, Non-Status Indian, Métis, and Inuit. For the purposes of this analysis, only those people who identified themselves to be a member of one of these groups, as identified in the 1996 Census, were included. In 1996, 1.1 million Canadians identified themselves as having Aboriginal ancestry, while 799,000 reported themselves as members of an Aboriginal group or as having Registered Indian status.

Registered Indians and Non-Status Indians are generally people of North American Indian (First Nations) descent. People belonging to groups that had negotiated treaties with the Crown are generally Registered Indians, and many of these treaties included provision for the establishment of reserve lands, where members of these groups have historically lived. There were some 610,000 people on the Indian Register in 1996, but the 1996 Census enumerated only about 488,000 Registered Indians due to high undercoverage on[1] and incomplete enumeration of reserves.[2]

Non-Status Indians, numbering about 90,400 in the 1996 Census, are not registered under the Indian Act. As such, these individuals are for the most part not members of Indian bands (First Nations) (although some can be, depending on membership provisions), and relatively few live in reserve communities. In many cases, Non-Status Indians are descendants of mixed (registered and non-registered) parenting combinations, who are not eligible to be registered.[3]

The name *Métis* traditionally refers to those persons of Aboriginal ancestry who are descended from the historic Red River Métis community of Western Canada, a population that was the product of Aboriginal and European cultures. The term is now also used to refer to persons who report Métis ancestry or identity. About 210,000 persons identified themselves as Métis in the 1996 Census.

The Inuit are the Aboriginal people of northern Quebec, the Northwest Territories, Nunavut, and Labrador. There were 41,000 people who identified themselves as Inuit in the 1996 Census.

Geographic Definitions

For the purposes of studying the migration flows of Aboriginal people in Canada, four mutually exclusive and exhaustive geographies are defined. Places of residence can be divided into urban census metropolitan areas (CMAs), urban non-CMAs, reserves and settlements, and rural areas. Census metropolitan areas are large cities, defined as urban agglomerations with a core population of at least 100,000, and exclude rural fringes and reserves in urban areas. Urban non-CMAs are smaller cities; they are defined as census agglomerations (CAs) with an urban core of between 10,000 and 100,000, and also do not include rural fringes. A reserve is legally defined in the Indian Act as a tract of land that has been set aside for the use and benefit of an Indian band or First Nation. For the most part, reserves are inhabited by Registered Indians. Settlements include Crown land and other communities with Aboriginal populations as defined by the Department of Indian Affairs and Northern Development (DIAND), and include some Métis and Inuit communities. These settlements and communities are distinct from reserves in that they do not have the same legal distinction as reserves, nor any rights or benefits.[4] For the purpose of analyzing flows by origin and destination, reserves and settlements are combined as one geography, although they are analyzed separately in terms of community type. Rural areas are sparsely populated areas lying outside of urban areas.

Reserve communities are of particular importance for the study of migration of the Registered Indian population in Canada. There are certain rights and benefits associated with Registered Indian status, especially on reserves. These benefits may include such things as access to funding for housing, postsecondary schooling, and tax-exempt status, as well as land and treaty rights. Aboriginal populations in off-reserve Métis and Non-Status Indian communities do not have legal access to the same rights and benefits as Registered Indians on reserves. For these reasons, the distinction between reserve and off-reserve geographies is important in terms of understanding the push-and-pull factors associated with the migration patterns of Registered Indians.

Migration Measurement and Concepts

Census migration data used in this analysis are obtained from the five-year mobility question, which asks about an individual's residence five years earlier.[5] "Non-movers" are those people who responded that they lived five years ago in the same residence as on Census Day. Those whose place of residence was not the same are "movers," and these can be divided into two types. Migrants are movers who lived in a different community (Census sub-division, or CSD), while non-migrant movers are people who lived in a different residence, but in the same community, five years ago. These people can be referred to as "residential movers." There are some limitations associated with mobility and migration data from the census mobility questions. Demo-graphic, marital status, and socio-economic characteristics can change over time, and the characteristics as measured in the census may not necessarily be the same as at the time of migration. For example, age is measured at the time of the census, which is the end of the migration interval. As such, the age at the census may not represent the age at which people actually moved.[6] Another limitation is that the moves of people who leave and return during an interval, those who made several moves during the interval, and those who died during the interval are not captured.

Geographic Distribution of Aboriginal Populations

Aboriginal groups differ significantly among themselves in their degree of urbanization as well as from the non-Aboriginal population in general. Figure 5.1 illustrates these differences. The most urbanized Aboriginal groups were the Non-Status Indians and the Métis, with 73% and 66%, respectively, living in urban areas (although living in urban areas was still less common for these groups than for the non-Aboriginal population, which had 80% in urban areas). Aboriginal off-reserve communities, including those of the Métis, Non-Status Indians, and Inuit, would fall within the rural classification of residence, such

Figure 5.1   Geographic distribution of Aboriginal and non-Aboriginal populations, 1996

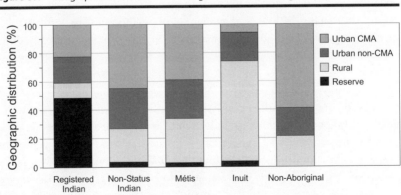

Sources: Norris et al. 2000, based on census data.

that some of the 30% of Métis and 23% of Non-Status Indian populations who were in rural areas would be residing in Aboriginal communities.

In contrast to the Métis and Non-Status Indians, the Inuit tend to be the least urbanized, with less than 30% residing in urban areas. Relatively few Inuit live in communities that have been designated as settlements by Indian and Northern Affairs Canada (INAC).

In the case of residential distribution, Registered Indians are distinct from the other Aboriginal groups in that they can reside on reserves.[7] Data from the 1996 Census indicate that the Registered Indian population was split fairly equally between on- and off-reserve residence; it should be noted, however, that the proportion on reserve is understated due to undercoverage and the incomplete enumeration of reserves and settlements.[8] Registered Indians are less urbanized than the Non-Status Indian and Métis groups, with some 40% in urban areas (overstated), but more urbanized than the Inuit. Registered Indians most commonly live on reserves, but about 10% are located in rural areas off reserve. While some reserves are in urban areas, the majority are located in rural areas.

Factors Involved in Population Growth

Migration can play either a significant or a negligible role in the population growth of any geographic area, depending on the net impact of the migration flows to and from that area relative to the population size of that area. The size of the Aboriginal population in Canada, and its distribution between rural areas, urban areas, and Aboriginal communities, has changed considerably since the 1960s. As Guimond (2000) indicates, the total population of Aboriginal ancestry has increased dramatically, and most of this growth *appears* to have occurred in urban areas.

It is important to consider all the various factors that can affect growth generally and those specific to the different Aboriginal groups themselves. These other factors include fertility, natural population growth, legal changes that affect growth, and ethnic identification change or ethnic mobility/drift.

Fertility

It is well known that the fertility of Aboriginal people tends to be higher than that of the general Canadian population. The highest fertility rates are found in the Aboriginal communities and in rural areas, but off reserve, even in urban areas, where Aboriginal fertility is lower than in Aboriginal communities, it still remains significantly higher than that of the non-Aboriginal population (see Figure 5.2). This high fertility, combined with high but decreasing mortality, has contributed to the growth of the Aboriginal population for all geographies (Bobet 1989). Thus, the role of fertility and hence natural increase

Figure 5.2   Estimated fertility rates in Aboriginal and non-Aboriginal populations, 1991

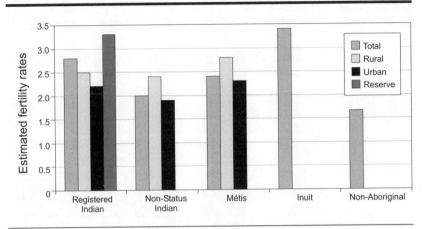

Source: Norris et al. 2000, based on census data.

(births minus deaths) is one factor in the growth of Aboriginal populations in urban areas.

There are also factors unique to the different Aboriginal groups that must be considered in addition to migration and natural increase.

Legislation as a Component of Growth

Much of the growth in the urban Aboriginal population has been among Registered Indians. The distribution of the Registered Indian population has changed between 1985, when more than 70% of Registered Indians were living in reserve communities, and 1996, when nearly half were living off reserve, with most off-reserve residents living in cities.

Registered Indian status is legally defined, however, and because of this, the size of the population can change with legal definitions. This is discussed in detail in Chapter 3. The impact of the 1985 amendments to the Indian Act has been a large increase in the Registered Indian population in urban areas and a smaller increase in the on-reserve population.

Ethnic Mobility as a Component of Growth

While the size of the Registered Indian population is a product of legislative definition, there is no such definition of the Métis, Inuit, or Non-Status Indian populations. As a result, the population of those who identify themselves as members of these groups on the census is subject to change with changing patterns of ethnic identification (Hull 1984). Furthermore, the intercensal growth of any population can be affected not only by migration, natural increase, and legislation but also by the coverage and measurement issues discussed

Figure 5.3   Estimated crude birth rate and total growth rate of the population of Aboriginal origin, 1971-81 to 1991-96

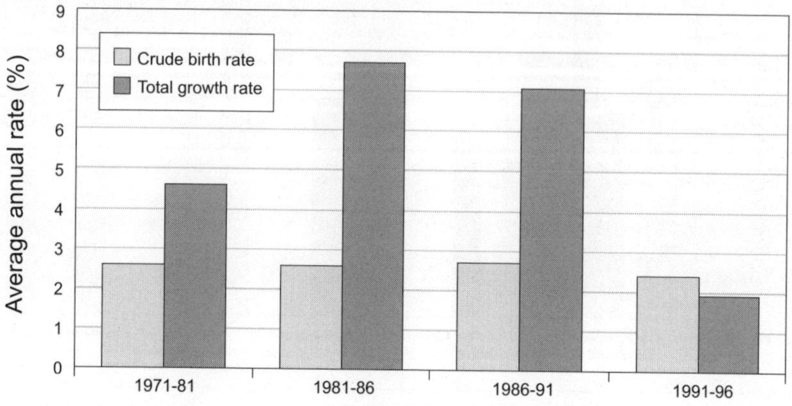

Source: Norris et al. 2000, based on census data.

above. In Chapter 4, Eric Guimond considers all the various possible factors that could contribute to population change at both the national and subnational levels. He concludes that intercensal changes in population are attributable not only to natural increase but also to ethnic mobility or "drift," which he defines as a change in the reporting of one's ethnic affiliation (ancestry and/ or identity) or from one census to another, or between generations. We can see in Figure 5.3 that the growth from births explains only a small proportion of overall Aboriginal population growths. At the subnational level, ethnic mobility has occurred especially off reserve in urban areas (where inter-ethnic contacts are more frequent), and migration is, in fact, currently not the major contributing factor to population growth.

Guimond (2000) has explored the contribution of ethnic mobility to the size of the different Aboriginal populations, and has found it to be a major factor in the considerable growth in the Métis-identity population over the 1991-96 period, growth that could not be explained by the demographic processes of migration or natural increase.

Migration as a Component of Growth

The popular belief that the urban Aboriginal population has grown because of current net in-migration to cities from Aboriginal communities is not supported by the data. Legislative change and ethnic mobility appear to be the major components affecting recent urban growth.

Figure 5.4 shows the net migration rates by place of residence (reserves, rural areas, urban CMAs and non-urban CMAs) for Registered Indians for the

Figure 5.4   Net migration rates of Registered Indians, by place of residence, 1966-96

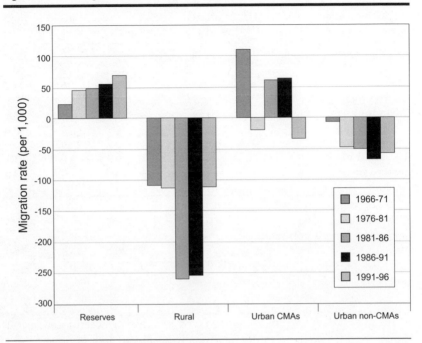

Source: Norris et al. 2000, based on census data.

1966 to 1996 Census periods. Throughout the 1970s and 1980s, a pattern of positive net migration to both reserves and cities continued, with the migrants to reserves from urban areas outnumbering those leaving reserves (Norris 1992). Both rural non-reserve areas and smaller urban areas experienced a continued net loss of Registered Indian migrants between 1986 and 1991. From the 1996 Census, the pattern of net migration between reserve, rural, and urban areas over the 1991-96 period was largely similar to that observed in previous censuses in terms of five-year net migration flows, except that both large and small urban areas experienced net outflows of migrants, whereas only smaller cities experienced this in the 1986-91 period.

Origin-Destination Flows

An important aspect of the migration patterns of Registered Indians that distinguishes them from other Aboriginal groups is their movement to and from reserves. While urban areas are attractive destinations, the stream of migration from reserves to cities is smaller than the flow from cities to reserves. Reciprocal moves between on- and off-reserve locations accounted for about a third of the 87,340 Registered Indians who were recorded as migrants over the 1991-96 period, while only 3% moved between reserves (see Table 5.1).

Table 5.1   Percentage distribution of Aboriginal migrants by origin-destination, 1991-96

Origin-destination flows	Registered Indian (%)	Non-Status Indian (%)	Métis (%)	Inuit (%)
Urban to urban	37.1	59.1	52.5	24.2
Urban to rural	9.7	18.2	22.5	19.3
Rural to urban	13.7	12.1	15.5	24.7
Rural to rural	3.8	5.8	6.8	27.9
Urban to reserve	19.6	2.3	1.4	0.3
Reserve to urban	6.9	1.2	0.4	0.6
Reserve to reserve	3.1	0.2	0.0	–
Reserve to rural	1.4	0.4	0.2	2.1
Rural to reserve	4.8	0.7	0.5	0.8
Total	100.0	100.0	100.0	100.0
Total no. of migrants aged 5+	87,340	20,130	37,460	4,760
Total population aged 5+	424,765	77,505	162,925	34,085
% migrants in total population aged 5+	20.6	26.0	23.0	14.0

Sources: Statistics Canada, 1991 and 1996 Censuses of Canada, special tabulations (author calculations).

As many as 64% of migrants were involved in moves between locations off reserve. Nearly two-thirds of the migration between on- and off-reserve locations involved migration from urban areas to reserves, and well over half of the migration between off-reserve areas was between urban areas. Seven out of ten Registered Indian migrants over the 1991-96 period can be classified into one of three major flows: urban to urban (37%), urban to reserve (20%), and rural to urban (14%). Flows from reserves to urban areas (CMA and non-CMA) accounted for only 7% of the migration volume.

For other Aboriginal groups, the urban-to-urban stream is also the largest, but it represented significantly higher shares, accounting for 59% and 52%, respectively, of Non-Status Indian and Métis migrants, compared with just 37% for the Registered Indian population. While the share of migrants from rural to urban areas is about the same for all three groups, ranging from 12% to 15%, the proportion of migrants moving from urban to rural areas (some of which would include the "city-to-Aboriginal-community" movement) is significantly higher for Non-Status Indians (18%) and Métis (23%) compared with Registered Indians (just 10%). Of course, part of this difference is attributable to the urban-to-reserve flow of 20% for Registered Indians, representing their "city-to-Aboriginal-community" flow. Contrasts are even more pronounced with the Inuit group, the least urbanized population, for which the rural-to-rural stream represents the largest share of Inuit migrants at 28%, a sharp contrast to all the other groups, for which it is one of the smaller flows. It is also interesting to note that for all four Aboriginal groups, about 20% of migrants are contained in the flow that would include movement from city to Aboriginal community.

Net Migration Flows

The net migration flows between the four geographies represents the net loss or gain of population to a geography resulting from exchanges in migration flows with other geographies. For Registered Indians, the net migration flows between 1991 and 1996 show that reserves and settlements gained over 14,000 migrants during the period, mainly through the exchange of migrants with CMAs and smaller urban areas, and to a lesser extent from rural areas. Consistent with the net out-migration rates discussed above, rural and smaller urban areas saw net outflows of 6,385 and 4,405 migrants, respectively. While some of this net out-migration was to CMAs, and from rural to small urban areas, the strongest net flows were to reserves and settlements (see Figure 5.5).

As with Registered Indians, there was a small net out-migration of Non-Status Indians from urban areas,[9] as shown in Figure 5.6. Unlike Registered Indian migrants, however, 1,155 more Non-Status Indian migrants moved into rural areas than left during the period. The largest net gain of Non-Status Indian migrants was experienced by rural areas, where a proportion of the destinations would be off-reserve Aboriginal communities.

The net migration patterns of Métis people between 1991 and 1996 were most similar to those of Non-Status Indians. Rural areas and reserves and settlements gained migrants during the period, while both CMAs and smaller urban areas saw net out-migration (Figure 5.7). As with Non-Status Indians, rural areas gained the most Métis people through net in-migration, while large cities experienced the greatest net losses.

Figure 5.5   Net migration flows for Registered Indians aged 5 and over, 1991-96

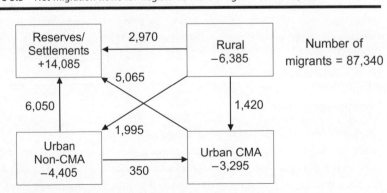

Source: Norris et al. 2000, based on census data.

Figure 5.6   Net migration flows for Non-Status Indians aged 5 and over, 1991-96

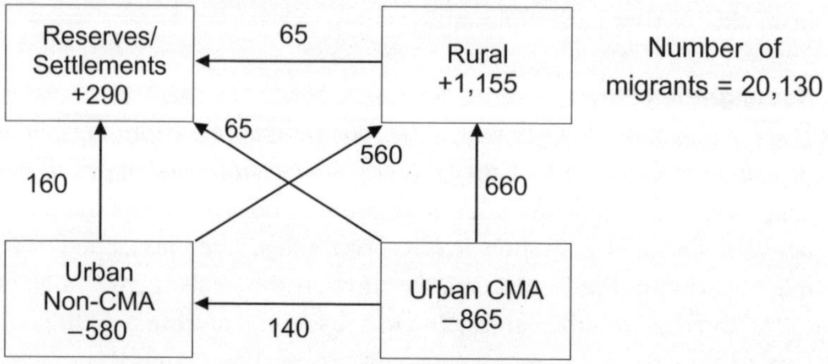

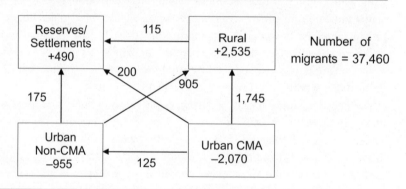

Source: Norris et al. 2000, based on census data.

Figure 5.7   Net migration flows for Métis aged 5 and over, 1991-96

Source: Norris et al. 2000, based on census data.

   The Inuit differ in their pattern of net migration from the other groups, recording a positive flow of 245 people to non-CMA urban settings during the period. CMAs saw no measurable change in the size of the Inuit population through migration, implying that net migration patterns over the 1991-96 period contributed little to the redistribution of the Inuit population.[10]

Net Migration Rates

The Relative Impact of Migration by Geography

While the net flows into and out of the four geographies can give an impression of the amount of population gain or loss in these areas due to migration, the significance of that impact is captured in the net migration rates. Net migration rates by geography vary by Aboriginal group. For example, in the case of Registered Indians, the impact of net migration on population was most pronounced in rural areas experiencing significant population loss, while the most positive impact on population was experienced by reserves. From this analysis of flows and rates, it would seem that while the major focal points in Registered Indian migration continue to be urban areas and reserves, the impact in terms of net gain or loss of population is felt most significantly in rural areas, which have lost Registered Indian population through migration mainly to urban areas (Figure 5.5). On the other hand, large inflows to urban areas are overshadowed by larger outflows to reserves. In rural areas, the high rate of population loss for Registered Indians contrasts sharply with the rate of population gain for Non-Status Indians and Métis (see Figures 5.6 and 5.7). The populations of all groups in large cities experience a low rate of net out-migration.

The Relative Impact of Migration by Community Type

Analyzing the flows of the Aboriginal population by reserve, rural, and urban origin-destinations provides one perspective on the similarities and contrasts in migration, but not at the level of community. Another way to look at migration is in terms of migration flows to and from different types of Aboriginal communities, which could provide some perspective on the push-and-pull factors associated with different community types. Four different community types are considered: reserves, settlements, Métis communities, and Inuit communities.

In the origin-destination geography, the only community type that is represented are reserves (combined with settlements). Although Métis and Inuit communities would fall within the rural geography classification, not all of the flows of Aboriginal migrants to and from rural areas represent movement to and from Aboriginal communities. We therefore treat reserves and settlements separately in this analysis. This is necessary because the different community types have legal distinctions that are reflected, among other things, in benefits and entitlements. While reserves and settlements are geographically and separately defined in 1996 through the census variable "CSD Type" with populations largely consisting of Registered Indians, other Aboriginal communities are not so clearly defined. Métis and Inuit communities were defined for the analysis on the basis of the group's size and share of the population in a given CSD. In the case of Non-Status Indians, there did not appear to be CSDs with sufficient concentrations to warrant "Non-Status Indian" communities; the vast majority, 73%, of Non-Status Indians live in urban areas, with only 4% on reserves and settlements, and the remaining 23% – representing a

Figure 5.8   Migration rates for First Nations, Métis, and Inuit communities, 1991-96

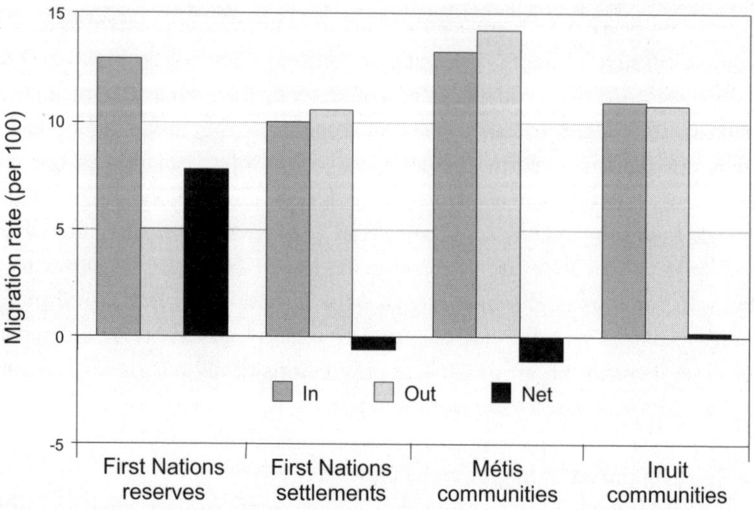

Source: Norris et al. 2000, based on census data.

population of some 20,000 – were distributed in rural areas across Canada. In contrast, the Métis and especially the Inuit tend to have higher shares of their populations in rural areas (31% and 70%, respectively), representing populations that are much more regionally concentrated than the population of Non-Status Indians.

Using 1996 Census data, Norris et al. (2000) calculated in-, out-, and net migration rates for the four different types of Aboriginal community. Shown in Figure 5.8, these rates give some measure of the relative impact of in-, out-, and net migration in these communities, and demonstrate the contrast between reserves and other community types. While each of the four types of Aboriginal community saw similar rates of migration, reserves were distinct, having significantly lower out-migration rates than in-migration rates. For the other three community types, out-migration rates were very similar to in-migration rates, such that the net impact of migration was almost nil.

Mobility and Migration Status

The percentage of migrants or movers in a population gives a sense of the amount of mobility in a population relative to its size, without reference to the origins or destinations of the moves. The amount of migration between communities, and mobility within communities, can have important consequences for the general stability and cohesion of a community as well as for ties between communities.

In general, Aboriginal people were more mobile than non-Aboriginal people, with over half of the Aboriginal population having changed residences between 1991 and 1996. In comparison, about 43% of non-Aboriginal people changed residences in the same period. Among the non-Aboriginal population, residential movers made up slightly more than half of all movers. On the other hand, among Aboriginal movers, residential movers made up almost three-fifths of all migrants.

Mobility Status by Place of Residence
Comparing the mobility of Aboriginal and non-Aboriginal people by place of residence yields even greater differences between the two groups, especially when we look at large cities. More than 70% of Aboriginal census metropolitan area (CMA) residents changed residences between 1991 and 1996, and more than 45% moved within the same community. Non-Aboriginal residents of CMAs moved to a much lesser extent during the period, with under 50% having moved. Residential movers made up a smaller proportion of non-Aboriginal movers. Residential mobility was highest in urban CMAs and lowest in rural areas for both Aboriginal and non-Aboriginal people. Outside of urban areas, Aboriginal people changed residences in reserve and rural areas at rates that were similar to the rates for non-Aboriginal people.

Among Aboriginal groups, Registered Indians living off reserve, Non-Status Indians, and Métis generally share similar levels of residential mobility, and

Figure 5.9   Residential mobility rates for Aboriginal and non-Aboriginal people, by location of residence, 1991-96

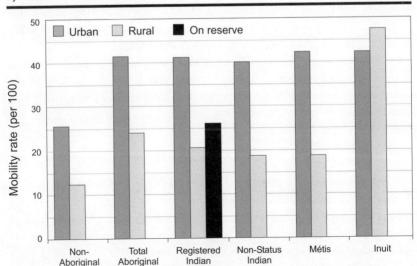

Source: Norris et al. 2000, based on census data.

Figure 5.10   Five-year residential mobility rates for Aboriginal and non-Aboriginal people, by age, 1991-96

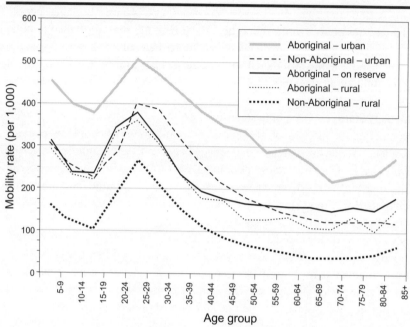

Source: Norris et al. 2000, based on census data.

display particularly high mobility in urban areas (Figure 5.9). People who identified themselves as Inuit and who were living in rural areas were much more likely to have made a residential move than were members of other Aboriginal groups, as were Inuit in smaller urban settings.

We examined the age-specific rates of residential mobility and found that a pattern of higher residential mobility among young people, peaking in the young adult age groups, is common to all populations (see Figure 5.10). The data also indicate the generally higher mobility rates in urban areas, and the higher mobility rates of Aboriginal people compared with non-Aboriginal people in those urban settings.

Age and Gender-Specific Migration Patterns by Origin and Destination

An analysis of the age and gender-specific rates of migration for particular groups can help our understanding of the demographic characteristics of those who chose to move. We focus on the age and gender patterns of the migrants for the following flows: between on and off reserve (for Registered Indians only) and between rural and urban areas for all four groups except the Inuit.[11]

Figure 5.11   Reserve to off-reserve migration rates of Registered Indians, by age and gender, 1991-96

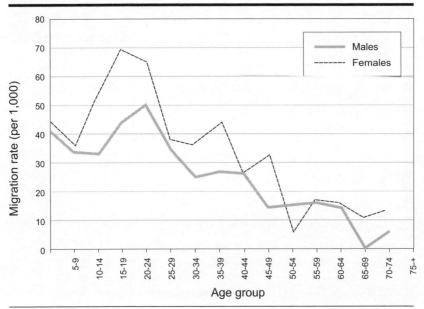

Source: Norris 2002.

Registered Indians

The migration rates for Registered Indians moving from reserve communities to off-reserve areas show a clear age pattern, in which young adults are the most mobile (see Figure 5.10). The higher rates among young adults are common to almost all human migration (Shaw 1975), as mobility can often accompany education, entry to the labour force, and marriage. Among these young adults, women have higher rates of mobility from reserves, with approximately 70 migrants per 1,000 women aged 20-24, compared with fewer than 50 per 1,000 men in the same age group (Figure 5.11). It should also be noted that urban populations have higher than average single parents per capita.

In the opposite direction of migration, from off-reserve to reserve communities, the age pattern is less pronounced and the gender patterns appear reversed, with working-age men experiencing higher migration rates to reserves (Figure 5.12). The high rates of mobility in both directions among children from 5 to 15 years, suggests that many moves are being made by young adults with children. In terms of rural-urban migration, the higher outmigration of women from rural to urban areas is similar to that observed for reserve to off-reserve flows. In the case of the flow from urban to rural areas, however, the pattern of higher migration rates for men observed in the flow to reserves does not occur.

Figure 5.12   Off-reserve to reserve migration rates of Registered Indians, by age and gender, 1991-96

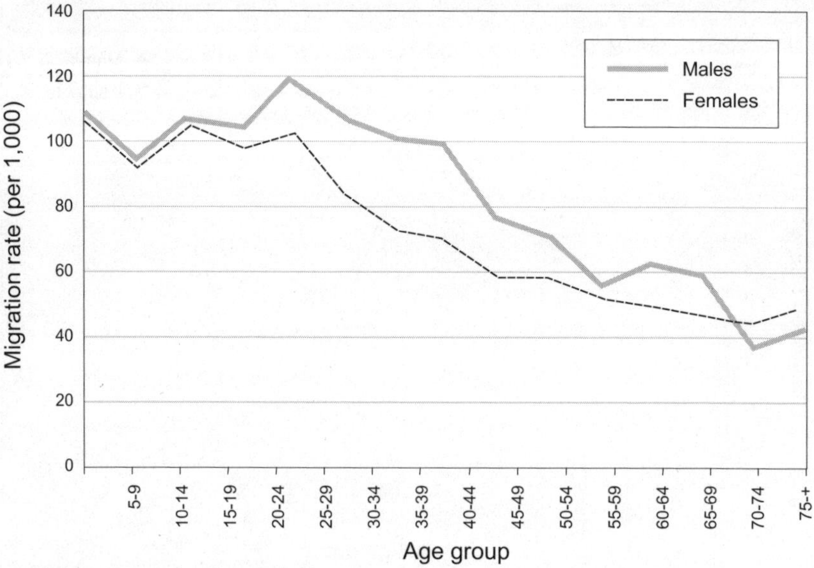

Sources: Norris 2002.

Non-Status Indians and Métis

The age and gender-specific mobility rates for Non-Status Indian and Métis from rural to urban areas have some similarities to Registered Indian migration from reserve communities to off-reserve areas, and from rural areas to cities. The high rates of young adult age groups, especially among young women, again suggest that there are factors that affect males and females differently, and that migration of Non-Status Indians to the city might accompany labour force entry. As with reserve communities, the higher mobility of young women suggests that there are push-and-pull factors between Aboriginal communities and cities that affect women differently than men. In contrast, the migration rates from cities to rural areas for Non-Status Indians do not show the clear age or gender patterns that can be seen in the rates of migration into cities. Some of the reasons for these age and gender patterns are discussed next.

Migration and Cities: Registered Indians versus Other Aboriginal People

An understanding of the high mobility between reserves and cities of the Registered Indian population can be developed through comparison with the mobility of other Aboriginal groups, and the dynamics of migration between off-reserve Aboriginal communities and cities. The high in- and out-migration rates for Registered Indians, relative to those of other Aboriginal people and non-Aboriginal Canadians, suggest that there are important differences between the migration of Registered Indians and other Aboriginal groups. In- and out-migration of Registered Indians appears to be especially high for cities with larger reserve populations nearby. For example, 27% of the Registered Indian migrants to Winnipeg during the 1991-96 period came from reserves, while almost half (47%) of out-migrants from Winnipeg moved to reserves. In the case of Winnipeg, this migration to and from reserves accounts for most of the difference in migration rates between Registered Indians and other Aboriginal groups.

While Registered Indians had higher in- and out-migration rates to and from urban areas, there does not appear to be much difference between the residential mobility status of Registered Indians, Non-Status Indians, and Métis. This suggests that, although reserves may have important effects on the migration patterns of Registered Indians, each of the four Aboriginal groups appears to experience similar pressures in urban areas, leading to high residential mobility.

Discussion and Conclusion

Several important patterns in the migration of Aboriginal people have been identified. Whereas the Aboriginal population in urban areas has certainly grown, migration does not appear to have a large impact on the distribution of the Aboriginal population. In fact, as we have seen, migration between 1991 and 1996 had a net negative effect on the Aboriginal population in urban areas. This appears to be generally consistent with previous findings (Siggner 1977; Norris 1985; Clatworthy 1996; Clatworthy et al. 1997). Other factors, including ethnic mobility and legislative changes affecting the Registered Indian population, appear to have been more important in the growth of the urban Aboriginal population.

First Nations reserves contribute significantly to differences in migration between Registered Indians and other Aboriginal people. Compared with the mobility of Non-Status Indians, Métis, and Inuit people between rural areas and cities, the high mobility of Registered Indians between reserves and urban areas suggests that reserves provide a unique set of factors for potential migrants. Whereas other Aboriginal communities experienced net out-migration during the period, reserves posted net gains of Registered Indian migrants. Also, the higher rates of in-migration to reserves among males is not a pattern seen in migration to other Aboriginal communities, or for that matter in the migration from urban to rural areas among Registered Indians.

The patterns of high mobility among young people, particularly of women, from reserves replicate the patterns taking place between rural and urban areas generally (Clatworthy 1980; Clatworthy and Hull 1983). Previous studies found that in some urban centres, there was a large proportion of Aboriginal women who were lone parents. This suggests that women with children may be more likely to move out of reserve communities, and may be responding to different push-and-pull factors than men. This may be related to the lack of employment for women in Aboriginal communities, as well as the possibility of better social services and educational institutions in cities. Peters (1994) suggests that Aboriginal women tend to move in a family context, while men are more likely to respond to economic factors in their decisions to migrate. Clatworthy (1996) has found that men tend to move to the city for employment, while women tend to cite issues related to the quality of community. Return migration by Registered Indian men to reserves may therefore reflect the lack of appropriate employment opportunities in the city, while the lower rates of migration of women to reserves might indicate the importance of social conditions on some reserves as factors that lead women with families to remain in the city.

The high rates of residential mobility in urban areas experienced by each of the four groups have been related to a general lack of available quality housing in the city and to the low rates of home ownership among Aboriginal people in the city. Aboriginal people tend to live in older and often deficient housing (Clatworthy 1996, 24). Barsh (1997) has found that Aboriginal people in the city tend to have greater difficulty finding suitable housing than non-Aboriginal people, because of discrimination as well as lower average incomes.

Clatworthy (1996) has found that among Registered Indians moving off reserve, family was most often given as the reason for migration, followed by employment, housing, and education. For those moving to reserves, family-related reasons were also the most common, but movement to improve housing conditions was more common than among migrants leaving reserves. Reserves are different from other Aboriginal communities in that Registered Indians who are members of an Indian band might have the option of living in band-provided housing on reserve. Whereas each of the four Aboriginal populations appears to experience the same difficulties leading to high residential mobility in the city, moving back to a reserve is an alternative that is generally available only to Registered Indians.

Reserves may also differ from other Aboriginal communities in their closeness and sense of community. Being legally defined communities, usually with clear rules for membership and residency, reserves may have greater importance as homelands, and as places where one can find the support of kin and friends and a more or less homogeneous culture (Lurie 1967). Because they have less permeable boundaries than other Aboriginal communities, members of Indian bands or reserve communities might return or stay for some perceived greater sense of closeness than other Aboriginal communities. There may also be differences between reserve communities and other Aboriginal communities in terms of their location and distance from cities. This remains to be investigated. Such factors may be particularly important in the case of Inuit communities in the North, which tend to be relatively isolated. As Gerber (1984) has found, geographic distance is an important factor in migration from Aboriginal communities, as is institutional completeness, or the ability of people to satisfy their economic, social, and material needs within their community. It might be that reserve communities differ in the opportunity that appears to be available in the nearby urban setting. This may cause out-migration, which then is not successful in achieving the desired outcomes. The reserve then exerts a pull, as it is easier to return because of the proximity and the draw of the legal status and benefits available to residents.

Migration may not have very sizeable effects on the distribution of the Aboriginal population, but high population turnover between reserves and cities, and high residential mobility within cities, may have implications for communities in urban areas as well as for First Nations communities on reserves. A constant turnover of population between two areas is with little doubt socially disruptive, depending on the length of time people spend away (Gould and Prothero 1975, 45). In the case of the urban Aboriginal population, this pattern can affect service delivery and have negative implications for the development of strong urban Aboriginal community institutions. For reserve communities, high population turnover may also affect community institutions and social cohesion. Within cities, high residential mobility rates may be an indicator of housing need, but might also affect community institutions. Future research on the migration of Aboriginal people clearly needs to focus on the turbulence in urban communities caused by high rates of residential mobility and the turnover between reserves and urban areas.

Clearly, as noted in the introduction to this part of the book, there are policy implications that arise from the research presented here and the research that is indicated by our study.

Notes

1 Historically, the Census of Canada has had problems with undercoverage of Aboriginal people, and the extent and nature of this undercoverage can change between censuses (Hull 1984; Statistics Canada 1993, 1998; Wright 1993). There are several reasons for undercoverage in the census. The census uses the long form (the "2B") to ask people about their ethnicity, mobility, and other questions, and this form is administered to a sample of the total census population, not including people living in institutions such as prisons, hospitals, rooming houses, or barracks. This "missed" population could be problematic because of the high incarceration rates among Aboriginal people, particularly in the western provinces. Other sources of undercoverage

include the high concentrations of Aboriginal people living in rooming houses in urban centres, high levels of residential mobility among Aboriginal people and differentials in coverage across censuses, and changes in the census questions that define and measure Aboriginal identity and ancestry. Another source of undercoverage is that some First Nations communities have refused to participate in the census for a variety of reasons, including as an expression of their sovereignty. Also, changes in geography such as new reserves being created from census year to census year, and the geographic designation of census geography, can affect measures of the geographic distribution and movement of the population. For these reasons, some caution must be used in comparing census populations over time.

2 Maxim and White of the University of Western Ontario First Nations Cohesion Project have determined that the communities that did not participate in the census are not unique in their characteristics and can therefore be assumed not to present a potential major bias to the analysis (Maxim and White 2001).

3 In 1985, amendments to the Indian Act restored Registered Indian status to those who had lost status as a result of provisions of earlier versions of the act (see Chapter 3).

4 There are Métis settlements in Alberta that have some special relationships with the provincial government.

5 While the results presented in this analysis use data based on the five-year mobility question, the census also includes a one-year mobility question.

6 The one-year migration data may have some advantages in that individual characteristics at the time of migration can be more precisely identified. However, the shorter period and the relatively small size of the Aboriginal populations leads to instability in rates and flows computed from one-year migration data.

7 While only an extremely small percentage of other Aboriginals, less than 5%, lived in reserve communities in 1996, it is worth noting that Non-Status Indians living on reserves could increase in the future due to out-marriage and the consequences of status inheritance.

8 We estimate that it is more likely closer to 60%.

9 There was minor activity involving reserves and settlements that resulted in a small net in-migration.

10 Caution should be used when interpreting the patterns, given the small numbers involved.

11 Because of the overall small numbers of migrants, stable age and gender-specific rates could not be computed for the Inuit.

References

Barsh, R.L. 1997. Aboriginal people in the urban housing market: Lethbridge, Alberta. *Canadian Journal of Native Studies* 18(2): 203-14.

Bobet, Ellen. 1989. Indian mortality. *Canadian Social Trends* 15 (Winter): 11-14.

Clatworthy, S.J. 1980. *The Demographic Composition and Economic Circumstances of Winnipeg's Native Population.* Winnipeg: Institute of Urban Studies.

–. 1996. *The Migration and Mobility Patterns of Canada's Aboriginal Population.* Prepared for the Royal Commission on Aboriginal Peoples. Ottawa: Canada Mortgage and Housing Corporation, and the Royal Commission on Aboriginal Peoples.

–. Forthcoming. *Registered Indian Migration between On- and Off-Reserve Locations, 1986-1996: Summary and Implications.* Report prepared by Four Directions Consulting Group for Research and Analysis Directorate, Indian and Northern Affairs Canada.

Clatworthy, S.J., and J. Hull. 1983. *Native Economic Conditions in Regina and Saskatoon.* Winnipeg: Institute of Urban Studies.

Clatworthy, S.J., J. Hull, and N. Laughren. 1997. *Implications of First Nations Demography*. Report prepared by Four Directions Consulting Group for the Research and Analysis Directorate, Indian and Northern Affairs Canada. Ottawa: Department of Indian Affairs and Northern Development.

Gerber, Linda M. 1984. Community characteristics and out-migration from Canadian Indian reserves: Path analyses. *Canadian Review of Sociology and Anthropology* 21(2): 145-65.

Gould, W.T.S., and R.M. Prothero. 1975. Space and time in African mobility. In *People on the Move*, edited by L.A. Kosinski and R.M. Proethero. London: Methuen.

Guimond, E. 2000. Ethnic mobility and the demographic growth of Canada's Aboriginal population from 1986-1996. In *Report on the Demographic Situation in Canada, 1998-1999*. Catalogue no. 91-208-XPE. Ottawa: Statistics Canada.

Hull, J. 1984. 1981 Census coverage of the Native population in Manitoba and Saskatchewan. *Canadian Journal of Native Studies* 1(1): 147-56.

Lurie, N.O. 1967. The Indian moves to an urban setting. In *Resolving Conflicts: A Cross Cultural Approach*. Winnipeg: University of Manitoba Extension and Adult Education Department.

Maxim, Paul, and Jerry White. 2001. *Assessing the Data Effects of Non-Participation in the Census by Aboriginal Communities*. Working paper, First Nations Cohesion Project. London: University of Western Ontario.

Norris, M.J. 1985. Migration patterns of Status Indians in Canada, 1976-1981. Paper prepared for the Demography of Northern and Native Peoples in Canada session at Statistics Canada, June 1985.

–. 1992. New developments and increased analytical possibilities with mobility and migration data from the 1991 census. Paper prepared for the Annual Meeting of the Canadian Population Association, Charlottetown, PE, 2-5 June 1992.

–. 2002. *Registered Indian Mobility and Migration: An Analysis of 1996 Census Data*. Ottawa: Indian and Northern Affairs Canada.

Norris, M.J., D. Beavon, E. Guimond, and M. Cooke. 2000. Migration and residential mobility of Canada's Aboriginal groups: An analysis of census data. Poster prepared for the Annual Meeting of the Population Association of America, Los Angeles, March 2000.

Peters, Evelyn. 1994. Demographics of Aboriginal people in urban areas. In *Aboriginal Self Government in Urban Areas*. Kingston, ON: Institute of Intergovernmental Relations, Queen's University.

Shaw, R.P. 1975. *Migration Theory and Fact: A Review and Bibliography of the Current Literature*. Philadelphia: Regional Science Research Institute.

Siggner, Andrew J. 1977. *Preliminary Results from a Study of 1966-1971 Migration Patterns among Status Indians in Canada*. Ottawa: Indian and Eskimo Affairs Program.

Statistics Canada. 1993. *1991 Aboriginal Data: User's guide*. Ottawa: Statistics Canada.

–. 1998. 1996 Census: Aboriginal data. *The Daily*, 13 January, 2-7.

Wright, Robert E. 1993. Using census data to examine Aboriginal issues: A methodological note. *Canadian Journal of Native Studies* 19(2): 391-07.

PART 3

Confronting Culture with Science: Language and Public Policy
Jerry P. White

Language is not simply a way to communicate, although that certainly plays a core role in its construction, use, and understanding. Languages are fundamental to all human cultures, and, understood as such, we see them play a role in defining the existence of those cultures, differentiating them from others, and acting as an evolutionary universal (Parsons 1964). Few Canadians would have trouble recognizing the importance of language given the decades-long controversy over the use and maintenance of language in Quebec. Language has played a similar role in Europe, from the Mongols of the East to the Belgians or the Welsh of the West. Everywhere language and national identity have been linked. This linkage means that the collectivities of peoples, whether community or country, have real attachments and altered experiences as a result of their language retention or lack of it.

A nation is a collectivity that shares some geography, has a common history, culture, and language, and wishes to be identified as a nation. If we understand nations to have these characteristics, then we also have to see collectivities that are deprived of any of these characteristics as losing their nationhood, losing their identity as a nation. The result of the loss of one's land or one's language can come about gradually or abruptly, but experience tells us that it is always resisted. The resistance to the loss of nation, or even the perception of some threat to one's existence as a nation, is a defining point of our human history in the past century. Whether we look at the Hutu and Tutsi, the Afghan and Russian, the Palestinian and Israeli, the Serb, Albanian, and Croatian, or even the French Canadian and English Canadian, in all cases we find an element of the disagreement that relates to the protection of nation. Part of that core disagreement is language.

Nationalism relates to the model we presented in Chapter 1, but it is a two-edged sword. Nationalism has a positive side, where a people can cohere and in that process achieve great feats through collective effort. The first leader of the People's Republic of China, Mao Tse-tung, credited nationalism with playing a key role in defeating the Japanese aggression and occupation in the Second World War. On the other hand, Ramsay Cook is certainly right when he pointed to how nationalism creates the basis of war, as people engage in conflict about who belongs where and with whom (Cook 1995). For the member of a First Nation, the maintenance of a language may be a dear project, and the redevelopment/reintroduction of a past language may be seen as life giving: "Native languages embody indigenous people's identity and are the most important element in their culture. They must be revived and protected as symbols and sources of nationhood" (Alfred 1999, 136).

To a policy maker, the issues are undoubtedly different. Can the language continue? Is it continuing and why? Can public spending on language protection or reintroduction bring returns? Is it desired and desirable from the First Nations perspective and from societal viewpoints? Does the maintenance of a language have an effect on the socio-economic well-being of the people? Sound research can provide a foundation for weighing the pros and cons of the real world.

Part of that foundation is provided by Erin O'Sullivan in Chapter 6. She takes on a politically and ideologically charged controversy and, in her chapter, asks for one thing from those who study the issue and those who make policy: that they leave ideologically driven simplicities aside and try to look at the complexity of the issue. O'Sullivan finds that there is no clear answer to the long-standing debate over integration versus positive self-identity. On the one hand, integrationists argue that maintenance of language separation from the dominant economic groups in society is a cause of lower socio-economic development. On the other hand, as O'Sullivan points out, those opposed to assimilation argue that the maintenance of identity (language is a key part of that) is the essence of nationhood and creates a cohesion that allows collective growth. She finds that Aboriginal language use is associated with nonparticipation in the dominant culture and dominant economy. However, it is less profoundly related to success when such involvement in the economy is already initiated and language is reintroduced. She feels that neither the integrationist nor the cohesion position is universally valid or completely explanatory. The data for First Nations communities provide some support for instances where it is positive to reintroduce a language that has become endangered or even nearly lost, while in several scenarios that she examines, it appears that the separation created by maintaining a traditional language can suppress socio-economic development. The conclusion we can draw is that you cannot draw hard and fast conclusions. "I hesitate to conclude that Aboriginal language use is a ghettoizing force," she writes.

There are indications that the duality of language functions may be a key. The language, functioning as the means of communication, may tend to disadvantage a group, while languages that function as symbols of the group's sameness and shared culture may be positive. Her development of this view is the greatest contribution of Chapter 6. It gives us an interesting framework for explaining why this issue of maintenance versus abandonment is so complex. If we go back to the model developed in Chapter 1, it would appear that maintenance of traditional language might be a contributor to cohesion (Alfred 1999), and it might probably operate through the increasing levels of social capital that can be generated by sharing a cultural attribute such as language. Regardless, the cohesion would likely increase due to the ties to the older generations, the passage of myths and norms of the group, and increased symbolic and communicative interaction.

So why does the O'Sullivan piece find that there are stronger indications of a negative relationship? It is conceivable that language retention does improve cohesion, but that positive outcome is undermined by the negative relationship between human capital development and the saturation of traditional language. O'Sullivan asks, "Why is language saturation high in very low human capital communities?" This is perhaps the key relationship. We know that human capital attainment is lower in the Aboriginal communities than in the general population (see Chapter 10), and we can see here that language saturation has a relationship with communities at the lower end of the human capital spectrum. Perhaps that is how the model works its way through this issue of language, communicative and symbolic. The decline in human capital in Aboriginal communities that is associated with language retention undermines the positive cohesive properties.

Policy implications are manifest. Polls and anecdotal information indicate that the Canadian public is quite prepared to support spending on problems related to the Aboriginal condition. They do, however, appear to demand accountability, both from the First Nations and the government. The demand is that there be a return on any investment. In a constellation of choices about priorities, what is the measured effect of the spending that is made against the projected aims of that investment? This is difficult in the realm of social policy, but is nonetheless expected by the taxpayer. Is it rational to spend money on language reintroduction? Will that work to bring back a language? Is it wise or even possible to protect endangered Aboriginal languages? Will it actually help the First Nations in some way? The public questions us, but researchers and policy makers have few answers. The O'Sullivan piece is part of the puzzle. Chapter 7, by Mary Jane Norris and Karen MacCon is another part of that puzzle.

Norris and MacCon's study brings us the most complete review of how languages are maintained as well as why some are disappearing while others are more robust. It also contributes to the discussion that follows from

O'Sullivan over what motivates peoples to maintain languages. Norris and MacCon begin with the understanding that while loss of a language may not doom a culture, it can handicap the transmission of that culture. That cultural maintenance is very positive is taken for granted in the chapter. This is truly a Canadian policy attribute. The authors concur with the Royal Commission on Aboriginal Peoples declaration that the transfer of language from old to young is critical in the process of maintaining an Aboriginal language, but they find that "even for some of Canada's more viable Aboriginal languages, there is erosion of language use in the home. There are only a few viable languages that the overwhelming majority of children continue to speak at home." They conclude that "most of Canada's Aboriginal languages that are currently considered viable may experience growing problems of continuity with younger generations, accelerating the process of language erosion. In the case of already endangered languages, extinction appears to be only a generation away."

The finding that many of Canada's Aboriginal languages have suffered serious decay or extinction may not be surprising to the First Nations peoples, but it is important to clearly define and understand. Norris and MacCon show us how the current social trends toward linguistic intermarriage of Aboriginal speakers with non-Aboriginal speakers as well as the large number of single-parent families have had devastating effects on language maintenance. They point out that these social processes will continue to undermine even the more robust of the viable languages over the coming years. The learning and use of Aboriginal languages that are reintroduced (usually as second languages) are not positive in the process of protecting traditional languages, according to the authors. Linguistic endogamy, more limited migration, and measures to encourage family stability will be necessary to increase the potential for languages to survive. These are difficult if not impossible issues to influence. The thought of socially engineering marriage patterns is not desirable in any way. Any actions related to language retention will demand the infusion of funds. It is clear that the calls by First Nations for human capital development within the rubric of the traditional language are going to increase. These are very difficult problems that really cry out for an assessment of existing research, and even more extensive research and analysis, prior to policy development.

The lessons for policy, research, and Aboriginal communities here are somewhat clear. The development of demands for action and the policy development to deal with those demands is best done away from simplistic preconceptions. The problem of language retention should not be avoided in research simply because it raises so many political and social difficulties. Policy-relevant research can have some very dynamic and controversial sides.

In Chapter 6, O'Sullivan notes: "It may therefore be the case that the death of Aboriginal languages is certain, and to oppose that death may simply be to postpone the inevitable." She says this at the conclusion of her extensive review of the debates over the advisability and viability of promoting language maintenance. Good policy-relevant research raises even the most controversial problems and confronts orthodoxy. Just as Part 2 of this book examined the limits of our knowledge and challenged our understanding of who is an Aboriginal person in Canada, this part of the book turns toward tough questions where feelings run high and passion may override science.

How can we marshal our resources effectively and achieve some measure of success in dealing with the acknowledged problems across the many issues that face the First Nations? How can we be accountable without abandoning people's heartfelt desire to protect language and nation? Is it possible to create the conditions to protect even the currently viable languages, given the social practices among the peoples themselves that mitigate success?

These questions are not answered in this book; they are simply raised. It is our collective responsibility to pursue them to find better answers than we have today. That may involve trying to understand what the affected people actually want. The Ekos survey (Ekos Research Associates 2001) of First Nations on reserves did not find a significant interest in language retention. The major issues were more pragmatic, including health and education. This does not mean that culture is not important, but with finite fiscal resources Aboriginally defined priorities could be one of many tools with which to make decisions.

References

Alfred, Taiaiake. 1999. *Peace, Power, Righteousness*. Toronto: Oxford University Press.

Cook, Ramsay. 1995. *Canada, Quebec and the Uses of Nationalism*. Toronto: McClelland and Stewart.

Ekos Research Associates. 2001. *First Nations Survey on Reserve*. Ottawa: Department of Indian Affairs and Northern Development.

Parsons, Talcott. 1964. Evolutionary universals in society. *American Sociological Review* 29(3): 339-40.

6
Aboriginal Language Retention and Socio-Economic Development: Theory and Practice

Erin O'Sullivan

Of late, interest has increased in the potential of culture to resolve the social ills of First Nations communities. Correspondingly, many are demanding that measures be taken to repair the deterioration of Canada's Aboriginal languages (see Chapter 7 of this book). Unfortunately, reparation efforts are fraught with numerous difficulties of their own. These impediments, coupled with the opposition of those who continue to champion assimilation as the expedient route to minority success, have rendered Aboriginal language programming vulnerable to abandonment. From a policy point of view, governments are cognizant that the public wants more accountability for funds and measurements or indicators of return on investment. This makes it important to determine whether money spent on reparation of language is the best way to improve the Aboriginal condition.

The research presented in this chapter attempts to ascertain what impact Aboriginal language use has on socio-economic status (SES) in First Nations communities. Specifically, using a multifaceted measure of language use, logistic regression is applied to various SES indicators in an attempt to assess the relative value of the cohesion and ghettoization perspectives. According to the former, Aboriginal language use promotes identification with and pride in the Aboriginal ethnic identity, which in turn improves SES in Aboriginal communities. The latter position, however, doubts the cohesive capabilities of Aboriginal language use, and suggests that it will reduce SES in Native communities by isolating them from mainstream social and economic arenas.

Arguments for Language Maintenance

Probably the most common argument in support of language maintenance suggests that language is a fundamental component of ethnic identity. That is, speaking a particular language gives one the sense that he or she "belongs" to the group with which that language is associated. Proponents of the perspective include prominent researcher Joshua A. Fishman, as well as Pool,

Herder, and countless others. Norris (1996, 125) congruously reports that "in 1996, practically all (99 percent) of the [Canadian] populations with an Aboriginal mother tongue or home language or knowledge of Aboriginal languages (98 percent) reported an Aboriginal identity." Unfortunately, such empirical evidence is relatively rare, as the importance of language to identity is largely taken for granted. While the basic connection is assumed, however, the question of how and why language can produce a sense of identity is debated zealously. Edwards's distinction (1984) between the *symbolic* and *communicative* functions of language lies at the heart of the dispute.

Language as Symbol

There are multiple interpretations regarding the significance of language as a *symbol* of ethnic identity. I identify two recurring questions: Is language a particularly important symbol, or is it just one of many that may be employed to define one's ethnic identity? For language to be effective as a symbol, how fluent must group members be?

Many researchers suggest that language retention is not essential for the retention of ethnic or cultural identity. That is, other symbols of ethnic identity may be used in lieu of language without any discernible loss of group unity. Drapeau (1995), for example, refers to the loss of Gaelic in Ireland, where a sense of Irish identity nonetheless remains strong. Eastman (1985) similarly discovered that Alaska's Haida attach greater cultural significance to one's ability to identify culturally relevant items than to one's knowledge of the Haida tongue. The notion of the interchangeability of cultural symbols is supported by Barth's assertion, now widely accepted, that ethnic identity has "a subjective basis rather than objective cultural content" (Drapeau 1995, 17). He insists that ethnic identity is all about social comparison and the definition of in-group and out-group boundaries, and that the compositions of these groups is really a non-issue. If this is the case, it certainly seems reasonable that, as long as a culture has other symbols by which to differentiate itself from out-group members, the abandonment of an ancestral language should not precipitate any identity crises.

There are, however, some important flaws in this argument. It may be the case, as Ross (in Giles and Coupland 1991, 107) suggests, that "in the process of self-definition, the group myths and cultural values, including language ... may be substantially revised, altered, and reinterpreted so as to fit with changing conditions." One should not assume, however, that groups may alter their traditions *consciously*. A group does not decide to stop caring for its language because it is too burdensome, suggesting that language loss might be inconsequential to group identity only in the unlikely event that the group did not notice its disappearance. Essentially, the arbitrary nature of culture, while theoretically interesting, is less practically important than many tout it to be. As Fishman (1989, 212) suggests: "The scholars' determination that [ethnic] identities are composed of great slices of fabrication and imagination are beside the point, in the same way that all rational empiricism is beside the point when emotional needs are uppermost."

Besides the practical difficulty of applying the notion of the interchangeability of symbols, the idea is conceptually flawed. Edwards (1984) suggests that overt displays of ethnic identity may be abandoned, without fear of identity degradation, in favour of subtler symbols that pose fewer obstacles to social mobility. This position raises a very important question: can these alternative symbols (chosen perhaps for their "discretion" or even their "cost-effectiveness"), besides fostering a sense of identity, foster a sense of *pride* in that identity? This is not an insignificant question, for, as Giles and Coupland (1991, 105) indicate, "the knowledge of our category memberships, *together with the values (positive or negative) attached to them,* is defined as our social identity" (emphasis added).

Consider, for example, the slaves of colonial America. While it is probable that they identified themselves as blacks or slaves, it is less likely that they were very impressed with their lineage. In light of this consideration, Edwards's suggestion that whether or not cultural symbols are prominent or discrete has no implications for one's sense of cultural identity seems in error. Fishman's ideas (1989, 471) about the use of minority languages in the educational system appear to more correctly reflect the importance of the distinction between private and public symbols: "The use of the disadvantaged language in the school is a symbolic statement ... of public legitimacy on behalf of populations that possess few other modes of symbolic entree into the public realm." In essence, while symbols attached to a culture are possibly equal insofar as they prompt *identification* with a culture, they are *not* equal in terms of the ameliorative or pejorative flavour they will lend to such identification. Whether a negative sense of identity can produce positive effects, such as the motivation to excel economically, is an important, and often overlooked, question.

Like the question of the interchangeability of symbols, the relationship between fluency and linguistic identity is widely debated. Pool (in Eastman 1981) suggests that one's level of fluency in a language is directly related to the degree of identification one has with the language community. Others, however, insist that the relationship is less straightforward. Eastman (1981, 51) suggests that "language is not only an entire repertoire but also a set of speech elements which reflect culturally specific items." De Vos (in Giles and Coupland 1991, 100) indicates that "group identity can even be maintained by minor differences in linguistic patterns and by style of gesture."

Congruously, Eastman (1985) reports that a small band of Alaskan English-speaking Haida maintain a clear sense of linguistic identity by using a specific selection of Haida terms. This behaviour appears akin to the jargon that frequently emerges *intralinguistically* within subcultures. "Hippies," "surfers," "rappers," and so on all add their own unique list of terms to their otherwise common English vocabulary, identifying in-group and out-group members by their ability to "talk the talk."

Eastman and De Vos actually suggest that a group may utilize a common language as a symbol without actually having to know *any* of it. De Vos (in Giles and Coupland 1991) refers to Welsh and Breton, which, although spoken by few, are still a very highly valued component of ethnic identity. Congruously, although programming for Adnyamathanha (an Australian tongue) failed to increase its pool of 20 speakers, the very notion that it was worth reviving made the language a boon to ethnic pride.

Language as Communication

As indicated earlier, language-as-symbol arguments threaten the currently accepted notion that endangered languages must be retained as living languages. Other symbols may be equally useful sources of ethnic pride, and even where language is regarded as an irreplaceable symbol, fluency among those who revere it may not be necessary. There are programmatic implications attached to these possibilities. The resources required to retain language as a "token" or symbol of identity, as opposed to a full-fledged form of communication, would be substantially less. Some, however, insist that the communicative function of language plays an essential role in the construction of ethnic identity. At the heart of these arguments is the notion that the substance of a language, and not just its existence as a whole, has cultural significance. Many claim that an ancestral language is necessary for the transmission of cultural knowledge. Proponents of this view indicate that it is difficult to pass along cultural knowledge if the younger generation has no idea what its predecessors are saying. As one young Inuit woman remarks: "If we didn't speak Inuktitut how would we speak to my aunts and uncles? Like there's knowledge that my grandparents have but if they can't pass it on to me, what use is it?" (in Crago et al. 1998, 86). The situation is particularly dire for Aboriginal languages, owing to the swiftness with which the languages have been lost. In many groups, bilingualism did not exist long enough for legends, cultural knowledge, and so on to be translated into English or French.

Some deny the possibility of cultural transmission even where there is a common form of communication across generations. According to instrumentalists, languages are mere tools, and the association of a particular language with a particular culture in no way implies that the former can express the conventions of the latter any more successfully than any other language (Skutnabb-Kangas 2000). Indeed, linguists generally agree that all languages are logical and that all are ultimately capable of expressing any concept (Skutnabb-Kangas 2000). There is, however, considerable evidence of the difficulty of translation. For example, several authors have indicated that attempts to translate such legal terms as "guilty" and "not guilty" into the Aboriginal semantic system have been unsuccessful (Fettes 1998). Similarly, one Native man indicates that the relationships among his people cannot be expressed in English (Fettes 1998). In addition, recent theoretical work suggests that language is simply too complicated for exact translation. Forrester (1996, 10) remarks upon the Derridean perspective: "Nobody can step outside language and somehow attain a pre-semiotic intuition ... no sign exists somehow on its own and every signified has the potential for being another's signifier." Essentially, language is conceptualized here as a system in which each element is irrevocably connected to every other element. The definition of a single word can never end, implying that the things we perceive to be elements of reality are really just subjective constructions of our respective cultures.

Related to the translatability issue is the dispute over whether or not language affects cognition. According to the Whorfian perspective, different languages impose unique structures and systems of meaning upon reality, thus reflecting and perpetuating different "ways of seeing the world" (Eastman 1981, 49). The "primordialist" version posits that one's perceptions are indelibly structured by one's mother tongue, and that, for example, native speakers of English could never "understand" a translated French concept in the way those did who learned it in its original form (Skutnaab-Kangas 2000). Alternate versions of the Whorfian perspective suggest that while cognitive function is not irretrievably set by one's mother tongue, languages do reflect and preserve specific worldviews. A general linguistic phenomenon known as "markedness" is often considered in conjunction with the Whorfian perspective (Khosroshahi 1989, 505). The elemental word is called "unmarked," and represents the "positive and neutral norm" (Kangas 2000, 143). Marked forms of the word, however, such as those containing suffixes or prefixes, represent deviations from the norm. The English words "heir" and "heiress" are examples of the unmarked and marked forms, respectively, and are said to exemplify the androcentric nature of the English language that is often faulted for the perpetuation of sexism among anglophones (Spolsky 1998). Even if this accusation is justified, however, it is still unclear whether translation would be hindered because of fundamentally differing worldviews or whether it would fail simply because translators do not notice these types of subtle connotations. Essentially, unless one accepts primordialism, the usefulness of the worldviews concept is uncertain. The latter may simply be another way of saying that language is really complicated.

Ironically, despite the profusion of debate over the theoretical possibility of translation, the material world renders the question somewhat moot. As Skutnabb-Kangas (2000) notes, regardless of whether or not cultures can be translated into other languages, they never have nor ever will. The resources that would be necessary to perform such a momentous task are simply not available. Practically, then, for a culture to maintain all of its elements, it seems that it must maintain its language. This is particularly true for groups like the Canadian Aboriginals. Lacking as they do a literary tradition, they also lack sufficient time to conduct translations. Every day their languages change, leaving little evidence of their origins.

There are numerous other arguments for language retention that are unrelated to the question of how such retention can benefit minority communities directly. The notion that diversity is intrinsically good and worthy of preservation has gained followers in academia (especially among the postmodern thinkers) as well as in popular culture. Dascal (in Skutnabb-Kangas 2000), for example, suggests that diverse elements complement and even constitute each other, and that the loss of elements is the loss of points of opposition for all other elements, ultimately reducing the richness of each individual. As Crawford (1998) points out, however, the evidence in favour of the intrinsic good of diversity is hardly strong. After all, what is intrinsically wrong with the whole world speaking the same language? Among the authors who support diversity, there is an alarming number whose endorsements stem from nothing but the belief that diversity "makes the world more interesting." Few seem interested in the question of whose interest is being piqued, and at whose expense. From a policy perspective, these issues are critical.

Arguments against Language Maintenance

Some suggest that language maintenance or efforts to that end may actually work to divide, rather than unite, a community. First, as Giles and Coupland (1991, 104) indicate, "there is often heterogeneity in language attitudes and behaviors across different factions of the same group." Correspondingly, in the 1991 Census of Canada, only 65% of Canadian Aboriginals reported attachment to their ancestral language (Fettes 1998). There are several explanations for this, however, and some suggest that, owing to the discrimination perpetrated against them in the past, many Aboriginals denigrate their own heritage (see Milloy 1999) or fear persecution (see Crawford 1998), and therefore prefer assimilation. This disagreement is particularly problematic when coupled with the accusations of elitism often levied at language retention efforts (see Edwards 1984; Adams 1999).

Regardless of desire for language maintenance, language retention is not possible for all Aboriginals. Some languages are extinct or beyond revival. Wagamese (2000) eloquently describes the culturally corrosive potential of conflict over the necessity of language retention. From his perspective as an Aboriginal author, he discusses a lecture in which a prominent Aboriginal man proclaimed that one who does not know his ancestral language cannot rightly claim to be an Aboriginal. The author indicates, however, that his linguistic tradition was obliterated by residential schools, thereby rendering impossible his acquisition of his native tongue. He indicates that such an impossibility does not make his identification as an Aboriginal any weaker, nor should it deny him the right to his native identity. Essentially, if language retention becomes so widespread that it really becomes an integral element of Aboriginal identity, many may necessarily be relegated to out-group status. Considering that these "ousted" individuals would likely be members of groups whose languages had been forcibly taken, language as a necessary component of Aboriginal identity could even further alienate those Aboriginals already most victimized.

Language authenticity is also an issue. That is, what should a retained language "look like"? Should Aboriginal tongues be "modernized," updated in an attempt to make them competitive in mainstream socio-economic systems? Or should their traditional forms be preserved *in toto?* While the disagreement itself can promote factionalism, modernizing Aboriginal languages threatens to be divisive in a subtler manner. As Aboriginal languages are traditionally oral, they exhibit very strong local influences. The standardization involved in modernization threatens to erase these peculiarities, possibly alienating speakers in the process. To illustrate this point, consider the recent efforts to revive Ojibway traditions. According to Warry (1998), many of the Ojibway people denigrated the resulting "traditions." They felt that the ceremonies were not genuine, or "pan-Indian rather than local" (218). The elders, for example, did not participate in the sweat lodge ceremonies, nor did they identify with the powwows. One community member commented: "The powwows should be bringing us together. Right now [tradition] is dividing us" (218).

Another argument against language maintenance posits that bilingualism reduces proficiency in the dominant language, a skill identified by many researchers as related to socio-economic status (Balakrishnan and Gyimah 2000; Boyd 1999; Rumberger and Larson 1998). Many researchers, however, contest the legitimacy of the claim. Kangas (2000), for example, indicates that the means popularly cited by which bilingualism reduces dominant language competence are actually "fallacies." Aboriginal language use produced no decline in English language ability among the Rough Rock Navajos, according to McCarty (1998). Still, the possibility that dominant and minority tongue proficiency are negatively related must not be prematurely dismissed. The case of the Maori schools in New Zealand is illustrative. Dixon (1997, 111) indicates that the Maori children have begun to speak in "a developing Maori-English creole," rather than restricting themselves to either of the "pure" languages. In addition, many authors indicate that reduced use of a minority language from bilingualism reduces fluency in that tongue (Balakrishnan and Gyimah 2000, 2). It seems unreasonable to suppose that the same effect would never be observed in a majority language.

A final argument against minority language retention proposes that a shift from minority to dominant language is a positive, evolutionary process with which we would be unwise to interfere. The "triumphalists" or "linguistic Darwinists" who champion this view are often criticized for the essentialist flavour of their argument, their implicit assumption that certain languages and, by extension, certain cultures are intrinsically inferior and therefore undesirable (Crawford 1998). Others similarly dispute the notion that language maintenance efforts are "devolutionary" or "anti-progress." Not surprisingly, many language maintenance advocates deny that they are retrogressive. Fishman, for example, compares "RLS-ers" (reversal-of-language-shift-ers) to people who wish to raise the standards of cleanliness in their neighbourhoods to a level enjoyed in the past, insisting that a state of being is not undesirable simply because it has ceased to exist. Fishman fails to recognize, however, that language is a means (to social cohesion, etc.) and not an end. The question is not "Is the past state better?" but rather "Is the means by which the past state was achieved still appropriate for achieving that state in the present?" To extend Fishman's analogy, in the modern context, a cleaner community would be more effectively achieved by hiring additional sanitation workers than by reducing the population to past levels and outlawing the modern consumption patterns that produce so much trash.

Saving Aboriginal Languages

Unfortunately, even given consensus over whether or not Aboriginal languages should be saved, debate continues over whether salvation is possible. Many researchers believe, for example, that dead languages cannot be revived. While the propagation of Hebrew is often cited as a successful instance of revivification, many dispute the assertion that the language was ever truly extinct (see Dixon 1997). Rigsby indicated in 1987 that he knew "of no successful revival programs in North America or Australia" (Drapeau 1995, 20). Dixon (1997) extends this assertion to the world as a whole. Other authors claim that even decline cannot be stopped indefinitely. According to Drapeau (1995, 31), "the only way to make absolutely sure a language will survive is to restore complete cultural autonomy," meaning that there must be "maintained or recreated the existence of a sizable body of monolinguals who live without using or being exposed to dominant language."

Moreover, the necessity of tailoring language planning efforts to individual communities is being increasingly recognized. As Fettes (1998) notes, the viability of Native languages is extremely varied even intralinguistically at the community level. The Whitefish reserve in Saskatchewan, for example, has largely retained its native Cree, while the language is almost lost on the Atahkakop reserve only fifty kilometres away. Fishman's (1990) eight-stage model for reversing language shift helps to illustrate the enormous variability that language programs will necessarily exhibit, depending on the strength of the tongue in the community for which they are designed. The stages include such actions as language codification; the use of the language in special cultural events; "family-, neighborhood-, community reinforcement"; the expansion of literacy in the minority language; teaching of minority languages in schools; use of the minority tongue in the workplace beyond the community; use of the minority language in the lower levels of government and local mass media; and finally use in higher levels of education, government, and media. While the value of this typology is debatable, it does demonstrate that measures to retain a language must be tailored to suit its current level of vitality. Micro-programming of this sort necessitates that, rather than one federally regulated body arguing over the necessary components of a language program, there will be multitudinous, unregulated, and likely inexpert bodies debating the issue.

Consider Fettes (1998, 122), who cites lack of coordination and expertise as a major cause of the failure of formal education programs: "The evolving network of band-controlled and federal schools has been plagued by a lack of both expertise and consistency. In terms of language policy, each Aboriginal community and school board has essentially set about reinventing the wheel, usually with little technical or financial support." Problems associated with the theoretical dubiousness of minority language retention and the extreme complexity of language program formation and implementation are greatly exacerbated by a single fact. As Drapeau (1995, 30) notes, "all efforts, means and measures geared towards Aboriginal language conservation/ revitalization will have to be permanent. They cannot be thought of as a transitory stage. Language endangerment is a permanent predicament and will thus require permanent efforts. Speaking of reversing the tide is mistaken in that the negative undertow is there to stay." As language programs are extremely vulnerable to funding cuts, uninterrupted programming is unlikely. It may therefore be the case that the death of Aboriginal languages is certain, and to oppose that death may simply be to postpone the inevitable.

In summary, we should be aware that both the means and the utility of Aboriginal language propagation are surrounded by uncertainty. Before we step into the minefield of language programming, we need solid empirical evidence that its successful navigation will be worth the effort. This research is an initial attempt to determine whether such evidence exists.

The Current Research

This study examines the relationship between Aboriginal language use and the low socio-economic status of Canada's First Nations (see Warburton 1997). I assess the relative value of the two competing perceptions of the costs and benefits of language maintenance. As indicated earlier, many claim that language is an integral part of ethnic identity. Many adhering to this perspective go on to suggest that the lack of such identification may have a negative impact on socio-economic status. Crawford (1998, 163), for example, states that "language loss can destroy a sense of self-worth, limiting human potential and complicating efforts to solve other problems such as poverty, family breakdown, school failure, and substance abuse." Tawney (1998) suggests that language loss reduces self-respect among community members, which in turn has a negative impact on the socio-economic status of the group. Lee (1992) similarly suggests that loss of identity may disorganize a community and members' motivation to strive for economic success. In their recent works, White et al. (2000) suggest that Native languages may be an important element of the social capital that forms the bases of more cohesive, and thus more prosperous, communities. This perspective, which I will call the "cohesion perspective," is efficiently summarized in Crystal (2000, 31): "Local languages are seen to be valuable because they promote community cohesion and vitality, foster pride in culture, and give a community (and thus a workforce) self-confidence."

Alternately, there is the "ghettoization perspective," which regards minority languages as detrimental to the socio-economic status of their users. As indicated earlier, many contest the claim that Aboriginal languages can really foster the sense of community unity of which such great things are expected. Others insist that minority language use is related to majority language incompetence, which is, in turn related to inferior levels of socio-economic status. Still others suggest that Aboriginal tongues, specifically, may be incompatible with capitalist enterprise. McArthur (1980, 16), for example, questions the conventional wisdom with which Aboriginal economic development has traditionally been approached: "A whole network of concepts, 'development,' 'progress,' 'master,' 'man over nature,' that reflect the confidence, the dynamism, and the aggressiveness of the industrial system, of capitalism, completely pervade our language and our thoughts ... we think my inability, and others' inability to understand these issues of economic development stems, in part, from the pervasiveness of those philosophical assumptions, and our ignorance of that fact."

Similarly, Armstrong (1989) suggests that the past/present orientation of Native cultures, and their emphasis on general work skills over specialization and on equitable distribution, may be incompatible with modern capitalism. If one accepts Whorfianism, this assertion has grave implications for the utility of Aboriginal language use.

In the early 1970s, Jonathan Pool wrote an influential article about language diversity. A comment in that article perfectly synopsizes the ghettoization perspective: "A planner who insists on preserving cultural-linguistic pluralism had better be ready to sacrifice economic progress" (in Nettle and Romaine 2000, 155).

Much of the research into the relationship between minority language use and socio-economic status supports the ghettoization perspective: minority language speakers are more likely to drop out of school (Anaya 2000), francophones in New Brunswick have significantly lower incomes than anglophones (Grenier 1997), and Spanish-speakers in the United States are less successful than English-speakers in the labour market (Bloom and Grenier 1996). While little empirical support exists for the cohesion perspective, several studies, including one on Canadian Aboriginals (Robinson 1985), indicate that socio-economic status and minority language retention are completely unrelated. Cook and Jordan (1997) found that the income of Hispanic, female-headed households in Washington relative to white, female-headed households is not affected by whether those households use English or Spanish. Wolbers and Driessen (1996) found that the scholastic success of immigrants to the Netherlands is unrelated to home language. Stevens and Garrett (1994) discovered that, while Spanish-language communities in New Jersey are economically disadvantaged, Asian and Pacific Island-language communities are not. The inconsistency of these findings highlights the complexity of minority language use, and suggests that its effects may be very context-dependent.

The Data

The data employed in this study describe 543 communities and are derived from the 1991 Aboriginal Peoples Survey (APS).[1] The population addressed in the APS includes those Canadians registered under the Indian Act as well as those who identify with their Aboriginal origins. The complete questionnaire, however, was administered only to those who actually identified with their Native roots. A representative sample was drawn from each of two domains within each province. The first consisted of communities with high concentrations of Aboriginals, and was the domain from which the data described herein were drawn.[2] The response rate for this domain was 79%.[3]

The Dependent Variables: Measures of Socio-Economic Status (SES)

The variables I examine in relation to Aboriginal language use may be divided into three categories: educational attainment, employment, and income. While not an exhaustive list of the components of SES, the political significance of these variables is undeniable, and they do provide a good starting point from which to begin assessing economic well-being in Aboriginal communities.

Education

The importance of education to SES is now widely accepted and research into Canadian Aboriginal people reveals that the relationship holds for this subpopulation (see Robinson 1985; White and Maxim 2000). The first of two education variables employed in this study describe the proportion of community members with eight years of schooling or less. Armstrong's research (1989) reinforces the suitability of this educational level as a component of low SES. He utilizes an education level of less than grade 9 as a proxy for functional illiteracy, indicating that "literacy is a basic qualification for many sorts of work" (7).

The second education variable describes the proportion of elementary school graduates who have completed some form of postsecondary education.[4] The particular importance of postsecondary education to SES is indicated by Odekirk (1993). White and Maxim (2000), moreover, suggest that Aboriginal Canadians, relative to non-Aboriginal people, actually receive a "greater return" on their postsecondary educational achievements.

Unfortunately, while language saturation is based upon all community members over 15 years of age, the education variables include only those aged 15 to 65. This introduces the possibility that results may be somewhat biased. It is not conceivable that communities that otherwise speak English or French may contain populations of elders among whom Native languages are very prevalent. The age categorizations also pose a problem for the analysis of postsecondary educational attainment. That is, individuals typically do not graduate from postsecondary programs until they are at least 19 or 20. An overabundance of 15- to 18-year-olds, therefore, may give a community the appearance of a less educated population than it actually boasts.

Analysis of postsecondary graduation levels may be problematic for another reason. Arguably, an analysis of language use against postsecondary graduation rates would produce not an assessment of the impact of the former on the latter but of the impact of the latter on migration. That is, postsecondary graduates may be likely to leave their less prosperous communities in search of the more gainful employment afforded to them by their diplomas and degrees.

Labour Force Status

This indicator consists of three variables. The first is labour force participation. The second, the proportion of employed labour force participants, pertains to whether those seeking employment have found it.[5] The third variable in this category is the proportion of community members who worked for income in 1990 or 1991. This third variable may appear superfluous. Unlike the first two, however, which reflect labour force status only for June 1990, this last variable is not subject to problems of seasonality. I think it desirable to extend this time line given the association of Aboriginal work with natural resources (such as lumber and fishing), the extraction of which is often dependent upon climatic conditions.

A related variable, the proportion of a community receiving social assistance, is also examined. An important issue in and of itself, this variable can help to ascertain whether or not possible fluctuations in income are offset through non-monetary means (such as hunting or barter). This is an important consideration as the Eurocentrism implicit in much research is increasingly being recognized and questioned.

Also related to labour force status is entrepreneurialism, the fifth variable included in this study. A recent study of Aboriginal entrepreneurialism lauds the practice, indicating that it holds considerable future promise for Aboriginal communities and that through self-employment, Native peoples are leading their own way to a brighter economic future (Anderson 1999). For example, the study estimates that "one in four new Aboriginal jobs can be attributed to self-employment" (8), as entrepreneurs create industries and hire Native employees. I have decided, therefore, to include entrepreneurialism levels as an indicator of the level of economic opportunity and prosperity present in Aboriginal communities.[6]

Income

The proportion of a community earning less than $10,000 is examined to determine whether employed members of communities with high levels of Aboriginal language saturation have "better" jobs than those in communities with low saturation levels.[7] Ten thousand dollars is the most appropriate of the available income levels for several reasons. First, it is closest to the 1991 Low Income Cutoff established by Statistics Canada (Paquet 2001). The distribution of the data is also a factor. Cases were distributed relatively evenly on either side of the $10,000 mark, suggesting that this is an appropriate point to

Table 6.1 Excluded communities and modified sample sizes for the dependent variables

	Number of excluded communities		
	Zeros	Undefined[a]	Modified N
Proportion with 0-8 years of education	79	0	465
Proportion of elementary school graduates who have completed postsecondary education	148	0	396
Proportion not in labour force	17	0	527
Employed proportion of the labour force	78	17	449
Proportion that worked for income in 1990 or 1991	2	0	542
Proportion receiving social assistance	18	0	526
Proportion that own or operate a business	403	0	141
Proportion earning less than $10,000 in annual employment income	29	13	502

a Zero in denominator.

capture the distinction between relatively well-off Native peoples from the less affluent.[8] See Table 6.1 for a summary of the sample size modifications for each of the dependent variables.[9]

The Independent Variable: "Language Saturation"

Language use is operationalized in this study as a scale with six components. These include the proportions of community members who speak an Aboriginal language (1) in the home, (2) in "other places," or (3) at work, as well as those who can (4) read an Aboriginal language or (5) write an Aboriginal language, and finally who (6) have received services in an Aboriginal language. The overall purpose of this model of language use is to measure the degree to which a community is "saturated" by an Aboriginal language – to determine the intensity of language use within and across the social dimensions of a community. Recall that the exact mechanism through which language is supposed to affect its speakers remains a great point of contention. Recall, particularly, the proposition that a language may unite the members of its associated ethnic group even if that group does not actually *speak* the language. Despite these disputes, however, language planning seems consistently targeted to the tasks of language maintenance and reversing language shift. In Chapter 7, Mary Jane Norris and Karen MacCon clearly identify the goals of language planning in Canada.

Essentially, language-planning efforts in this country appear largely directed toward large-scale language use across different spheres. I feel it prudent to initiate the study of Aboriginal languages with a conceptualization of language use similar to that held by those with the power to effect real change.

Figure 6.1   The language saturation model

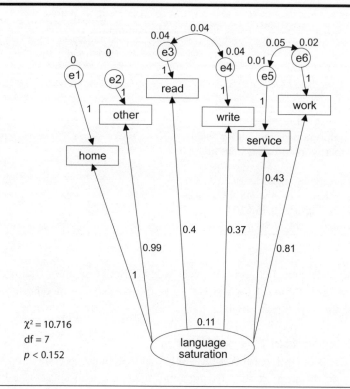

$\chi^2 = 10.716$
df = 7
$p < 0.152$

Confirmatory factor analysis generated the weights applied to each of the indicators in the model. In this method, the measurable variables are conceived of as *manifest variables* influenced by an underlying, or *latent, variable* (or variables) (Maxim 1998).[10]

The congeneric model in this study, unlike the parallel measurement models associated with traditional summated scales, allows both item lambdas and error variances to vary, thereby producing a better "fit" between model and data (Maxim 1998). According to this model, Aboriginal language use at home and in "other places" should be allotted approximately 20% more weight than Aboriginal language use at work, and just over twice the weight of the remaining three variables. See Figure 6.1 for a graphic depiction of the language saturation model.

The desirably small, insignificant chi-square value of this model basically indicates that the observed covariance matrix and the one estimated by the model are not significantly different (i.e., they are similar, or the model "fits" the data) (see Maxim 1998).

The Control Variables

Isolation

The possible confounding nature of geographic isolation on investigation of the language retention/economic development relationship is widely recognized. As argued above and by Norris and MacCon in Chapter 7, isolation contributes to language retention.[11] The average straight-line distance, in kilometres, between a given community and the nearest 100,000 people is therefore included as a control in this analysis.[12]

Reserve Status

In Armstrong's study (1989) of Aboriginal economic success, he notes the influence of legal barriers associated with reserves. Specifically, Indian reserve lands are protected from seizure and alienation, and therefore cannot be used as collateral. These restrictions impede surety bonding and the acquisition of capital investment. Several other regulations pertaining to reserves also create "a development milieu different from (creating uncertainty for potential investors) and more restrictive than that associated with non-reserve lands" (Armstrong 1989, 9). Similarly, the Royal Commission on Aboriginal Peoples (RCAP) (in Cairns 2000) indicates that SES is considerably higher in urban areas than on reserve. As Cairns also notes that language use is greater on than off reserve, I have included reserve status as a control variable in these analyses.

Traditionalism

As indicated earlier, some suggest that Aboriginal culture is incompatible with mainstream economic pursuits. As Aboriginal languages are affiliated with Aboriginal cultures, the former may be related to socio-economic status solely through their relationship to the latter. To account for this possibility, "participation in traditional activities" is included among the control variables. Unfortunately, this operationalization of the degree to which a community is "traditional" is somewhat flawed. Most significantly, it includes post-contact elements such as fiddle playing. This is not problematic if we are simply concerned with traditionalism as a symbolic feature, as symbolic importance may be assigned to items or events that are only perceived to be traditional. However, if one wishes to address the possibility that the fundamental principles of Native culture are incompatible with capitalist pursuits, then the inclusion of European-inspired "traditions" presents grave difficulties.

Age

Age, operationalized as the proportion of the population over the age of 65, is included as a control variable in three of the modelled relationships. The first is labour force participation. As Norris (1996) notes, Native tongues are more common among the elderly, who are likely to have retired from the labour force. For the same reason, age is included in the modelled relationship between language saturation and employment in 1990-91. Age is also considered in relation to social assistance, as those aged people who do not work may more often require government allocations as an alternate means of sustenance.

Education
As indicated earlier, education is related to SES. If language is related to education, therefore, the former is necessarily related to the other two SES indicators currently being examined. To determine whether language is related to labour force status and income in any way other than through its relationship to education, the latter is included as a control variable in a second run of the controlled model.

   Educational attainment is once again operationalized as the proportion of the population having eight or fewer years of education. Whether this is an ideal operationalization is debatable, but Armstrong (1989) utilizes the 0-8 years of education level in his model of economic development, suggesting that completion of these early years is the most critical to economic success.

Data Analysis
The first of three logistic models is a basic bivariate regression of language saturation and each of the eight dependent variables. The second model includes, as control variables, isolation, traditionalism, reserve status, and age.[13] In addition to these variables, the third model also controls for education. The logistic model required that the data be transformed.[14] Concordantly, this research is conceptualized as the analysis of the relationship between language saturation and SES indicators in those communities whose levels of the latter are non-zero.

Missing Data
Missing data from the education, income, and labour force fields in the original data set came already imputed in this community-level compilation. Missing data appear not to have been a problem for any of the independent variables, or for the dependent variables documenting social assistance and 1990-91 employment. Because of uncertainty with respect to the number of individuals between the ages of 56 and 64, two additional cases were missing from the education data.

Where the denominators used to produce the proportions are equal to zero, the proportions are undefined. For the affected dependent variables, these cases are unproblematic since the analyses being conducted simply do not apply (for example, you cannot examine the determinants of employment income in a community where no one is employed). This issue was more contentious, however, in the construction of the language saturation model. The variable describing the proportion of the population receiving services in an Aboriginal language was undefined in about eighty cases (i.e., in eighty communities, no services, in an Aboriginal language or otherwise, were received). These data were replaced in two stages. First, a value of zero was applied to the thirty-two communities with no Aboriginal language use in any of the other five areas comprising the saturation model. Presumably, services in an Aboriginal language would not be provided in a community where no one spoke it. Mean substitution was utilized for the forty-eight communities that did exhibit some measure of Aboriginal language use.

Undefined levels of language use in the workplace were also replaced with the mean value of that variable. As there were only three cases that required this modification, the possibility of its introducing bias is negligible.

Conversion of Results from Logits to Proportions

To make logistic regression results more intelligible, they are converted from logits to proportions. Prior to conversion, one enters specific values of the independent variables into the linear regression equation: $\hat{y} = B_o + BX_1 + \ldots + BX_k$. One then inserts the resultant logit ($\hat{y}$) into the following equation: $p = 1/(1 + \exp^{-\hat{y}})$.

The proportion represented by p reflects the level of the dependent variable expected in a community that exhibits the levels of the independent variables entered into the linear equation described above.

As calculating the expected proportions of all the independent variables for all possible levels of language saturation would be overly arduous, only the highest (3.61), and lowest (0) levels of language saturation are addressed. From both model 2 (which does not control for education) and model 3 (which does control for education), I derive the highest and lowest expected levels of language saturation, holding constant at their means[15] any significant[16] control variables. These values address the following question: "Other things being equal, what is the difference in socio-economic status between those communities with high Aboriginal language saturation and those with low saturation?" A discussion of the significant control variables, while certainly desirable, is beyond the scope of this chapter. A complete discussion may be found in O'Sullivan (2001).

Results

Education

The uncontrolled model predicts that 55.1% of a heavily saturated community would have eight or fewer years of schooling, while only 14% of a minimally saturated community would occupy this lowest education category (a difference of over 40% and a relational fourfold difference). The slope of language saturation is only minutely affected by the introduction of the controls in model 2.

The relationship between language saturation and completion of postsecondary education is comparatively very weak. Maximally and minimally saturated communities differ on this variable by only about 4%.

Labour Force Status

In model 1, all of the five variables comprising this category, with the exception of employment among those in the labour force, are significantly related to language saturation. In general, the relationships are relatively weak.

The control variables in model 2 vary in significance among the dependent variables. In no case, however, does the influence of control variables diminish in any notable degree the influence of language saturation. In most cases, in fact, the slope associated with language saturation increases slightly when controls are introduced.

In model 3, language saturation is again related to all five areas of labour force status, except the employed proportion of the workforce. The introduction of education, however, invariably weakens these relationships. The control variables remain unchanged in terms of relationship significance and direction, although some small variations in strength inevitably occur.

Model 1 indicates that 63.6% of a minimally saturated community will have worked for income in 1990 or 1991. In a maximally saturated community, a level of 43.3% is expected. The difference between the extreme saturation levels actually increases by a few percentage points when the model 2 control variables are introduced. The inclusion of education in model 3 decreases, by about 10 percentage points, the impact of language saturation on 1990-91 employment levels.

The bivariate model indicates that labour force participation in a minimally saturated community should exceed that of a maximally saturated community by about 20 percentage points. Again, the introduction of the model 2 control variables increases the disparity slightly. The introduction of education in model 3, however, has quite a large effect, decreasing the disparity by 15 percentage points.

Interestingly, in none of the three models is language saturation significantly related to employment levels among labour force participants. When the model 2 control variables are introduced, only isolation is significantly (and positively) related at the 0.05 level.

Communities with high and low levels of language saturation are expected to have entrepreneurialism levels of 4.8% and 8.9%, respectively.

Bivariate analysis indicates that 45.2% of a highly saturated community will be recipients of social assistance, as opposed to 30.1% of a minimally saturated community. This disparity increases almost 10 percentage points with the introduction of the model 2 control variables. Again, the addition of education as a control in model 3 attenuates the relationship between language saturation and social assistance. The 24-percentage-point difference described above shrinks to about 14 percentage points.

Income
Bivariate analysis uncovers a weak relationship between language saturation and employment income. A highly saturated community should have about 10% fewer higher earners than a community with low language saturation. The introduction of the model 2 control variables has a negligible effect on this relationship. With the introduction of education as a control variable, however, the relationship between income and language saturation disappears.

Summary of Results
In the simple, bivariate regressions, all significant relationships are consistent with the ghettoization perspective. Communities with higher levels of language saturation are expected to have fewer labour force participants, fewer members employed in 1990 or 1991, fewer entrepreneurs, more recipients of social assistance, more members with lower employment incomes, more members with very little education, and fewer members with higher education. What minor differences were produced by the introduction of the model 2 control variables generally enhance rather than attenuate the bivariate relationships.

In model 3, the relationships between language saturation and the SES indicators are weaker than their counterparts in model 2, but still support the ghettoization perspective across labour force participation, employment, entrepreneur rates, and levels of social assistance.

Discussion
In all three models, where language saturation is significantly related to the SES indicators, it is a negative influence on SES. Of particular interest, however, are the implications associated with the way the significant relationships are patterned. Language saturation is related to labour force participation, but not to employment among participants. The relatively small relationship

between income and language saturation further reinforces the idea that, once in the labour force, Aboriginal and dominant language speakers have relatively similar levels of success. This is especially interesting when we see that the very strong relationship between language saturation and minimal education does not exist between language saturation and postsecondary education. This combination of relationships suggests that perhaps Aboriginal language use is associated with non-involvement in the dominant culture, but is less profoundly related to success when such involvement is attempted. Of course, the possibility of individual-level effects remains.

One possibility is that it is not Aboriginal language use per se that is negatively associated with socio-economic status. Rather, it may be that ineptitude in English or French is the real culprit. Aboriginal language use may decrease dominant language proficiency knowledge in a community, thereby decreasing the motivation of community members to master or maintain it. In fact, even in the absence of such a causal relationship, the two variables are almost necessarily correlated. If people cannot speak English or French, after all, they are still going to speak *something*. If a person is Aboriginal, the default language will almost certainly be a Native tongue. This inherent relationship means that anything affecting dominant language proficiency can automatically be attributed to Aboriginal language retention. Essentially, it may be the case that a lack of English or French proficiency, associated with Aboriginal language use, inhibits socio-economic success, while those who do gain dominant language skills are not hindered by the fact that they *also* speak an Aboriginal tongue.

As expected, less-educated communities have lower SES. As education appears in a separate model, and as it is only this model in which the effect of language saturation is seen to become attenuated, one may reasonably conclude that some of the effects of the language are actually rendered by education. If, as Robinson (1985) asserts, lack of education produces Aboriginal language maintenance, as opposed to vice versa, language saturation may still be said to affect socio-economic status in a manner independent of its relationship to educational attainment.

The Language Saturation Model and Implications for Future Research

The language saturation model employed in this analysis is limited in that it fails to distinguish between several very important facets of language use. This leaves us with an agenda for future research. First, it does not distinguish between the communicative and the symbolic functions of language. Is Aboriginal language use associated with lower income because the language cannot produce the motivating pride promised by maintenance advocates, or is the pride produced simply insufficient to overcome the language barrier between Aboriginals and the economic mainstream? Note that this conflation of functions is not necessarily a flaw. As indicated earlier, programmers generally do not distinguish between language as symbol and language as communication. A spokesperson for the RCAP, for example, recognizes that languages serve this dual purpose, but fails to recognize that this duality has implications with respect to *how* Aboriginal languages should be used: "Hence, the motivation to revive the ancestral language is not communication, since the dominant language fulfils that need, but stems from the desire to revive or protect a tangible emblem of group identity" (in Norris 1996, 168). This spokesperson fails to recognize the possibility that a language may serve as a symbol even where it is hardly spoken. The results of this research imply that using an Aboriginal language to communicate is negatively related to SES. A distinction between the communicative and symbolic functions is now necessary in order to determine whether language in a noncommunicative capacity may be retained or revived so that any symbolic benefits may still be reaped.

Second, this model does not address shift at the language level. As is suggested of traditionalism, the symbolic value of an altered language should not be affected so long as its speakers believe in its authenticity. Corruption of a language, however, may produce effects through its use as a tool of communication. Essentially, failure to document changes in the languages themselves negates the possibility of positively identifying "Whorfian" effects. As indicated earlier, language is considered by many to embody and perpetuate specific worldviews. Additionally, the Aboriginal worldview is thought by many to be incompatible with capitalism. A language that has been substantially altered to resemble a dominant tongue, then, could conceivably be far less detrimental to Aboriginal SES than an Aboriginal language that has retained its original character. Unfortunately, unlike the other complications of language analysis, the resolution of the Whorfian issue seems unlikely. Considering limitations of time and resources, distinguishing which features are native and which are "imported" for each of the Aboriginal languages is all but impossible.

Third, this model does not distinguish language maintenance from language revival and revivification. Language maintenance, or retention, refers to the preservation of Aboriginal languages in those communities where these languages are currently used. Language revival and revivification, respectively, refer to the increase of Aboriginal language use in those communities where the tongues are declining or extinct (Drapeau 1995, 19). Essentially, communities wherein the language already exists on a relatively large scale must be distinguished from those in which it has already been largely lost. Coulmas's assertions (1992) help to illustrate the necessity of this differentiation. She does not deny that ethnic pride can effect positive change, but insists that it cannot do so unless the community in question already possesses a sound economic foundation. In order to achieve the latter, however, some degree of assimilation is necessary. Basically, Coulmas's argument suggests that Aboriginal language use may encourage economic prosperity in communities where the foundation for expansion has been laid by the integration that originally included the loss of the Native tongue. While Aboriginal language *retention* may reduce SES, therefore, Aboriginal language *revival* or *revivification* may increase it. If this is the case, the conflation of these two types of language use must obfuscate the true significance of both.

Fourth, the basis of this model on cross-sectional research may be problematic. As indicated above, Aboriginal languages are in a state of relatively rapid decline, and the introduction of revival programs is a relatively recent development. It is very possible, therefore, that the socio-economic status statistics analyzed in this research reflect states of language saturation that are quite different from those with which they appear to be associated. For example, a traditionally wealthy community whose language has vanished over the last thirty years would have accumulated its wealth, and the infrastructure that currently sustains it, during a period of high language saturation. In this analysis, however, such a community would contribute to the conclusion that SES and language saturation are negatively related.

Additionally, cross-sectional data do not allow for the assessment of causality. While I have included language saturation in this analysis as an independent variable, its status as such is by no means certain. As indicated earlier, whether language affects educational attainment or vice versa is debatable. Does Aboriginal language use disengage Natives from the dominant culture and its economic benefits, or does contact with the dominant culture through economic activities promote a shift to dominant languages?

A related issue concerns the relationship between language decline and social change. As Nettle and Romaine (2000, 79) note: "Where language use changes, there is an underlying social upheaval that may have environmental, economic, or political causes." As Armstrong (1989, 8) indicates, "breakdown of traditional cultures can result in destructive behavior and social pathologies ... limiting the potential of individuals and communities." This is also an implicit argument made by White and Maxim (Chapter 1, this volume) in their cohesion model. It is possible that some of the effects of language per se implied by my results are actually the result of the social disorganization associated with change. For example, it may be that communities with higher language saturation levels have more recently begun to experience major social change. Their lower SES levels may simply be the result of their having had insufficient time to adjust to this change. Arguably, if the decline of their language is halted, their SES will improve because their economic expansion will no longer be impeded by the disempowering spectre of cultural breakdown. Essentially, the relative importance of language use in itself, and *change* in language use (and related cultural changes), must be ascertained. Such information would be most effectively supplied by longitudinal research.

Conclusions

Aboriginal languages in Canada are deteriorating. The widespread belief that this loss will negatively affect First Nations communities has led to various efforts to protect and restore Aboriginal tongues. This study examines whether Aboriginal language use is truly a boon to the socio-economic standing of First Nations communities. While, overall, the analyses suggest that it is not, I hesitate to conclude that Aboriginal language use is a ghettoizing force. First, language saturation seems to be more associated with participation in modern institutions than with success once participation has been attempted. I suspect that this relationship pattern could just as well be the result of a negative relationship between levels of ineptitude in dominant languages and SES.

Even if language saturation per se is related to SES, whether the pattern of relationships uncovered by these analyses reinforces the ghettoization perspective depends on several additional questions. Most importantly, *why* is language saturation high in very low human capital communities and communities with low labour force participation? On the one hand, it is argued by assimilationists and integrationists that language saturation connects these communities to a more traditional mentality that eschews the material accomplishments so valued in the modern West. If this is the case, then the pejorative term "ghettoization" seems inappropriate. On the other hand, the cause of this withdrawal may be more sinister. There are multiple ways in which Aboriginal language can have a negative effect on community morale. If, for example, nonparticipation in the labour force is caused by high rates of illness, injury, depression, and so on brought on by lowered community morale, then language saturation may rightly be accused of ghettoizing Aboriginal communities.

The other consideration that prevents me from proclaiming victory for the ghettoization perspective is the relative weakness of the relationships when education is controlled. That is, if the relationship between Aboriginal language use and SES is the result of the spurious influence of education on both of these variables, then the findings indicate that the residual effect of language is not terribly large. Recall the differences in income and labour force activity levels between the communities with high and low language saturation. Levels of nonparticipation in the labour force, employment in 1990-91, entrepreneurialism, and social assistance differ between minimally and maximally saturated communities by 9, 16, 4, and 14 percentage points, respectively.

Overall, I cannot claim to have produced any definitive evidence that Aboriginal languages either help or hinder the communities in which they are used. The current research may be invoked only as evidence that increasing Aboriginal language use in Native communities is not the economic panacea that many advocates believe it to be. Language use is a very complex issue. Until its nuances are recognized and understood, its effects on other areas of life cannot be adequately assessed.

Notes

1 Quebec communities, as well as a few from other regions, are excluded owing to a lack of data on key control variables.
2 As the second domain is not germane to this research, I will not review its particulars.
3 The survey was administered through personal interviews with sampled persons, although about 17% of adult cases were surveyed through another household member. Most information pertaining to children was also gathered by proxy.
4 This operationalization distinguishes those who fail to complete postsecondary school because they have not acquired its prerequisite from those who do not complete higher education for other reasons.
5 Note that seventy cases have undefined values for this variable, and were therefore excluded from the analysis.
6 This indicator includes community members who operate businesses in addition to those who actually own them. In addition, it must be noted that some contest the claim that entrepreneurialism is a boon to Native communities, as Aboriginal entrepreneurs are highly under-represented in more modern, capital-intensive fields (Aboriginal Entrepreneurs 1998).
7 In order to allow for the production of a logit, and to maintain the shape of the residuals distribution, seven cases with values of 1 were set to 0.95.
8 Note that thirteen undefined cases were removed from the analysis. These are communities in which no employment income was reported.
9 Note that, in model 3, two additional cases are missing as a result of incomplete data on education. In addition, twenty-nine cases are missing from the age variable. Regressions omitting this variable demonstrate that the impact on the relationships described herein by the loss of these cases is negligible.
10 An equation linearly relates each empirical referent (denoted Y) to the latent variable(s) (denoted F) through an estimable parameter (denoted λ): $Y_1 = \lambda_1 F + e_1$.
11 Somewhat counterintuitively, however, Armstrong (1989) found that isolation is positively correlated with economic success in First Nations communities. Jerry White and Paul Maxim of the University of Western Ontario are currently attempting to unpack this relationship.
12 This variable was derived from a separate file produced by Statistics Canada, which was matched by community identification number to the cases in the community-level APS file. This was produced by the University of Western Ontario First Nations Cohesion Project.
13 Where applicable.

14 The logistic model required that the data be converted according to the following equation: $= \log_{10}O = \log_{10}\{(P)/(1-P)\}$. Essentially, this means that the logit is the log (base of 10 logarithm) of the population having a certain characteristic (such as employment) divided by the proportion of the population that lacks that characteristic. Unfortunately, logistic transformation alone was unable to adapt the data to regression assumptions. Further diagnostics revealed that those communities with Y-values of zero formed distinct patterns in the dependent variables' residuals. The existence of these patterns implies that separate analyses are required for these extreme cases. Cases with proportions equal to zero were therefore excluded from the regression analyses. Cases with a score of 1 (instead of zero) are excluded from the variable indicating the level of employment among labour force participants. This difference is not substantive, but is merely an effect of the way in which the information is framed (100% employed is equal to 0% unemployed).

15 As the distribution of the isolation variable is highly skewed, the median is used in place of the mean.

16 Significance for all relationships is defined by the 0.05 alpha level.

References

Adams, H. 1999. *Tortured People: The Politics of Colonization*. Penticton, BC: Theytus Books.

Anaya, H.D. 2000. The determinants of school dropout in the United States. *Dissertation Abstracts International: The Humanities and Social Sciences* 61: 773-A.

Anderson, R.B. 1999. *Economic Development among Aboriginal People in Canada: The Hope for the Future*. North York, ON: Captus Press.

Armstrong, R. 1989. Factors of Indian economic development on-reserve: An initial analysis. In *Native Socio-Economic Development in Canada [Microform]: Adaptation, Accessibility, and Opportunity*, edited by University of Winnipeg Institute of Urban Studies. Winnipeg: University of Winnipeg.

Balakrishnan, T.R., and S. Gyimah. 2000. Language maintenance among ethnic groups in Canada. Paper presented at the annual meeting of the Population Association of America, 23-25 March 2000, Los Angeles.

Bloom, D.E., and G. Grenier. 1996. Language, employment, and earnings in the United States: Spanish-English differentials from 1970 to 1990. *International Journal of the Sociology of Language* 121: 45-68.

Boyd, M. 1999. Integrating language, gender, and race. In *Immigrant Canada: Demographic, Economic, and Social Challenges*, edited by Shiva S. Halli and Leo Driedger. Toronto: University of Toronto Press.

Cairns, A.C. 2000. *Citizens Plus: Aboriginal Peoples and the Canadian State*. Vancouver: UBC Press.

Cook, A.K., and M.W. Jordan. 1997. Explaining variation in income between Hispanic and white female-headed households in Washington. *Hispanic Journal of Behavioral Sciences* 19: 433-45.

Coulmas, F. 1992. *Language and Economy*. Cambridge: Blackwell Publishers.

Crago, M.B., Clair Chen, Fred Genesee, and Stanley E.M. Allen. 1998. Power and deference: Bilingual decision making in Inuit homes. *Journal for a Just and Caring Education* 4: 78-95.

Crawford, J. 1998. Endangered Native American languages: What is to be done, and why? In *Language and Politics in the United States and Canada*, edited by Thomas Ricento and Barbara Burnaby Lawrence. Mahwah, NJ: Erlbaum Associates.

Crystal, D. 2000. *Language Death*. New York: Cambridge University Press.

Dixon, R.M.W. 1997. *The Rise and Fall of Languages*. Cambridge: Cambridge University Press.

Drapeau, L. 1995. Perspectives on Aboriginal language conservation and revitalization in Canada. In *Public Policy and Aboriginal Peoples 1965-1992*. Ottawa: Royal Commission on Aboriginal Peoples.

Eastman, C.M. 1981. Language planning, identity planning, and world view. *International Journal of the Sociology of Language* 32: 45-53.

–. 1985. Establishing social identity through language use. *Journal of Language and Social Psychology* 4: 1-21.

Edwards, John. 1984. Language, diversity and identity. In *Linguistic Minorities, Policies and Pluralism,* edited by J. Edwards. London: Academic Press.

Fettes, M. 1998. Life on the edge: Canada's Aboriginal languages under official bilingualism. In *Language and Politics in the United States and Canada,* edited by Thomas Ricento and Barbara Burnaby Lawrence. Mahwah, NJ: Erlbaum Associates.

Fishman, J.A. 1989. *Language and Ethnicity in Minority Sociolinguistic Perspective.* Cleveland: Multilingual Matters.

–. 1990. What is reversing language shift RLS and how can it succeed? *Journal of Multilingual and Multicultural Development* 11: 5-36.

Forrester, M.A. 1996. *Psychology of Language.* Thousand Oaks, CA: SAGE Publications.

Giles, H., and N. Coupland. 1991. *Language: Contexts and Consequences.* Pacific Grove, CA: Brooks/Cole Publishing.

Grenier, G. 1997. Linguistic and economic characteristics of francophone minorities in Canada: A comparison of Ontario and New Brunswick. *Journal of Multilingual and Multicultural Development* 18: 285-301.

Khosroshahi, F. 1989. Penguins don't care, but women do: A social identity analysis of a Whorfian problem. *Language in Society* 18: 505-25.

Lee, B. 1992. Colonialization and community: Implications for First Nations' development. *Community Development Journal* 27: 211-19.

McArthur, T. 1980. *Comments on Indian Economic Development in Ontario.* Toronto: Oasis Policy Research Group.

McCarty, T.L. 1998. Schooling, resistance, and Amerindian languages. *International Journal of the Sociology of Language* 132: 27-41.

Maxim, P.S. 1998. *Quantitative Research Methods in the Social Sciences.* Toronto: Oxford University Press.

Milloy, J.S. 1999. *A National Crime: The Canadian Government and the Residential School System 1879-1986.* Winnipeg: University of Manitoba Press.

Nettle, Daniel, and Suzanne Romaine. 2000. *The Extinction of the World's Languages.* Toronto: Oxford University Press.

Norris, M.J. 1996. Aboriginal peoples: Demographic and linguistic perspectives. In *Visions of the Heart: Canadian Aboriginal Issues,* edited by David Alan Long and Olive Patricia Dickason. Toronto: Harcourt Brace Canada.

–. 1998. Canada's Aboriginal languages. *Canadian Social Trends* (Winter): 8-16.

O'Sullivan, Erin. 2001. Aboriginal Language Use and Socio-Economic Status. MA thesis, Department of Sociology, University of Western Ontario.

Paquet, B. 2001. Low income cutoffs from 1990 to 1999 and low income measures from 1989 to 1998. Statistics Canada, <http://www.statcan.ca/english/research/75F0002MIE/75F0002MIE00017.pdf>.

Robinson, P. 1985. Language retention among Canadian Indians: A simultaneous equations model with dichotomous endogenous variables. *American Sociological Review* 50: 515-29.

Rumberger, R.W., and K.A. Larson. 1998. Toward explaining differences in educational achievement among Mexican American language minority students. *Sociology of Education* 71: 68-92.

Skutnabb-Kangas, T. 2000. *Linguistic Genocide in Education or Worldwide Diversity and Human Rights?* Mahwah, NJ: Erlbaum Associates.

Spolsky, B. 1998. *Sociolinguistics*. Toronto: Oxford University Press.

Stevens, G., and N. Garrett. 1994. Migrants and the linguistic ecology of New Jersey, 1990. In *Keys to Successful Immigration: Implications of the New Jersey Experience*, edited by Thomas J. Espenshade. Washington, DC: Urban Institute Press.

Tawney, R.H. 1998. The status of third languages. In *The Practice of Language Rights in Canada*, edited by C. Michael MacMillan. New York: Oxford University Press.

Wagamese, R. 2000. Reflections on the Native tongue. *Ottawa Citizen*, 13 April, A5.

Warburton, R. 1997. Status, class, and the politics of Canadian Aboriginal peoples. *Studies in Political Economy* 54: 119-41.

Warry, W. 1998. *Unfinished Dreams: Community Healing and the Reality of Aboriginal Self-Government*. Toronto: University of Toronto Press.

White, J., and P. Maxim. 2000. *Dispersion and Polarization*. Working paper. London: University of Western Ontario.

White, J., P. Maxim, and P.C. Whitehead. 2000. *Social Capital, Social Cohesion and Population Outcomes in Canada's First Nations Communities*. Working paper. London: University of Western Ontario.

Wolbers, M., and G. Driessen. 1996. Social class or migration? Determinants of differences in educational careers between nonindigenous students in secondary education. *Sociologische Gids* 43: 349-66.

7
Aboriginal Language Transmission and Maintenance in Families: Results of an Intergenerational and Gender-Based Analysis for Canada, 1996

Mary Jane Norris and Karen MacCon

Language transmission from one generation to another is the major factor in Aboriginal language maintenance. Unlike other minority heritage language groups in Canada, Aboriginal languages cannot rely on immigration flows for maintaining the population of speakers.[1] Like other minority languages, Aboriginal languages today are subject to the forces of modernization, where the prevalence of more dominant languages in everyday life contributes to the decline in their use. Historical factors, such as the discouragement of Aboriginal language use in residential schools, have ruptured the transmission of language from one generation to another. Also, the fact that most Aboriginal languages were predominantly oral may have affected their chances of survival.

Study Objectives and Approach

The study described in this chapter explores the patterns of intergenerational transmission of Aboriginal languages within families, where at least one parent has an Aboriginal mother tongue.[2] Within the context of family structure and gender, analysis is directed at the passing of Aboriginal languages to the next generation and the relationship between transmission and marriage type. Linguistic intermarriage (husband-wife endogamous and exogamous couples) and lone-parent families are of particular interest. The findings will provide insight into the future with respect to language continuity and ability to speak, and further reinforcement for the recommendations of the Royal Commission on Aboriginal Peoples concerning the survival of Aboriginal languages. Our aim is to sketch out the research foundations on which policy can be better informed and developed with regard to Aboriginal language preservation.

Background on Aboriginal Languages[3]

The variety in Aboriginal culture and identity is reflected in Canada's Aboriginal languages, which are many and diverse. Today, some fifty individual languages belong to eleven Aboriginal language families or isolates, ten First Nations and Inuktitut. Most language families consist of separate but related member languages (for example, the Algonquian language family consists of individual languages such as Cree, Blackfoot, and Algonquin, among others). Each individual language can also have separate dialects (such as Swampy Cree, Woods Cree).

The range in the size of the eleven Aboriginal language families in Canada is considerable. In terms of mother tongue populations, the largest family by far is the Algonquian language group. According to the 1996 Census,[4] there were 147,000 persons in the Algonquian mother tongue population, whereas counts of the smallest families, such as Haida or Tlingit, are a few hundred persons or less. In 1996, the three largest families – Algonquian, Inuktitut (28,000), and Athapaskan (20,000) represented 93% of persons with an Aboriginal mother tongue. The other eight language families accounted for only 7%.

Population Size and Intergenerational Transmission[5]

Among Canada's Aboriginal languages, only three out of some fifty languages have sufficiently large population bases to ensure survival over the long term, based on the understanding that the larger the population of speakers, the greater the chance for survival. Cree, Inuktitut, and Ojibway, the largest, most widespread, and flourishing of Aboriginal languages, have significantly large mother tongue populations of 87,600, 27,800, and 25,900, respectively (Table 7.1). These languages are also highly likely to be passed on to the next generation, as indicated by high continuity indices that measure the ratio of home language[6] speakers to the population with that particular language as a mother tongue. Inuktitut has a relatively high continuity index[7] of 86 persons per 100 speaking Inuktitut mother tongue, followed by continuity indices of 72 and 55 for Cree and Ojibway, respectively. The state of these three languages demonstrates viability (Table 7.1).

In sharp contrast, many of the smaller languages, often with far fewer than a 1,000 speakers, have very low prospects for continuity and can be considered endangered. Many British Columbia First Nations have small populations. For example, as of 1996, there were only 240 persons with a Haida mother tongue, and the continuity index is only 6 (see Table 7.1). Even the larger languages, such as the Nishga of British Columbia, with a mother tongue population of 800 persons, have low chances of passing the language on to the next generation.[8]

The use of a language at home has important implications for the prospects of transmission to the next generation, and hence its continuity. A language no longer spoken at home cannot be handed down as a mother tongue to

Table 7.1 Selected indicators for Aboriginal language vitality, based on total Canadian population, 1996

| Aboriginal language | Mother tongue[a] | Index of continuity, HL/MT[a] | % children in mixed marriages | Index of ability, Kn/MT[b] | Average age of population with | | | Status of language[c] |
					Knowledge of Aboriginal language	Aboriginal mother tongue[a]	Aboriginal home language[a]	
Algonquian Family								
Cree	146,635	70	34	117	30.5	30.9	28.8	**Mostly viable**
Ojibway	87,555	72	31	117	29.9	30.2	27.9	Viable large
Montagnais-Naskapi	25,885	55	47	122	34.9	36.2	34.4	Viable large
Mi'kmaq	9,070	94	19	104	25.1	25.2	24.8	Viable small
Oji-Cree	7,310	72	43	111	29.5	29.9	29.2	Viable small
Attikamek	5,400	80	27	114	25.7	26.3	26.8	Viable small
Blackfoot	3,995	97	7	103	21.8	21.9	21.5	Viable small
Algonquin	4,145	61	50	135	36.4	39.7	40.6	Viable small
Malecite	2,275	58	50	119	29.8	30.7	31.4	Viable small
	655	37	83	148	40.5	44.0	44.8	Viable small
Algonquian NIE	350	40	75	159	47.2	52.2	46.7	Uncertain
Inuktitut Family	27,780	86	19	109	23.9	23.9	23.3	**Viable large**
Athapaskan Family	20,090	68	41	117	31.4	32.5	30.0	**Mostly viable**
Dene	9,000	86	28	107	24.4	24.8	24.1	Viable small
South Slave	2,620	55	45	124	35.6	37.8	38.4	Viable small
Dogrib	2,085	72	29	118	28.3	29.8	30.6	Viable small
Carrier	2,190	51	70	130	37.5	41.4	40.5	Viable small
Chipewyan	1,455	44	82	128	39.4	40.2	40.7	Viable small
Athapaskan NIE	1,310	37	70	129	41.6	44.7	44.2	Uncertain
Chilcotin	705	65	55	130	32.2	37.0	36.9	Viable small
Kutchin-Gwich'in (Loucheux)	430	24	67	114	53.0	53.1	56.8	Endangered
North Slave (Hare)	290	60	36	116	38.3	39.1	39.8	Endangered
(Dakota) Siouan Family	4,295	67	49	111	31.0	31.9	28.0	**Viable small**

Salish Family	3,200	25	79	132	42.0	48.7	47.2	Endangered
Salish NIE	1,850	24	80	130	43.0	49.7	48.5	Endangered
Shuswap	745	25	80	134	38.7	46.3	42.9	Endangered
Thompson	595	31	80	135	43.1	48.6	48.3	Endangered
Tsimshian Family	2,460	31	71	132	43.2	48.0	49.6	Mostly endangered
Gitskan	1,200	39	76	123	41.4	45.2	45.7	Viable small
Nishga	795	23	70	146	41.8	47.5	57.6	Endangered
Tsimshian	465	24	83	132	50.5	55.9	52.7	Endangered
Wakashan Family	1,650	27	79	118	47.3	51.3	51.1	Endangered
Wakashan	1,070	24	88	129	47.7	53.0	53.2	Endangered
Nootka	590	31	69	99	46.5	48.1	48.4	Endangered
Iroquoian Family[d]	590	13	88	160	36.4	46.5	52.0	Uncertain
Mohawk	350	10	100	184	36.6	46.1	60.5	Uncertain
Iroquoian NIE	235	13	80	128	35.8	47.0	41.4	Uncertain
Haida Family	240	6	100	144	46.7	50.4	64.6	Endangered
Tlingit Family	145	21	100	128	45.5	49.3	41.6	Endangered
Kutenai Family	120	17	67	200	37.1	52.3	41.2	Endangered
Aboriginal Ln NIE	1,405	28	68	176	43.0	47.0	45.8	Endangered
Total Aboriginal languages	208,610	70	34	117	30.4	31.0	28.3	Mix of viable and endangered

Notes: The indicators – index of continuity, index of ability, and average age of population with Aboriginal mother tongue and home language – are based on single and multiple responses (of mother tongue and home language) combined. Compared with multiple-based measures, the index of continuity is lower and the index of ability is higher for single responses. The average age of persons with a single Aboriginal mother tongue or home language tends to be higher, particularly for endangered languages, where the average age of those speaking only an Aboriginal language at home is much older than those speaking more than one language.

a Single and multiple.

b The index of ability (Kn/MT) compares the number of people who report being able to speak the language (Kn) with the number who have that Aboriginal language as a mother tongue (MT).

c The viability status of the *individual* languages is based on a classification in Kinkade 1991.

d Data for the Iroquoian family is not particularly representative due to the significant impact of incomplete enumeration of reserves for this language family. Other languages, such as those in the Algonquian, family may be affected to some extent by incomplete enumeration.

Sources: Adapted from Norris 1998; 1996 Census of Canada.

the younger generation. However, even with only a few thousand people, some of the smaller languages in Canada appear viable. For example, the Attikamek in Quebec have a mother tongue population of only 4,000 persons but a continuity index of 97. This means that there are 97 persons speaking Attikamek at home for every 100 persons with an Attikamek mother tongue. Clearly, the chances of transmitting Attikamek to the next generation are high.

Thus, even though some languages with 1,000 or more speakers are relatively small, they can be considered viable if their prospects for continuity are high. Languages such as Attikamek, Montagnais-Naskapi, Mi'kmaq, Dene, and Dogrib are considered viable. These languages tend to be spoken in isolated or well-organized communities with strong self-awareness. In these communities, language is considered one of the important marks of identity (Kinkade 1991).

Language Transmission and Maintenance[9]

The motivation to maintain or revive an Aboriginal language can be best understood by considering both the communicative and symbolic functions of language. Aboriginal languages, whether viable or endangered, not only serve as tools of communication but also remain important symbols of cultural and group identity. They are therefore critical components in maintaining and transmitting that culture and identity. While loss of language does not necessarily lead to the death of a culture, it can severely handicap the transmission of that culture. In cases where the group may be shifting from its ancestral language to the dominant language, the Aboriginal language may no longer be used as the main form of communication, but it still remains an important symbol of the group's identity. There are two processes that we can identify: language maintenance and language revitalization.

Language maintenance refers to the steps necessary to ensure that intergenerational transmission can be maintained for those viable languages in communities where the Aboriginal language is still both the mother tongue and the main language of communication.

Revitalization involves trying to "revive" languages that are effectively endangered in communities due to the developing shift to the dominant language. To revitalize a language, the capacity to transmit it from one generation to the next must be restored. It is not enough to increase the number of second-language speakers, but it is also necessary to increase the number of Aboriginal first-language speakers while restoring the transmission of that language from one generation to the next. The transmission of Aboriginal languages from older to younger generations becomes the critical factor in the continuation of any Aboriginal language.

In its recommendations concerning the revitalization of Aboriginal languages, the Royal Commission on Aboriginal Peoples (RCAP) indicated that intergenerational transmission is best effected through use of an Aboriginal language in everyday life in the home and in the community; formal instruction alone is not enough. Once intergenerational transmission is ensured, language usage can be extended into work, higher education, and government. "The continual exposure to the dominant language and the necessity to use it in every facet of daily life is a powerful catalyst for the decline of the Aboriginal language" (Royal Commission on Aboriginal Peoples 1996, 614-17). Language maintenance and revival are critical if currently viable languages are to continue to be transmitted from one generation to the next and if endangered languages are to survive.

Languages with Young Populations

The average age of those who have an Aboriginal mother tongue or speak it as a home language indicates the extent to which the language has been transmitted to the younger generation. The higher the average age of traditional language speakers, the relatively fewer young people have learned or still understand the language. This also affects the intergenerational communication between the youth and the older people who still speak their traditional tongue. If the language is not transmitted to the younger generations, then as these older persons continue to age and then die, so will the language. Viable languages such as Attikamek, Inuktitut, and Dene are characterized by relatively young mother tongue populations (average ages between 22 and 24 years) and corresponding high indices of continuity (between 86 and 97). In contrast, the endangered languages, such as Haida, Kutenai, and Tlingit, have typically older mother tongue populations (average ages between 40 and 65) combined with extremely low continuity indices of 21 or less. Notably in 1996, only 20% of children under 5 had an Aboriginal mother tongue, whereas 60% of those 85 years and over and 30% of those aged 40 to 44 had an Aboriginal mother tongue.

Language and Community Residence

It is reasonable to infer that the reserve environment of Registered Indians and the Northern communities of the Inuit would tend to support the maintenance and transmission of Aboriginal languages. In 1996, 52% of Registered Indians living on reserve and 67% of Inuit (most of whom live in Northern communities) reported an Aboriginal mother tongue, compared with only 18% of Registered Indians off reserve, 6% of Non-Status Indians, and 7% of Métis. Similarly, Registered Indians and Inuit have the highest ratio of Aboriginal language use in the home among all groups, with continuity indices of 80 and 85, respectively. In contrast, Non-Status Indians and Métis (who tend to live off reserve and are more scattered throughout urban areas), as well as off-reserve Registered Indians, have lower levels (58, 50, and 40, respectively).

Language Maintenance and Life Cycle

Patterns of language transmission within the family and the relationship between language maintenance and life cycle changes are important. Analysis of past census data (1981-96) shows that the use of an Aboriginal language at home relative to the mother tongue population is related to stages in the life cycle. Language loss was most pronounced during the family formation years, and especially among women.

> As youth move out of the original family home, marriage, entry into the labour force, and a different, often large, urban environment can further accelerate their language decline. Without the support of a closely-knit community, and immersed in the language and culture of the dominant society, language erosion becomes difficult to resist. Indeed, the data show that language loss is most pronounced during the labour force years. While this holds for both men and women, it is particularly notable for women. Why this should be so is not clear, but contributing factors may include the fact that women are more likely than men to leave their reserves and marry non-Aboriginals. (Norris 1998)

The decline in use of an Aboriginal language at home was most pronounced among women between the age groups of 20-24 and 35-39. Because these are the very years during which women tend to bring up young children, this shift (from an Aboriginal home language to another home language) is all the more serious for the transmission of Aboriginal languages.

Aboriginal Language Transmission and Maintenance:
The Effects of Gender and Marriage Type

How does intermarriage affect the transmission of Aboriginal languages? According to Harrison (1997), the most recent censuses have shown an increasing tendency of Canadian couples to choose mates who differ from themselves, across many social dimensions. Marriages in the 1990s are more likely to involve people from different cultural, religious, and ethnic backgrounds than ever before (Harrison 1997, 290). Exogamy[10] may play a critical role in passing on Aboriginal language(s) to the next generation. In addition, gender roles within the context of family structure, particularly in lone-parent families and exogamous couples, may also have an impact on language transmission. This study attempts to determine how differences in marriage and family types – husband-wife, linguistically endogamous or exogamous couples, and lone-parent – affect that transmission, and whether the impact varies by gender of the parent.

Language transmission from one generation to the next is studied by comparing language characteristics of children in the age group 5-14 with those of their parents. This method of comparing mother tongues of children with those of their parents was pioneered in Canada by Réjean Lachapelle (see Harrison 1997).

The 1996 Census of Canada enables the researcher to compare language characteristics three ways. First, language can be transmitted as a mother tongue. Second, language can be passed on to the next generation as a home language. Finally, the third variable used to analyze language transmission is knowledge, or ability to speak a language well enough to conduct a conversation. In the case of Aboriginal languages, this is a relevant measure, as there is an ongoing concerted effort to provide instruction to children in their indigenous languages. "These include such measures as language instruction programs, Aboriginal media programming, and the recording of elders' stories, songs, and accounts of history in the Aboriginal language. Perhaps as a result, the number of people who can speak and understand an Aboriginal language has been on the rise" (Norris 1998).

Data Considerations and Methods

Canada is one of the few countries to collect language data relating to both language use and language ability. The national census includes questions on mother tongue, home language, and knowledge of official and non-official languages. The unit of analysis is based on children derived from the family data file. This permits the comparison of the language characteristics of children with those of their parents, yielding an assessment of the extent to which languages are passed from one generation to the next, either as the mother tongue or as a second language.

Data on children with knowledge of an Aboriginal language (ability to speak), with an Aboriginal mother tongue, or with an Aboriginal home language are analyzed by family status, focusing particularly on husband-wife and lone-parent families where at least one of the parents has an Aboriginal mother tongue. Data are also presented, for each individual Aboriginal language or language family, according to the mother tongue of the parent or parents.

It should be noted that for retrieval purposes, children are identified as having an Aboriginal mother tongue or home language, or having an ability to speak at a general level, that is, the child's specific Aboriginal language was not retrieved. It is assumed that if both child and parent have an Aboriginal mother tongue, then it will be the same language. For example, if a child has an Aboriginal mother tongue and the parent's mother tongue is Cree, it is reasonable to assume that the child's mother tongue would also be Cree.

Endogamous couples were defined in relation to both the husband and wife having the same Aboriginal mother tongue (for example, Cree). Practically all of the exogamous couples consisted of Aboriginal/non-Aboriginal languages, and cases of exogamous Aboriginal language couples (e.g., Cree/Ojibway) were few. Therefore, distinctions were not made in the analysis between mixed Aboriginal and Aboriginal/non-Aboriginal couples.

It should also be noted that in this study, the retrieval and analysis of data were restricted to the Canada level, without a breakdown by residence on or off reserve. Further understanding of transmission patterns could be gained with analysis of residence on and off reserve where population size permits, and possibly by regions.

The study population consists of children residing in Canada with at least one parent who has an Aboriginal mother tongue (in either husband-wife or lone-parent families). The study population does not include non-children who report an Aboriginal mother tongue or home language, or those who have the ability to speak an Aboriginal language, if they do not have a parent with an Aboriginal mother tongue. The numbers of children so affected are relatively small with respect to mother tongue (325) or home language (550). In the case of children having the ability to speak an Aboriginal language,

Table 7.2 Number of children aged 5-14 years with an Aboriginal mother tongue or home language, or with knowledge of an Aboriginal language, by family structure and gender, 1996

Family structure	Knowledge of an Aboriginal language	Aboriginal mother tongue	Aboriginal home language
Parent(s) with Aboriginal mother tongue			
Endogamous families	28,890	20,115	16,995
Exogamous families	12,730	1,640	695
By husband	6,150	440	250
By wife	6,580	1,200	455
Lone-parent families			
Male parent	1,715	855	655
Female parent	10,429	4,455	3,220
Parent(s) without Aboriginal mother tongue	11,900	325	550
Total number of children	65,664	27,390	22,115

Source: Statistics Canada, census data, special tabulations (author calculations).

however, there are close to 12,000 whose parent(s) do not report an Aboriginal mother tongue (Table 7.2). This group could have one of three origins. It is likely many of these children are learning an Aboriginal language as a second language. It is also possible that a small number of these children (particularly those with an Aboriginal mother tongue or home language) could have been adopted, since one's mother tongue or home language is usually transmitted through that of the parent(s). Finally, it is also possible that their parent(s), while not having an Aboriginal mother tongue, may have learned an Aboriginal language as a second language and passed on that knowledge.

Characteristics of the Study Population

Among the nearly 59,000 children in the study population, the majority, 45,850 (78%), are in husband-wife families, with the remaining 22% residing in lone-parent families. As Table 7.3 indicates, most lone-parent families (86%) are headed by females. The fact that there are more female than male lone parents with an Aboriginal mother tongue is consistent with the ratios in the general Aboriginal population. In 1996, 18% of Aboriginal women in Canada aged 15 and over were heading families on their own, compared with only 3% of Aboriginal men (Tait 2000, 253-54).

In terms of intermarriage, just over half (52%) of the children in the study population are represented in endogamous marriages.[11] Just over a quarter (26%) are in exogamous marriages, and 22% belong to lone-parent families. Within husband-wife families, the majority of children, some 66%, have both parents with the same Aboriginal mother tongue (Table 7.3). It is possible that intermarriage, residence, and fertility considerations affect these findings.

Table 7.3 Distribution of children aged 5-14 years, by family structure and gender, 1996

Family structure	Number of children	Share of total (%)	Distribution by type and gender (%)
Children in husband-wife families	45,850	78.0	100.0
Endogamous families	30,490	51.9	66.5
Exogamous families	15,360	26.1	33.5
By husband	7,640	13.0	16.7
By wife	7,720	13.1	16.8
Lone-parent families	12,925	22.0	100.0
Male parent	1,820	3.1	14.1
Female parent	11,105	18.9	85.9
Total number of children	58,775	100.0	

Source: Statistics Canada, census data, special tabulations (author calculations).

It is highly probable that most of the husband-wife families that are endogamous in terms of language are located in Aboriginal communities, including reserves and settlements, whereas exogamous families are more likely residing off reserve. Given that the maintenance and continuity of Aboriginal languages is significantly higher on reserve than off reserve, parents on reserve are more likely to have an Aboriginal language as a mother tongue in the first place. Second, intermarriage is more likely to occur off reserve, given that the probability of choosing a mate with an Aboriginal mother tongue is significantly lower where either English or French is the dominant language.[12] The effect of the relatively small population size of mother tongue groups on their degree of endogamy has been documented in the literature. Some of the explanations offered include the dimensions of "availability" and "desirability" of certain characteristics in a mate and their interaction. There are also a number of considerations with respect to language being a barrier in marriage formation, the tendency for "like to marry like," and the relative population size that play out differently between on- and off-reserve locations. The impact of higher fertility on reserve than off reserve, combined with the fact that parents with an Aboriginal mother tongue are more likely to reside on reserve, suggests that endogamous couples probably have larger family sizes than mixed couples.

Passing on the Language to the Next Generation

Focusing on children of parents who have an Aboriginal mother tongue, we can assess transmission of the language to the next generation. Table 7.4 shows the children in families[13] and, for each Aboriginal language, the percentages of children who have an Aboriginal mother tongue or home language or who are able to speak the language. Variation in these indicators across the different language groups reflects their earlier classifications regarding the viability of the language, based on continuity and population size.

Knowledge of, or Ability to Speak, the Language

The overwhelming majority of children in the study population – some 54,400, or 93% – are reported to have knowledge of an Aboriginal language (Table 7.4).[14] The proportion of children having the ability to conduct a conversation in an Aboriginal language varies across different Aboriginal languages.[15] For most of the viable languages, at least 85% of children are able to speak the language, whereas among some of the endangered languages, only about half of the children are able to speak the language.

There are, of course, variations within viable and endangered languages themselves. Practically all of the children (at least 95%) are reported to speak the language in marriages involving mother tongue populations of Cree, Montagnais-Naskapi, Mi'kmaq, Attikamek, Inuktitut, and Dogrib. In the case of the endangered languages, some caution is required in their interpretation, given that the numbers are small and hence more subject to effects of sampling variability. For example, there are less than 100 children in husband-wife families involving parents with Haida, Tlingit, or Kutenai mother tongues combined, for which some 60% report an ability to speak the language. In the case of the children with Salish or Tsimshian parents, both the numbers (each around 600 children) and the proportions able to speak the language (about 70% and 90%, respectively) are higher than for other endangered languages, including Wakashan. In this latter case, of the 300 children with Wakashan parentage, just over half have the ability to speak an Aboriginal language. These findings for endangered languages appear to be consistent with the younger average ages of the populations able to speak Salish and Tsimshian (around 42 years, versus 47 years for Wakashan and Haida). These figures suggest that transmission of the language to children, even as a second language, may go some way toward preventing or at least slowing down the extinction of these languages.

Mother Tongue

The reported number of children[16] with an Aboriginal mother tongue as indicated in Table 7.4 (overall 47%) is significantly lower than the proportion reporting an ability to speak an Aboriginal language (93% overall). Among children of parents whose mother tongue belongs to the largest viable First Nation language, Cree, 97% have the ability to speak an Aboriginal language but only 45% report an Aboriginal mother tongue. The second largest First Nation language, Ojibway, demonstrates an even greater contrast, with 87% reporting an ability to speak that language yet only 25% having an Aboriginal mother tongue. In the case of Inuktitut, only slightly smaller than Ojibway in number but far more viable in terms of continuity, the difference between ability to speak the language and mother tongue is least (98% of the children have the ability to speak and 79% indicate an Aboriginal mother tongue).

For endangered languages, there are sharp contrasts between the proportion of children who know an Aboriginal language and the proportion that actually have an Aboriginal mother tongue. For example, only 10% of children with Salish and Tsimshian language parentage have an Aboriginal mother tongue, although 70% and 90%, respectively, report an ability to speak one. In the case of children with Wakashan parentage, only 3% report having an Aboriginal mother tongue, while 52% have some knowledge of the language. There still appears to be a relatively strong tendency among parents to transmit knowledge of their mother tongue, but a very weak tendency to pass on

Table 7.4 Children aged 5-14 years of parent(s) with an Aboriginal mother tongue, by possession of Aboriginal mother tongue or home language or knowledge of Aboriginal language, 1996

Aboriginal languages	Number of children	% with knowledge of an Aboriginal language	% with Aboriginal mother tongue	% with Aboriginal home language	Index of continuity, HL/MT	Index of ability, Kn/MT	Status of language
Algonquian Family	**41,925**	**92.8**	**43.2**	**33.1**	**77**	**215**	
Cree	24,795	96.7	60.3	35.7	59	160	Viable large
Ojibway	8,065	87.1	24.9	16.0	64	350	Viable large
Montagnais-Naskapi	2,015	98.5	87.3	81.1	93	113	Viable small
Mi'kmaq	1,895	96.0	49.3	30.9	63	195	Viable small
Oji-Cree	1,465	90.1	58.0	41.3	71	155	Viable small
Attikamek	970	96.9	93.3	90.7	97	104	Viable small
Blackfoot	1,505	91.0	8.0	5.0	63	1,142	Viable small
Algonquin	475	90.5	56.8	16.8	30	159	Viable small
Malecite	190	86.8	2.6	7.9	300	3,300	Viable small
Inuktitut Family	**7,580**	**98.1**	**79.0**	**68.4**	**87**	**124**	**Viable large**
Athapaskan Family	**5,585**	**90.5**	**41.3**	**32.8**	**79**	**219**	
Dene	2,425	94.4	66.8	57.3	86	141	Viable small
South Slave	715	92.4	28.7	20.3	71	322	Viable small
Dogrib	610	97.5	50.0	31.1	62	195	Viable small
Carrier	525	89.5	7.6	5.7	74	1,175	Viable small
Chipewyan	545	79.8	11.0	7.3	67	725	Viable small
Athapaskan NIE	285	80.7	12.3	3.5	29	657	Uncertain
Chilcotin	250	86.4	8.0	6.0	75	1,080	Viable small
Kutchin-Gwich'in (Loucheux)/North Slave	215	74.4	11.6	4.7	40	640	Endangered

(Dakota) Siouan Family	1,975	87.5	47.3	41.0	87	185	Viable small
Salish Family	605	68.6	9.1	0.8	9	755	Endangered
Tsimshian Family	590	89.8	10.2	1.7	17	883	Endangered
Wakashan Family	300	51.7	3.3	0.0	0	1,551	Endangered
Iroquoian Family	80	45.3	31.3	0.0	0	145	Uncertain
Haida Family–Tlingit–Kutenai isolates	85	58.8	23.5	0.0	0	250	Endangered
Total Aboriginal languages	58,570	92.5	47.0	37.5	80	197.1	

Source: Statistics Canada, census data, special tabulations (author calculations).

their own mother tongue to their children. Children are thus much more likely to learn endangered languages only as a second language.

Home Language

Few children, some 22,000, or 38% of the study population, use an Aboriginal language at home, even among the more viable languages. For example, only 36% of children with Cree language parentage spoke an Aboriginal language at home, even though 45% of them had an Aboriginal mother tongue. In the case of Ojibway, only 16% of children use an Aboriginal language in the home, even with 25% reporting an Aboriginal mother tongue. For Inuktitut, just over two-thirds (68%) of children with Inuktitut parentage speak the language at home, even though 80% state having an Inuktitut mother tongue. These findings suggest that even for some of Canada's more viable Aboriginal languages, there is erosion of language use in the home. There are only a few viable languages that the overwhelming majority of children continue to speak at home. Among children with Montagnais-Naskapi and Attikamek parentage, 81% and 91%, respectively, speak their Aboriginal language at home.

What is most significant is that among children whose linguistic parentage is one of the endangered languages, practically none speak an Aboriginal language at home. Children with parents whose mother tongues are Haida, Tlingit, Kutenai, or Wakashan do not speak an Aboriginal language. Only a negligible 1% and 2%, respectively, of children of Salish and Tsimshian descent speak an Aboriginal language at home. Given that there are few children speaking these languages at home, it is reasonable to expect that these languages could easily be close to extinction within a generation. While it is encouraging that children are learning an Aboriginal language as a second language, if they are not speaking the language at home, they are not likely to pass it on to their own children. Thus, in terms of passing the language on to the next generation, most of Canada's Aboriginal languages that are currently considered viable may experience growing problems of continuity with younger generations, accelerating the process of language erosion. In the case of already endangered languages, extinction appears to be only a generation away.

Family Structure, Exogamy, and Gender

Do the proportions of children with knowledge of an Aboriginal language, or with an Aboriginal mother tongue or home language, differ between husband-wife and lone-parent families? Overall, the proportion of children who are reported to have an ability to speak an Aboriginal language does not seem to differ by family structure, being similar between husband-wife and lone-parent (male or female) families (about 93% to 94%). As Table 7.5 indicates,

Table 7.5 Summary of language indicators for children aged 5-14 years of parent(s) with Aboriginal mother tongue, 1996

Family structure	Number of children	Index of continuity (HL/MT)	Index of ability (Kn/MT)	% of children with knowledge of Aboriginal language	% of children with Aboriginal mother tongue	% of children with Aboriginal home language
Endogamous families	30,490	85	144	96.9	67.4	57.0
Exogamous families						
By husband	7,640	56	1,376	79.8	5.8	3.2
By wife	7,720	52	543	85.2	15.7	8.2
Lone-parent families						
Male parent	1,820	66	201	91.2	47.0	31.0
Female parent	11,105	72	234	93.9	40.1	29.0
At least 1 parent with an Aboriginal mother tongue	45,275	81	194	93.9	48.2	39.0
Only 1 parent with an Aboriginal mother tongue	15,360	53	778	83.2	10.7	4.5

however, the proportions of children in husband-wife families with (at least one parent with) an Aboriginal mother tongue (48%) or home language (39%) are higher than the corresponding shares for children in female lone-parent families (40% and 29%, respectively), although closer to male lone-parent families (47% and 31%). This would suggest that family structure does play an important role in language use, although a clearer picture emerges when we consider the mother tongues of husband and wife.

Exogamy

Analysis of these husband-wife families by linguistically endogamous and exogamous couples indicates that children fare best in terms of Aboriginal language transmission or knowledge within endogamous marriages. Lone-parent families are the next most effective, and transmission is worst in exogamous marriages. Contrasts are most pronounced with respect to mother tongue and home language. The proportion of children with an Aboriginal mother tongue is 67% within endogamous marriages, compared with 40% in female lone-parent families and just 10% in mixed marriages. Furthermore, within exogamous marriages, less than 5% of children speak an Aboriginal language at home, a sharp contrast to the 57% of children with an Aboriginal home language living in endogamous marriages, and still significantly lower than the 29% of children in female lone-parent families.

Gender-Based Differences

Analysis of family structure and exogamy by sex suggests some interesting gender differences that warrant further exploration. For example, the proportion of children with an Aboriginal mother tongue in female exogamous marriages (involving the out-marriage of the mother) is 16%. This is significantly higher than the 6% of children in male exogamous marriages. However, the corresponding difference between female and male exogamous marriages in terms of the proportions of children speaking an Aboriginal language at home are 8% and 3%, respectively, not as great as the differential for mother tongue. Similarly the gender-based difference in the proportions of children with knowledge of an Aboriginal language is also not as pronounced. For lone-parent (female) families, 85% of the children report a knowledge of Aboriginal language, and for lone-parent (male) families, it is 80%.

Table 7.5 allows comparisons between male and female exogamous marriages using indices of language continuity and ability. For every 100 children with an Aboriginal mother tongue, relatively more children (56) in male exogamous marriages speak an Aboriginal language at home than in female exogamous marriages (52). So, even though children in female exogamous marriages are more likely to have an Aboriginal language as a mother tongue compared with their counterparts in male exogamous marriages, they are less likely to speak their Aboriginal mother tongue in the home. On the other hand, compared with children of mothers who have married out, ability indices suggest that children whose fathers married out are about two and half times more likely to learn an Aboriginal language as a second language rather than as a mother tongue.

In terms of Aboriginal language transmission and maintenance, children in male lone-parent families appear to fare slightly better than those with female lone-parents, with higher proportions having knowledge of an Aboriginal language or with an Aboriginal mother tongue or home language. For example, 47% of children in male lone-parent families have an Aboriginal mother tongue, compared with 40% for female lone-parent families; the corresponding proportions with respect to home language are 31% and 29%. Continuity indices suggest that children in male lone-parent families are more likely than children of female lone parents to speak their Aboriginal mother tongue at home, while children in female lone-parent families are slightly more likely to learn an Aboriginal language as a second language (Table 7.5).

Thus, children from endogamous marriages are most likely to have an Aboriginal mother tongue and to use their language at home, while those within exogamous marriages are least likely – most notably those in which the mother has married out (i.e., where the father does not have an Aboriginal mother tongue). With respect to language continuity and family structure, while children in lone-parent families do not fare as well as those in endogamous husband-wife families, they do have better prospects than those within mixed marriages. With respect to gender differences, women with an Aboriginal mother tongue in exogamous marriages or as lone parents are less likely than their male counterparts to have their children using their Aboriginal mother tongue in the home.

Some of these differentials in the transmission of language associated with intermarriage and gender can probably be explained in part by residential variations. As noted earlier, endogamous marriages are bound to be more common than mixed marriages in Aboriginal communities, where it is easier to retain indigenous language. With respect to gender, Aboriginal women are more likely than their male counterparts to live off reserve and have higher rates of out-migration from reserves. Similarly, Aboriginal women are much more likely than men to be lone parents or in mixed marriages, living off reserve, and more likely to be exposed to the dominant mainstream languages of English or French. Consequently, compared with their male counterparts, the challenges of maintaining the use of an Aboriginal language at home are probably greater for Aboriginal women who are lone parents, and especially so for those in mixed marriages.

Figure 7.1   Aboriginal language continuity and percentage of children from exogamous marriages, 1996

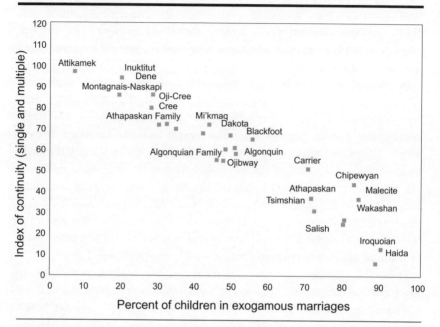

Overall exogamy and the continuity of language appear to be inversely associated. However, further exploration of the role of residence would be required to better understand the differentials in language continuity associated with intermarriage and family structure by gender.

Exogamy, Language Continuity, and Language Transmission

We examined the relationship between exogamy and language continuity as they relate to the transmission of the different Aboriginal languages. Language outcomes are compared across language groups by family structure and parent gender, as well as by exogamy. The visual presentation of Figure 7.1 provides a clear indication of the strong inverse linear association between language continuity (for all ages) and exogamy (percentage of children in mixed marriages) for Aboriginal languages. Exogamy generally reflects both the impacts of population size and the result of the integration process, such that as the degree of exogamy increases, the continuity of languages diminishes. This is consistent with Harrison (1997).

Viable languages with extremely high language continuity (>80%), such as Attikamek, Montagnais-Naskapi, and Inuktitut, and low exogamy rates (<20%) are in the top left corner of the graph. In contrast, endangered languages such as Haida, Tlingit, and Kutenai are in the lower right corner, with extremely low continuity levels of 20% or less and exogamy rates averaging some 90%. The largest First Nation language, Cree, is in the upper left quadrant, with continuity and exogamy rates of about 70% and 30%, respectively. Ojibway exhibits corresponding rates of 55% and 47%. A combination of both small viable and endangered languages can be found in the lower half of the graph. Small viable languages such as Carrier, Chipewyan, and Athapaskan have continuity rates in the 40%-50% range, with corresponding exogamy rates in the 70%-80% range.

Further details on the tendency to transmit the Aboriginal language to the next generation as children of linguistically exogamous couples are given in Tables 7.6 through 7.9, for different indicators, by separate Aboriginal languages and/or language families. Comparisons of language outcomes are provided for children of linguistically endogamous and exogamous couples and for lone parents by gender of parent. When both parents have the Aboriginal language as a mother tongue, the percentage of children who also have that mother tongue is quite high, particularly for viable languages, with over 60% for 10 of the 17 individual viable languages shown (at least 90% for Montagnais-Naskapi, Attikamek, and Inuktitut). In contrast, when the couple is linguistically mixed, especially when only the father has an Aboriginal mother tongue, the percentage of children who have that mother tongue is just 10% or less for 11 of the 15 viable languages. In the case of lone-parent families, the proportions of children that have an Aboriginal language as a mother tongue tend to be significantly higher than for children of mixed couples, but still significantly lower than for children of endogamous couples. In the case of endangered languages, because of small numbers, some caution must be used in interpreting differentials in language outcomes between endogamous and exogamous couples and lone parents. Generally, for both endogamous and exogamous couples, children in these language groups have the lowest tendency to have taken the Aboriginal language of their parent(s) as their mother tongue. The same is true for lone parents (Table 7.6).

Similar comparisons of language outcomes of children are made in terms of the percentage of children speaking a language at home (Table 7.7) and the percentage of children with knowledge of an Aboriginal language (ability to speak) (Table 7.8). Corresponding indices of continuity and ability[17] are compared among endogamous and exogamous couples and lone parents, by gender of parent (Table 7.9). For viable languages, the overall pattern appears to be one in which the tendency to use an Aboriginal language at home is clearly highest among children of endogamous couples and lowest among exogamous couples. Overall, as we saw earlier, the proportion of children with an Aboriginal home language in mixed-couple families tends to be higher

Table 7.6 Proportion of children with an Aboriginal mother tongue, by family structure, 1996

Aboriginal languages	Number of children with an Aboriginal mother tongue	Male lone parent (%)	Female lone parent (%)	Exogamous father couple (%)	Exogamous mother couple (%)	Endogamous couple (%)
Algonquian Family	**18,104**	**43.9**	**34.7**	**5.9**	**14.5**	**63.4**
Cree	14,959	45.5	33.4	5.1	14.3	93.9
Ojibway	2,005	25.4	18.2	5.4	5.9	45.7
Montagnais-Naskapi	1,760	90.9	83.0	14.3	65.7	98.7
Mi'kmaq	935	56.5	50.5	10.2	14.0	75.3
Oji-Cree	850	60.0	53.1	15.8	34.7	70.1
Attikamek	905	100.0	75.0	0.0	50.0	100.0
Blackfoot	120	12.5	3.6	4.4	0.0	15.0
Algonquin	270	50.0	88.2	13.6	31.3	79.0
Malecite	5	0.0	14.3	0.0	0.0	0.0
Inuktitut Family	**5,985**	**84.4**	**82.0**	**18.2**	**36.1**	**89.0**
Athapaskan Family	**2,305**	**40.0**	**49.5**	**4.6**	**6.1**	**63.7**
Dene	1,620	80.0	73.9	8.7	17.0	83.5
South Slave	205	0.0	31.3	4.2	3.2	50.0
Dogrib	305	0.0	57.1	25.0	14.3	62.9
Carrier	40	0.0	20.8	0.0	0.0	13.0
Chipewyan	60	50.0	12.0	0.0	0.0	53.3
Athapaskan NIE	35	33.3	0.0	0.0	0.0	42.9
Chilcotin	20	0.0	0.0	0.0	0.0	20.0
Kutchin-Gwich'in (Loucheux)/North Slave	25	0.0	25.0	0.0	0.0	16.7

(Dakota) Siouan Family	935	40.0	32.8	5.3	21.4	66.7
Salish Family	55	16.7	14.3	2.1	11.1	15.0
Tsimshian Family	60	0.0	30.8	4.1	13.6	10.4
Wakashan Family	10	0.0	6.3	0.0	0.0	11.1
Iroquoian Family	25	0.0	80.0	0.0	0.0	100.0
Haida Family–Tlingit–Kutenai	20	0.0	33.3	0.0	0.0	100.0
Total Aboriginal languages	27,500	47.0	40.1	5.8	15.7	67.4

Source: Statistics Canada, census data, special tabulations (author calculations).

Table 7.7 Proportion of children with an Aboriginal home language, by family structure, 1996

Aboriginal languages	Number of children with an Aboriginal mother tongue	Male lone parent (%)	Female lone parent (%)	Exogamous father couple (%)	Exogamous mother couple (%)	Endogamous couple (%)
Algonquian Family	**13,883**	**24.2**	**23.2**	**2.8**	**2.8**	**52.6**
Cree	8,840	29.7	21.6	2.8	6.8	55.1
Ojibway	1,290	18.6	8.6	1.0	2.8	32.6
Montagnais-Naskapi	1,635	0.0	80.0	14.3	45.7	96.6
Mi'kmaq	585	0.0	30.7	3.4	8.0	54.8
Oji-Cree	605	60.0	34.7	15.8	6.5	54.6
Attikamek	880	100.0	70.8	33.3	12.5	98.7
Blackfoot	75	0.0	3.6	1.5	2.0	9.2
Algonquin	80	50.0	23.5	0.0	0.0	29.0
Malecite	15	0.0	14.3	7.1	10.0	0.0
Inuktitut Family	**5,185**	**80.0**	**71.7**	**13.6**	**5.3**	**81.1**
Athapaskan Family	**1,830**	**31.3**	**42.2**	**2.7**	**2.8**	**50.7**
Dene	1,390	60.0	68.5	0.0	7.6	72.7
South Slave	145	0.0	25.0	12.5	0.0	32.4
Dogrib	190	0.0	28.6	0.0	0.0	45.7
Carrier	30	0.0	12.5	0.0	4.8	8.7
Chipewyan	40	50.0	8.0	0.0	0.0	33.3
Athapaskan NIE	10	0.0	0.0	9.1	0.0	7.1
Chilcotin	15	0.0	16.7	0.0	4.6	5.0
Kutchin-Gwich'in (Loucheux)/North Slave	10	0.0	0.0	0.0	0.0	11.1

(Dakota) Siouan Family	810	40.0	25.9	3.5	4.8	61.0
Salish Family	5	0.0	4.8	0.0	0.0	0.0
Tsimshian Family	10	0.0	0.0	2.0	4.6	0.0
Wakashan Family	0	0.0	0.0	0.0	0.0	0.0
Iroquoian Family	0	0.0	0.0	0.0	0.0	0.0
Haida Family–Tlingit-Kutenai	0	0.0	0.0	0.0	0.0	0.0
Total Aboriginal languages	21,950	36.0	29.0	3.8	5.9	57.0

Source: Statistics Canada, census data, special tabulations (author calculations).

Table 7.8 Proportion of children with knowledge of an Aboriginal language, by family structure, 1996

Aboriginal languages	Number of children with an Aboriginal mother tongue	Male lone parent (%)	Female lone parent (%)	Exogamous father couple (%)	Exogamous mother couple (%)	Endogamous couple (%)
Algonquian Family	**38,903**	**94.6**	**94.6**	**83.3**	**85.3**	**96.3**
Cree	23,971	95.9	100.0	88.2	88.7	99.3
Ojibway	7,025	88.1	85.3	75.8	79.6	96.5
Montagnais-Naskapi	1,985	109.1	98.0	85.7	94.3	100.0
Mi'kmaq	1,820	95.7	96.0	94.9	90.0	98.6
Oji-Cree	1,320	100.0	100.0	0.0	84.8	98.3
Attikamek	940	100.0	87.5	66.7	75.0	100.0
Blackfoot	1,370	87.5	94.5	86.8	72.0	100.0
Algonquin	430	100.0	105.9	72.7	75.0	100.0
Malecite	165	100.0	100.0	85.7	70.0	100.0
Inuktitut Family	**7,440**	**102.2**	**99.0**	**80.3**	**94.1**	**99.6**
Athapaskan Family	**5,052**	**88.6**	**93.6**	**75.0**	**85.9**	**95.8**
Dene	2,290	86.7	98.2	67.4	86.8	99.6
South Slave	661	100.0	100.0	75.0	87.5	98.5
Dogrib	595	100.0	100.0	75.0	95.0	100.0
Carrier	470	100.0	91.7	84.9	80.0	100.0
Chipewyan	435	100.0	96.0	55.8	84.9	93.3
Athapaskan NIE	230	66.7	57.1	63.6	86.4	100.0
Chilcotin	216	0.0	83.3	10.0	81.8	100.0
Kutchin-Gwich'in (Loucheux)/North Slave	160	100.0	75.0	66.7	80.0	72.2

(Dakota) Siouan Family	1,727	90.0	84.5	57.9	78.6	97.1
Salish Family	415	83.3	57.1	61.7	63.0	100.0
Tsimshian Family	530	80.0	92.3	89.8	86.4	93.1
Wakashan Family	155	200.0	25.0	61.9	38.5	77.8
Iroquoian Family	36	50.0	40.0	66.7	25.0	100.0
Haida Family–Tlingit–Kutenai	50	0.0	66.7	20.0	100.0	100.0
Total Aboriginal languages	54,196	94.2	93.9	79.8	85.2	96.9

Source: Statistics Canada, census data, special tabulations (author calculations).

Table 7.9 Indices of continuity and ability, by family structure, 1996

	Male lone parent		Female lone parent		Exogamous father couple		Exogamous mother couple		Endogamous couple	
	IC	IA	IC	IA	IC	IA	IC	IA	IC	IA
Algonquian Family	**55**	**216**	**67**	**273**	**48**	**1,423**	**54**	**588**	**83**	**152**
Cree	65	211	65	299	55	1,726	48	622	59	106
Ojibway	73	347	47	469	19	1,406	47	1,354	71	211
Montagnais-Naskapi	0	110	96	118	100	600	70	144	98	101
Mi'kmaq	0	169	61	190	33	933	57	643	73	131
Oji-Cree	100	167	65	188	100	0	19	244	78	140
Attikamek	100	100	94	117	0	0	25	150	99	100
Blackfoot	0	700	100	2,600	33	1,967	0	0	61	667
Algonquin	100	200	27	113	0	533	0	240	37	127
Malecite	0	0	100	700	0	0	0	0	0	0
Inuktitut Family	**95**	**118**	**88**	**121**	**75**	**442**	**51**	**261**	**91**	**112**
Athapaskan Family	**71**	**221**	**85**	**189**	**57**	**1,616**	**62**	**1,402**	**80**	**150**
Dene	75	108	93	133	0	775	44	511	87	119
South Slave	0	0	80	320	300	1,799	100	2,717	65	197
Dogrib	0	0	50	175	0	300	33	665	73	159
Carrier	0	0	60	440	0	0	0	0	67	767
Chipewyan	100	200	67	800	0	0	0	0	62	175
Athapaskan NIE	0	200	0	0	0	0	0	0	17	233
Chilcotin	0	0	0	0	0	0	0	0	25	500
Kutchin-Gwich'in (Loucheux)/North Slave	0	0	0	300	0	0	0	0	67	433

(Dakota) Siouan Family	100	225	79	258	67	1,101	56	367	91	146
Salish Family	0	500	33	400	0	2,910	33	567	0	667
Tsimshian Family	0	0	0	300	50	2,201	33	635	0	900
Wakashan Family	0	0	0	400	0	0	0	0	0	700
Iroquoian Family	0	0	0	50	0	0	0	0	0	100
Haida Family–Tlingit–Kutenai	0	0	0	200	0	0	0	0	0	100
Total Aboriginal languages	66	201	72	234	56	1,376	52	543	85	144

Note: IC = index of continuity (HL/MT); IA = index of ability (Kn/MT)
Source: Statistics Canada, census data, special tabulations (author calculations).

when it is the mother who has the Aboriginal mother tongue (6%) rather than the father (4%). However, there are some distinct reversals of this pattern. Perhaps residential differences among such mixed marriages may explain these variations. With respect to endangered languages, it is fair to say that practically none of the approximately 2,000 children whose parent(s) have one of the dozen endangered languages as a mother tongue speak an Aboriginal language at home, regardless of endogamy or family structure (Table 7.7).

In terms of the ability to speak an Aboriginal language, it is interesting to note that, generally, differentials in language outcomes are much less pronounced among children, whether in endogamous or mixed couples or in lone-parent families. While the tendency of parent(s) to transmit knowledge of the language to their children is highest in endogamous couples, differences in transmission are certainly not as significant as they are for passing on the language as a mother tongue or using it as a home language. The same patterns are replicated for the relationship between exogamy and language continuity and transmission. When we plotted the percentages of children in exogamous marriages against the corresponding percentages of children with an Aboriginal mother tongue and percentages with an Aboriginal home language, we found a strong inverse relationship between exogamy and transmission of an Aboriginal language as a mother tongue or home language, respectively. In contrast, there was a less pronounced inverse association between exogamy and transmission of the knowledge of (ability to speak) the language.

To summarize, the tendency of parent(s) to pass on their own Aboriginal mother tongue to their children as a mother tongue or as a second language, or to use it as a home language, varies depending on whether they form endogamous or exogamous couples or are lone parents. There are also gender differentials associated with these patterns. The indices of ability for most of the viable and endangered languages suggest that children in exogamous marriages – and more so for those of couples where the father has married – are much more likely to learn the Aboriginal language as a second language than children from endogamous marriages. The high ability indices for endangered languages indicates that only a small proportion of children in these marriages have an Aboriginal mother tongue. Furthermore, the continuity index shows that for children who do have a viable Aboriginal mother tongue, those in exogamous families are much less likely, especially where the mother has married out, to continue using their mother tongue as a home language than children of endogamous couples. In the case of children with an endangered mother tongue, there is no continuity at all, since none of them speak the language at home (Table 7.9). As noted earlier, strong continuity is essential if the language is to survive.

Implications of Language Transmission in the Younger Generation

Language outcomes of children are critical to the survival, maintenance, and revival of Aboriginal languages. Based on UNESCO's consideration that a language is endangered if it is not learned by at least 30% of the children in that community, it becomes critical that the language is spoken in the home in order for children to maintain that language and in order for there to be future generations of speakers (UNESCO 1996).

While it is reasonable to expect that among very young children mother tongue and home language should be one and the same, as children get older the two are not necessarily the same, as we have seen. The continuity of the language among children at least one of whose parents has an Aboriginal mother tongue tends to reflect the ratio of home language speakers to the mother tongue population for a given language. The continuity index for the study population of children appears to be positively associated with that obtained on the basis of home language and mother tongue populations of all ages. The relationship is less clear between corresponding measures of the ability index.

The percentage of children who have an Aboriginal mother tongue or home language will impact the overall average age of the populations that speak an Aboriginal language or have it for a mother tongue. The average age of traditional language speakers has been going up, which indicates that there has been less success in the transmission of language. The higher the average age, the fewer the young people who have learned or still understand the language itself, or the older the people who still speak it. When these older people die, so may the languages. We found an inverse relationship where the higher the proportions of children with the Aboriginal mother tongue, the lower the average age of the population with that mother tongue. The relationship is the same for home language speakers.

In terms of survival, the outlook is grim for many of the endangered languages when the average age of people speaking these languages at home is close to 50 years, while the proportion of children using the language at home is practically nil. On the other hand, the prospects are still encouraging for some of the more viable languages, such as Inuktitut, with an average age of home speakers of about 23 years and 68% of children using the language at home. In terms of knowledge, the association between the average age of persons with an ability to speak the language (knowledge) and the proportion of children with knowledge of the language is less pronounced, but the two measures are also inversely associated.

Overall, the continuity of a language is clearly related to the average age of its mother tongue population (as well as the age of home language speakers). There is a linear inverse relationship between the two measures, consistent with the observation that the younger the speakers, the stronger the language. For Aboriginal languages, the language outcomes of children are significant determinants not only of the maintenance of these languages but also for their very survival.

Unlike most Canadians, Aboriginal people are confronted with the issue that many of their languages are in the process of disappearing and nearing extinction. The implications of intergenerational language transmission and maintenance are much more profound for Aboriginal languages. According to Priest (1983) and Harrison (1997), for most other large minority groups such as Italians, Chinese, Spanish, and Punjabi, their languages are not in danger of extinction in Canada because of continuing immigration. Thus, while second-generation "new" Canadians may forsake their mother tongue for English or French in their homes, new waves of immigration will supplement the language patterns of the first-generation immigrants as they die off. For Canada's Aboriginal population, however, the luxury of immigration does not exist; there is no pool to draw upon to supplement their language patterns as this is their homeland.

Most of Canada's Aboriginal languages that are currently considered viable may experience growing problems of continuity with younger generations, accelerating the process of language erosion; in the case of already endangered languages, extinction appears to be only a generation away. For policy makers, this means that the issue of whether to save these languages is going to be very much part of the national dialogues of the near future. The RCAP made it clear that preservation is mandatory, but the research indicates that this will be difficult.

Acknowledgments
The authors would like to acknowledge with thanks the technical support provided by Lucette Dell'Osos of the Department of Indian Affairs and Northern Development (DIAND) and Ginette Sussault of Statistics Canada. Special thanks is also given to Réjean Lachapelle of Statistics Canada for facilitating access to data. The views expressed in this chapter are those of the authors and do not necessarily represent those of DIAND.

Notes
1 While there are Aboriginal languages in the United States, some of which are common to both Canada and the United States, census data show that the flows of Aboriginal people from the United States are not significantly large. On the other hand, for example, immigration spurred the growth of the Chinese mother tongue group from 95,000 in 1971 to 517,000 in 1991 (Harrison 1997, 292).
2 Mother tongue is defined as the first language learned at home in childhood and still understood by the individual at the time of the census.
3 This section is derived from Norris 1998, and the study is based on Norris 1998 and Harrison 1997.

4 Census data for some languages may be affected by the incomplete enumeration of reserves and settlements. Data for the Iroquoian family is not particularly representative due to the incomplete enumeration of Iroquoian reserves.

5 This section is derived from Norris 1998.

6 Home language is defined in the census as the predominant language spoken at home.

7 The index of continuity (HL/MT) measures language continuity, or vitality, by comparing the number of those who speak a given language at home (HL) with the number of those who learned that language as their mother tongue (MT). A ratio less than 100 indicates some decline in the strength of the language (i.e., for every 100 people with an Aboriginal mother tongue, there are fewer than 100 in the overall population who use it at home). The lower the score, the greater the decline or erosion.

8 With only 24 persons speaking Nishga at home for every 100 persons with a Nishga mother tongue.

9 This section is derived from Norris 2000.

10 Marriage occurring outside the group, as when someone with an Aboriginal mother tongue marries a person who does not have an Aboriginal mother tongue.

11 Endogamous marriages are those where both of the child's parents report an Aboriginal mother tongue.

12 Clatworthy's work (Chapter 3, this volume) on the intermarriage of Registered Indians with Non-Status individuals demonstrates that rates of intermarriage off reserve are significantly higher.

13 Families being of type husband-wife or lone-parent, with the parent(s) having an Aboriginal mother tongue.

14 Could speak and understand an Aboriginal language well enough to conduct a conversation.

15 It should be noted that answering the question on knowledge – "the ability to conduct a conversation" – is somewhat subjective in nature, and hence could contribute to some of the variation and comparability both within and across language groups.

16 $N = 27,400$.

17 The index of ability (Kn/MT) compares the number of people who report being able to speak the language (Kn) with the number who have that Aboriginal language as a mother tongue (MT). If for every 100 persons with a specific Aboriginal mother tongue, more than 100 persons in the overall population are able to speak that language, some clearly learned it as a second language either in school or later in life. This may suggest some degree of language revival.

References

Harrison, B.R. 1997. Language integration: Results of an intergenerational analysis. *Statistical Journal of the United Nations ECE* 14: 289-303.

Kinkade, M.D. 1991. The decline of Native languages in Canada. In *Endangered Languages*, edited by Robert H. Robins and Eugenius M. Uhlenbeck. Oxford: Berg Publishers.

Norris, M.J. 1998. Canada's Aboriginal languages. *Canadian Social Trends* 51 (Winter): 8-11. Catalogue no. 11-008. Ottawa: Statistics Canada.

–. 2000. Aboriginal peoples in Canada: Demographic and linguistic perspectives. In *Visions of the Heart: Canadian Aboriginal Issues*, edited by D.A. Long and O.P. Dickason, 2nd ed. Toronto: Harcourt Brace Canada.

Ponting, J.R. 1997. *First Nations in Canada: Perspectives on Opportunity, Empowerment, and Self-Determination.* McGraw-Hill Ryerson.

Priest, G.E. 1983. *Aboriginal Languages in Canada*. Ottawa: Housing, Family and Social Characteristics Division, Statistics Canada.

Royal Commission on Aboriginal Peoples. 1996. *Gathering Strength*. Vol. 3 of *Report of the Royal Commission on Aboriginal Peoples*. Ottawa: Minister of Supply and Services Canada.

Tait, Heather. 2000. Aboriginal women. In *Women in Canada*. Catalogue no. 89-503. Ottawa: Statistics Canada.

UNESCO (United Nations Educational, Scientific, and Cultural Organization). 1996. *Atlas of the World's Languages in Danger of Disappearing,* edited by Stephen A. Wurm. Paris, Canberrra: UNESCO Publishing and Pacific Linguistics.

Measuring and Predicting Capacity and Development

Jerry P. White

In this part of *Aboriginal Conditions*, we look at an important and complex question. Scientists and policy makers have long been faced with the problem of understanding the relative levels of human development and predicting the capacity of a community (or nation or people) to develop, given the resources they have at their disposal. Those interested in development have long sought to discover techniques for measuring social and economic progress. Even more challenging is trying to pinpoint the weaknesses in the mix of resources in order to increase the likelihood of success.

In the three chapters that make up Part 4, we approach this issue, taking the first steps toward finding some solutions. In Chapter 8, Dan Beavon and Martin Cooke present an innovative analysis of the human development of First Nations in Canada, relative to other Canadians and relative to the other countries of the world. In Chapter 9, Paul Maxim, Jerry White, and Dan Beavon present a detailed investigation of the relative income inequality faced by Aboriginal peoples in Canada, and for the first time assess intra-Aboriginal inequality as well as differences between Aboriginal and non-Aboriginal Canada. Chapter 10, by Paul Maxim and Jerry White, presents the first attempt to measure the capacity of First Nations communities to assume responsibility for devolved programs and to move forward their human development.

Beavon and Cooke point out that in the past decade, the United Nations Development Program's (UNDP) Human Development Index (HDI) has become one of the most commonly cited and used indices of well-being. Canada has consistently been ranked at or near the top of this index, making Canada one of the best places in the world in which to live. However, not all Canadians share the same high standards, as we can see from Chapter 9.

Despite the fact that Canadian social policy has focused for the last half-century on reducing inequalities through removal of economic barriers, the First Nations and other Aboriginal peoples face serious income inequalities.

The gap between Aboriginal and non-Aboriginal income remains very high, according to Maxim, White, and Beavon. The analysis they present goes much deeper than this comparison, however. They also examine intra-Aboriginal inequality. They point out that the disparity within Aboriginal communities has not been explored. Communities that were once homogeneous are now experiencing haves and have-nots, and the broadening income inequalities can weaken the social cohesion of the communities. Social cleavages and the lack of community cohesion may also undermine the ability of a community to become self-sustaining or to generate the initial level of economic activity that can lead to success in the long run.

This takes us back to the model presented in Chapter 1 and offers another dimension of the puzzle. As policy aimed at equality with non-Aboriginal society is put in place, the ability of the communities to develop could be jeopardized if intra-group differences are created. The capacity of a community to run its affairs and prosper can be undermined by dramatic inequalities within the group. Maxim and co-authors find that the Status Indian population has the greatest intra-group inequality, followed by the Inuit, Non-Status Indians, and Métis. They conclude that some of the causes of this dispersion and polarization of income are related to socio-demographic variables. They also conclude that some policies, such as transfers, may not be having the desired results. There are many implications for policy making, not the least of which is that we had better start looking carefully at the effects of the policies in place at present. What effect do the transfer policies have? In general, we have to investigate what is creating the inequality within communities. This will be an important part of the picture that allows us to create the conditions for First Nations to build their capacity and develop successfully.

Measuring the relative level of development is an important question, which Beavon and Cooke approach by utilizing a modified version of the UNDP Human Development Index. The HDI has been seen as a tool for diagnosing problems and ranking nations according to their relative human development. In the international context, the HDI may also be useful in identifying those countries that most need external assistance, and may perhaps provide some empirical basis for the levels of assistance required.

The measurement of the human development of the Registered Indian population allows us to gauge the disparity between that population and the rest of Canada on the dimensions included in the HDI. Particularly important is the chance to look at well-being or "quality of life," which, as Beavon and Cooke comment, "is in some ways a relative concept that can be understood only through comparison with other populations. The index provides a way of comparing the well-being of Aboriginal people in Canada with populations in developed and developing countries, in order to provide some understanding of their relative position on these indicators. It also allows us to see where First Nations on and off reserve rank in terms of the world.

Their study indicates there is a very significant difference between the general population and the First Nations. This suggests that we should be exploring, through research, the causes and outcomes of such differences. Beavon and Cooke recognize that the way to get at the root causes of these differences is the construction of a community-level indicator. The precursor to that indicator should be a community measure of HDI. As they indicate, however, there are no data reliable enough to accurately measure the HDI for First Nations communities. They write: "Such a community-level development measure might be a tool by which policy makers in Aboriginal, federal, and provincial governments could identify policies and models of development that have led to substantial improvement in community well-being. Such a measure may also be helpful in identifying those communities in which the need for external assistance is the greatest." They begin the process of measuring subgroups using the HDI and find that when the index is used to examine the development of First Nations or Registered Indians, it indicates that

> Registered Indians living off reserve in 1996 fared substantially better than did those living on reserve, in terms of total HDI scores and scores on each of the three subindices. However, the off-reserve population still had an estimated real GDP per capita that was less than half that of the total Canadian population. Registered Indians living off reserve also had approximately five years lower life expectancy at birth and 10% lower educational attainment index scores than the reference population ... Average levels of well-being in communities may be well above or below the individual averages, and it is possible that some First Nations may be comparable to the highly developed countries and some might rank considerably lower.

Maxim and White's Community Capacity Index (CCI) begins the process of measuring the capacity of communities to grow and develop. They start with the assumption, developed in the opening chapter of this volume, that communities are a key analytic level. Their studies of the human capital, occupational mix, and dependency ratios leads them to conclude that the communities have dramatic differential abilities to develop. If the HDI is diagnostic between countries and provides valuable comparisons and evaluation of Aboriginal conditions, then the CCI sets out a diagnostic framework to help guide policy in terms of differential resource allocations within the country.

If we compare Chapters 8 and 10, we find some consistency. Both HDI and CCI indicate that the reserve communities in the Prairies have the greater proportion of lower scores in well-being and community capacity. This finding is consistent with O'Sullivan's review of socio-economic development in Chapter 6. White and Maxim employ a test of their CCI utilizing financial audit information that also indicates that the model is robust. These consistencies may indicate that the CCI has validity and that the intra-regional community comparisons in the CCI may be a valuable tool in policy development. The validity issue is crucial, however, and, as Maxim and White note, there needs to be a new generation of CCI produced.[1] There remains much work to be done.

One conclusion we can draw is that the development of finer measures of well-being and community capacity are going to be fruitful in the diagnostic process and the policy development initiatives that flow from it. Beavon and Cooke note that "its [the HDI's] wide use and general acceptance as an international measure may help refocus Canadian attention on the inequalities that continue to exist within Canada despite Canada's high level of development." This is true, and the Maxim and White chapter indicates that intra-First Nation inequalities have to be explored in order to best focus our efforts to deal with the problems.

We need to develop better measures of the First Nations communities and tailor our programs and policies to match the reality of the country. We cannot, as Maxim and White say, download programs to communities that do not have the capacity to take them on. Nor can we have Canada-wide initiatives that do not target the intra-First Nation differences. We believe that the Canadian public is concerned and ready to address the kinds of problems and difficulties that face Aboriginal peoples. However, they also appear to want some assurance that the resources are apportioned where most needed and that they will have some success, given clear policy benchmarks and goals. The most cynical would say that this is a demand for the most "bang for the buck," while the most optimistic would say that they want to see more rapid improvement of Aboriginal conditions. The research we present here a first step in bringing that closer to reality.

Note

1 This is currently being done using much more detailed and sophisticated data compiled from the program data reported to the Department of Indian Affairs and Northern Development.

8

An Application of the United Nations Human Development Index to Registered Indians in Canada, 1996

Dan Beavon and Martin Cooke

For some time, economists and those studying economic development have been interested in techniques for measuring social and economic progress in developing societies. In the past decade, the United Nations Development Program (UNDP) Human Development Index (HDI) has become one of the most commonly cited and used indices of well-being. Canada has consistently scored at or near the top of the United Nations' ranking of countries based on the HDI scores. Canada's high life expectancy, per capita gross domestic product, and level of education have led many to conclude that, based on its HDI ranking, Canada is one of the best countries in the world in which to live.

It is clear, however, that not all in Canadian society share in our high average levels of human development. In particular, Aboriginal Canadians tend to have lower incomes, poorer health outcomes, and lower educational levels on average than other Canadians. This disparity in well-being has been articulated by former National Chief of the Assembly of First Nations Ovide Mercredi:

> The last thing we want to read is someone telling us that the United Nations has deemed Canada the best country in the world in which to live. It's not the best country for my people to live in ... Our young people should not be condemned to live in poverty indefinitely ... we should not have to be on welfare for the last 30 years of our lives. That is totally unforgivable in the wealthiest country in the world with the highest standard of life ... And people keep coming in here in great influx from all over the world to make a living, a good standard of life, which they do. In the meantime we live in third world conditions. It's not just the issues of land and treaties that people are ignoring. It's practical issues like a job, a house, good health, a good education. These are things that are absent in our communities.[1]

Speaking about Aboriginal communities in the North, Dr. Ian Gilchrist, the chief medical officer of the Northwest Territories, has reported that "a lot of patterns of illness you see in the North are like the patterns of illness in the Third World. They are related to lifestyle, they are related to few resources, low access to other services. They are related to populations under stress and development."[2]

Many Canadians perceive conditions in Aboriginal communities quite differently. In 1996, an Insight Canada poll found that nearly half of Canadians believed that the standard of living on reserves was as good as or better than the Canadian average. In the same poll, 83% of Canadians interviewed believed that conditions for Aboriginal people were either improving or staying the same (Insight Canada Research 1996). Part of the reason for these diverging perceptions of the conditions of Aboriginal people may be the lack of readily available and interpretable indicators of the well-being of Canadian Aboriginal populations.

This chapter is based on research that explores the current indices of development for Registered and Non-Status Indians, Inuit, and Métis, using adaptations of the UNDP HDI methodology. The purpose of this research is to measure the well-being of Aboriginal people in Canada relative to the general Canadian population, and to examine changes in well-being over time. In this chapter, the HDI rankings of Registered Indians and other Canadians are compared with the international scores published in the United Nations' 1999 *Human Development Report,* which uses data from 1996 and 1997. Gender and regional differences in human development among Registered Indians living on and off reserve are examined, and these levels of development are compared with those for the general Canadian population. We draw some conclusions about the relative well-being of Aboriginal peoples in Canada based on our research findings.

The United Nations Human Development Index

Since the 1970s, there have been many attempts to develop composite indicators to measure well-being or quality of life. Previously, economic indicators such as per capita GDP or income were used, with the rationale that GDP was a good proxy for the average power of citizens to fulfill their material needs, and that the fulfillment of these needs was a fundamental part of overall well-being. It has been increasingly recognized, however, that not all aspects of well-being are adequately captured by measuring consumptive ability. In particular, measures of average health are not always well predicted by GDP per capita, but clearly represent an important element of development. The incorporation of indicators of social development, as well as of economic progress, into indices of development has been the subject of considerable effort since the 1970s. One such index, the Physical Quality of Life Index (Morris 1979), was an effort to create a better measure of well-being by combining infant mortality, life expectancy, and literacy in a single index. Other composites, such as the Economic and Social Rank Index (Sivard, annual), attempt to form a more complete picture of a country's level of development by including more indicators of health and education, in addition to GNP per capita. One of the largest of these indices, the Index of Social Progress, combines as many as forty-four indicators across eleven subject areas in an effort to present as complete a picture of well-being as is possible using a quantitative index (Estes 1984).

Among the indices created as alternatives to purely economic measures of development, the HDI has become one of the most widely used and accepted. First published in 1990 in the *Human Development Report,* the new index characterized human development as "an expansion of choices" (UNDP 1990, i). Three aspects of well-being comprised the new index: health, knowledge, and access to material goods. These three dimensions are identified as necessary for the making of meaningful choices by individuals, which requires reasonable levels of health and longevity, literacy and some level of education, and a minimal level of material well-being.

The United Nations does not attempt to present the HDI as a perfect measurement tool for assessing human development, and minor changes are made in the index from year to year. It is a composite index of achievements in basic human capabilities, and three variables have been chosen to represent these dimensions: life expectancy, educational attainment, and income.

As well as capturing three dimensions that are fundamental to the United Nations' concept of human development, the HDI's relatively modest data requirements allow the index to be calculated for developing countries, for which data are sometimes lacking. Thus, it represents a balance between the use of a single indicator, such as per capita GDP, and more complex indices that may be difficult to apply to all countries or regions.

There has been a considerable amount of criticism of the construction of the Human Development Index. While some issues have been raised about the technical aspects of its calculation and weighting scheme and the quality of some of the particular measures used in the index (Saith and Harris-White 1999; Chowdhury 1991; Rao 1991), most debate has been about the choices of the dimensions of well-being in the index. Some writers have argued that the composite HDI offers little additional information over GDP alone, already widely used as a measure of development, and cite a high overall correlation between countries' GDP or GNP and their HDI scores as evidence of the redundancy of the index (McGillivray 1991). Others argue that the HDI is too restrictive and should include measures of environmental health, crime, and other aspects of overall well-being (Saith and Harris-White 1999).

While the correlation between GDP and HDI score, which includes GDP in its calculation, is typically high, it is precisely the lack of a perfect relationship that provides one of the uses of the HDI. Some countries have been able to attain fairly high levels of health and education despite low levels of national income, while others have failed to translate high levels of income into commensurate levels of human development. The 1990 *Human Development Report* suggests the use of the HDI in identifying the policy choices that affect how national income translates, or fails to translate, into broader human development (UNDP 1990, 1). In the international context, the HDI may also be useful in identifying those countries that most need external assistance, and may perhaps provide some empirical basis for the levels of assistance required.

In the case of Canada's Aboriginal population, some measures of well-being, such as this application of the HDI methodology, may be of similar use. Identification of regional differences in income, health, and educational attainment may allow the effects of different policies on the well-being of Aboriginal people to be better understood. While this chapter describes an application of the HDI to the Registered Indian population identified by the census, and not to individual communities, better community-level data could allow some future variation of the index to be applied to Aboriginal communities. Such a community-level development measure might be a tool by which policy makers in Aboriginal, federal, and provincial governments could identify policies and models of development that have led to substantial improvement in community well-being. Such a measure may also be helpful in identifying those communities in which the need for external assistance is the greatest.

Methodology

The methodology for creating the HDI involves calculating and combining three separate subindices: life expectancy, educational attainment, and GDP.[3] Each of these subindices is essentially a measure of the distance between the actually achieved scores and theoretical minimum and maximum scores.

The measure used in the *life expectancy index* is life expectancy at birth, with the minimum and maximum values being 25 and 85 years, respectively. Since 1995, the *educational attainment index* used in the HDI has included two measures to represent the knowledge required for an expansion of human choices: adult literacy rate and gross primary, secondary, and tertiary enrollment ratios. The adult literacy rate is given a two-thirds weighting within the educational attainment index. The gross primary, secondary, and tertiary enrollment ratio is the proportion of the appropriate age population that is actually enrolled in primary, secondary, or tertiary schooling. The gross enrollment index is given a one-third weight within the educational attainment index.

The *GDP index* is slightly more complicated than the other two indicators. Per capita gross domestic product is used in the HDI as a proxy for access to goods and services that are necessary for a decent standard of living. These goods are made available by the presence of a minimal level of income, for which per capita GDP is a proxy. The UNDP uses per capita GDP, expressed in Purchasing Power Parity dollars, in order to compare countries with different currencies and price levels. This value is then discounted using a log formula, to account for the diminishing marginal utility of income (UNDP 1999, 228-29).

Computing a Canadian Aboriginal Human Development Index

The population with which this chapter is primarily concerned is the *Registered Indian population,* which is the population of Canadians who are registered under the Indian Act of Canada. For the purposes of this chapter, the *reference population* refers to the Canadian population minus the Registered Indian population. *On-* and *off-reserve* residence refers to whether or not an individual was living on an Indian reserve or Crown land as defined by the Department of Indian Affairs and Northern Development (DIAND) (Statistics Canada 1997).

In general, the data required for the calculation of the education and GDP indices for the Canadian populations came from the 1996 Census of Canada, and were found in custom tabulations prepared by Statistics Canada for DIAND. Life expectancy estimates used were those developed by Statistics Canada for projections of the Registered Indian population, as well as those produced regularly for the Canadian population. The international index scores and rankings were obtained from the 1999 *Human Development Report* (UNDP 1999), which uses data from 1996 and 1997.

Income Data

Whereas the UNDP uses per capita GDP as a proxy for average individual income, gross domestic product is not available separately for Registered Indians. Instead, average individual income, as reported in the census, was used. This includes all sources of income, not just earned income, and so better reflects an average standard of living. Adjustments were also made to these averages to make them more appropriate for measuring well-being in the Canadian context. Statistics Canada generally calculates average incomes for those aged fifteen and over who earned income. However, the Aboriginal population in Canada is younger than the total Canadian population, and there tends to be a greater percentage of the Aboriginal population who report no income or negative income. This means that in the Aboriginal population there may be more people, including children, elders, and others with no income, who depend in some way on the incomes of others. If this is the case, the same average income earned by Aboriginal people and other Canadians would contribute less to the average level of well-being. To account for this, the mean individual incomes for the Registered Indian and reference populations were adjusted to include in their denominators those under fifteen years and those with no income (see Chapter 10).

Educational Attainment Data

While the UNDP uses the adult literacy rate and the gross primary, secondary, and tertiary enrollment ratios in the calculation of the educational attainment index, these measures did not apply particularly well to the Canadian case. Adult literacy estimates are not well developed for the Aboriginal populations in Canada, and the cross-cultural validity of adult literacy measures in general is questionable in any case, given the culturally specific construction and definitions of what it means to be literate (cf. Stromquist 1997; Hagell and Trudge 1998). Separate primary, secondary, and tertiary enrollment ratios were also not available for the Registered Indian population. Other problems with the use of gross enrollment measures have also been found to be unreliable for populations in which there tends to be a large proportion of adult students (Colcough and Lewin 1993). As a result, census educational attainment measures were substituted for the UNDP proxies for knowledge. The proportion of the population fifteen years and older that had attained less than grade 9 was substituted for adult literacy. The ratio of those that had attained high school or higher to the population aged nineteen years and older was substituted for the gross enrollment ratio.

The most serious problem with the census data on income and educational attainment is that of undercoverage of Aboriginal communities. Nonparticipation in the census by First Nations has historically been a problem, and was again in the 1996 Census (Statistics Canada 1998). Although this is to some extent dealt with by reweighting of the data by Statistics Canada, undercoverage will affect the results presented here to the extent that those who do not participate in the census differ from those who do, in terms of income or educational attainment.[4] The census also does not gather data on education, ethnicity, or income for the population living in institutions such as prisons or military barracks. Particularly in the western provinces, Aboriginal people are overrepresented in the institutional population.

Life Expectancy Data

Life expectancy at birth for Registered Indians has been calculated by Statistics Canada for use in their periodic *Population Projections for Registered Indians*. The Registered Indian life expectancies used in this report were the 1996 projections, assuming a moderate decline in mortality. The estimates for the Canadian population were derived from Statistics Canada life table estimates (Statistics Canada 1998). The life expectancies for the reference population were calculated by disaggregating the total Canadian life expectancy into a weighted average of those of the Registered Indian and reference populations.

Adjustment for International Comparison

The main purpose of this chapter is to highlight the differences between Registered Indians and other Canadians in their scores on the HDI and component indices. One way to present this information is to estimate where each of these populations would be placed among the countries ranked by the UNDP. In order to make the 1996 Canadian HDI figures comparable to international results published in the 1999 *Human Development Report,* the educational attainment and income indicators used in this study were adjusted by the ratio of the total Canadian population value on an indicator to the Canadian value used by the UNDP. While the indicators used in this chapter are not identical to the ones used by the UNDP, these indicators are valid proxies to the extent that they accurately estimate the relative gaps between the achievement of the Registered Indian and reference populations on the UNDP indicators. It should be stressed that these adjustments are only to allow international comparisons, and are not required in order to make comparisons between Canadian populations. Further, the relative gaps in achievement between Registered Indians and other Canadians hold, regardless of their international rankings.[5]

International Ranking

Human Development Index Ranking

In the 1999 *Human Development Report,* which uses data from 1996 and 1997, Canada was ranked first among the 174 countries included in the report, and had the highest overall Human Development Index score. Calculating HDI scores for Registered Indians, including those living on and off reserve, reveals a substantially lower HDI score for the Registered Indian population, which would be ranked about forty-eighth among the countries in the report. Accordingly, the reference population, or the Canadian population that is not registered under the Indian Act, scored slightly higher than the total Canadian population. This international ranking would place the Canadian Registered

Indian population with those countries that the UNDP considers to have achieved a "medium" level of human development, as shown in Table 8.1. The Registered Indian population scored substantially lower than the Canadian population on each of the educational attainment, income, and life expectancy subindices.

Table 8.1   Ranking of selected countries by the Human Development Index, 1996

HDI rank	Country	Real GDP per capita ($PPP)[a]	Educational attainment	Life expectancy at birth	HDI score
Selected countries with high human development					
Reference population		22,696	0.99	78.5	0.933
1	Canada	22,480	0.99	78.4[b]	0.932
2	Norway	24,450	0.99	78.1	0.927
3	United States	29,010	0.98	76.7	0.927
... 4-45 deleted					
Selected countries with medium human development					
46	Trinidad and Tobago	6,840	0.87	73.8	0.797
47	Hungary	7,200	0.91	70.9	0.795
Registered Indian		10,091	0.82	72.2	0.793
48	Venezuela	8,860	0.84	72.4	0.792
49	Panama	7,168	0.85	73.6	0.791
... 50-76 deleted					
77	Philippines	3,520	0.90	68.3	0.740
78	Saudi Arabia	10,120	0.67	71.4	0.740
On-reserve Registered Indian		8,720	0.73	69.6	0.739
79	Brazil	6,480	0.83	66.8	0.739
80	Peru	4,680	0.85	68.3	0.739
81	Saint Lucia	5,437	0.79	70.0	0.737
82	Jamaica	3,440	0.78	74.8	0.734
83	Belize	4,300	0.74	74.7	0.732
Countries with low human development					
140	Lao People's Democratic Republic	1,300	0.57	23.2	0.491
141	Congo, Democratic Republic of	880	0.64	50.8	0.479
... remaining countries deleted					

a Purchasing Power Parity dollars.
b The Canadian life expectancy at birth given in the 1999 *Human Development Report* (UNDP 1999) is 79 years. The Statistics Canada estimate for 1996 is 78.4 years (Statistics Canada 1998).
Sources: UNDP 1999; DIAND 1998; Statistics Canada CANSIM Table 102-006; Statistics Canada custom tabulations of census data; authors' calculations.

There appear to be important differences in the average level of well-being, as defined by HDI scores, between Registered Indians who live on reserves or Crown land and those who do not. Registered Indians living off reserve in 1996 fared substantially better than did those living on reserve, in terms of total HDI scores and scores on each of the three subindices. However, the off-reserve population still had an estimated real GDP per capita that was less than half that of the total Canadian population. Registered Indians living off reserve also had approximately five years lower life expectancy at birth and 10% lower educational attainment index scores than the reference population. As shown in Table 8.1, when taken as a whole, reserve residents would be about seventy-ninth among countries ranked by their HDI score. This would place these communities close to the ranks of Brazil and Peru. Of course, it should be remembered that these figures represent an average HDI score for Registered Indians living on reserve, and not an average level of development for Aboriginal communities. Average levels of well-being in communities may be well above or below the individual averages, and it is possible that some First Nations may be comparable to the highly developed countries and some might rank considerably lower. However, because of the limitations of the data, community-level indices could not be calculated.

Educational Attainment and Life Expectancy Index Ranking

Part of the reason for Canada's continued high ranking in the international Human Development Index has been its high score on the educational attainment index. Based on educational attainment index scores, Registered Indians would rank about seventieth in the world, with an index score of 0.82, as shown in Table 8.2.

The life expectancy at birth of Canadians put them in third place in the world in 1996, according to the UNDP. For Canadians who were not Registered Indians, life expectancy at birth was about 79 years for both sexes combined. Registered Indians, however, had an estimated life expectancy at birth of almost 7 years less than their fellow Canadians. Ranked internationally, their life expectancy of 72.2 years put them in fifty-fourth place, between those of Venezuela and Mexico (Table 8.3).

Real GDP Per Capita

In the 1999 *Human Development Report,* twelve countries scored higher than Canada, based on their per capita gross domestic product, in Purchasing Power Parity (PPP) dollars. Registered Indians had an estimated GDP per capita of $12,000 PPP less than the reference population, based on the average incomes of these populations in 1995. The international rank of Registered

Table 8.2 Educational attainment index ranking for selected countries, Registered Indians, and the reference population, 1996

Educational attainment rank	Country	Educational attainment index	HDI rank
Reference population		0.99	
1	Canada	0.99	1
2	Sweden	0.99	6
3	Australia	0.99	7
4	Norway	0.99	2
5	Netherlands	0.99	8
6	United Kingdom	0.99	10
67	Hong Kong	0.83	24
68	Mexico	0.83	50
70	Brazil	0.83	79
Registered Indians		0.82	
71	Libyan Arab Jamahiriya	0.82	65
72	Lebanon	0.82	69
73	St. Vincent and Grenadines	0.81	75

Sources: UNDP 1999; DIAND 1998; Statistics Canada CANSIM Table 102-006; Statistics Canada custom tabulations of census data; authors' calculations.

Table 8.3 Life expectancy index ranking for selected countries, Registered Indians, and the reference population, 1996

Life expectancy rank	Country	Life expectancy at birth	Life expectancy index	HDI rank
1	Japan	80.0	0.92	4
Reference population		79.1[a]	0.90	
2	Iceland	79.0	0.90	9
3	Canada	79.0[a]	0.90	1
4	Switzerland	78.6	0.89	12
5	Hong Kong	78.5	0.89	24
6	Sweden	78.5	0.89	6
7	Italy	78.2	0.89	19
52	Korea, Republic of	72.4	0.79	48
53	Venezuela	72.4	0.79	49
Registered Indians		72.3	0.79	
54	Mexico	72.2	0.79	50
55	Malaysia	72.0	0.78	51
56	Grenada	72.0	0.78	52

a The Canadian life expectancy at birth given in the 1999 *Human Development Report* (UNDP 1999) is 79 years. The Statistics Canada estimate for 1996 is 78.4 years (Statistics Canada 1998).

Sources: UNDP 1999; DIAND 1998; Statistics Canada CANSIM Table 102-006; authors' calculations.

Table 8.4 Real GDP per capita ranking of selected countries with high human development, Registered Indians, and the reference population, 1996

GDP rank	Country	Real GDP per capita ($PPP)[a]	GDP index	HDI rank
1	Luxembourg	30,863	0.96	17
2	Brunei Darussalam	29,773	0.95	25
3	United States	29,010	0.95	3
4	Singapore	28,460	0.94	22
5	Kuwait	25,314	0.92	35
6	Switzerland	25,240	0.92	12
7	Norway	24,450	0.92	2
8	Hong Kong	24,350	0.92	24
9	Japan	24,070	0.92	4
Reference population		**22,696**	**0.91**	
10	Denmark	23,690	0.91	15
11	Belgium	22,750	0.91	5
12	Iceland	22,497	0.90	9
13	Canada	22,480	0.90	1
14	Austria	22,070	0.90	16
40	Argentina	10,300	0.77	39
41	Saudi Arabia	10,120	0.77	78
Registered Indian		**10,091**	**0.77**	
42	Antigua and Barbuda	9,692	0.76	38
43	Mauritius	9,310	0.76	59
44	Uruguay	9,200	0.75	40

a Purchasing Power Parity dollars.
Sources: UNDP 1999; DIAND 1998; Statistics Canada CANSIM Table 102-006; Statistics Canada custom tabulations of census data; authors' calculations.

Indians, shown in Table 8.4, was about 41, which was higher than the ranking of this population on the other two indices, and which places this population among the countries with "high" human development, according to the UNDP. This indicates that when GDP is discounted, as it is in the UNDP methodology, the low ranking of Registered Indians in the overall HDI is due more to their scores on the educational attainment and life expectancy indices than to their GDP index score. As will be shown in the next section, however, there remains a large difference in the average individual incomes of the Registered Indian population and other Canadians.

Regional and Gender Differences
While it is clear that the Registered Indian population does not share the high level of human development enjoyed by other Canadians, it is also the case that the well-being of Aboriginal people is not uniform within Canada. In

Figure 8.1   Human Development Index scores for the reference population and for Registered Indians living on and off reserve, males and females, 1996

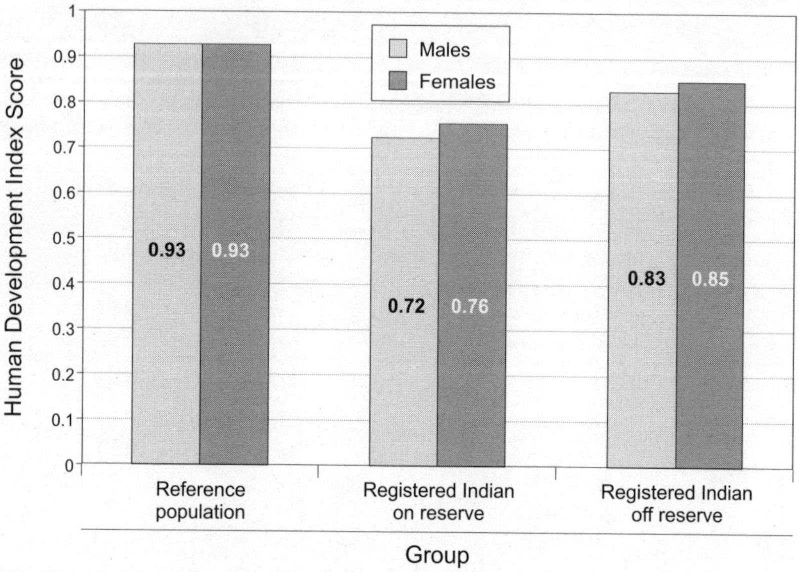

Sources: UNDP 1999; DIAND 1998; Statistics Canada, CANSIM Table 102-006; Statistics Canada, census data, special tabulations (authors' calculations).

particular, the HDI methodology can be extended to identify regional differences in life expectancy, educational attainment, and income among Registered Indians, and between Registered Indians and other Canadians. These indicators can also be used to identify differences in well-being between males and females, on and off reserve.

Figure 8.1 compares the HDI scores for the reference population with those for Registered Indians living on and off reserve, and shows that gender differences in well-being followed a somewhat different pattern for Registered Indians than for other Canadians. Whereas in the general Canadian population women tended to score lower than men on the Human Development Index, Registered Indian women had higher scores than their male counterparts. This result was due to advantages of Registered Indian women in both life expectancy and educational attainment compared with Registered Indian men.

The 1996 life expectancy at birth for Registered Indians was considerably lower than the life expectancy of other Canadians, as shown in Figure 8.2, and Registered Indians living on reserve had nearly a nine-year disadvantage in life expectancy compared with other Canadians. As in the Canadian population, however, Registered Indian women enjoyed an advantage over men of at

Figure 8.2   Life expectancy at birth for the reference population and for Registered
Indians living on and off reserve, males and females, 1996

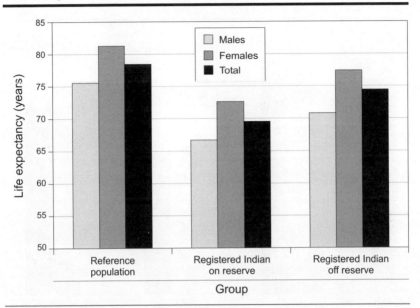

Sources: DIAND 1998; Statistics Canada, CANSIM Table 102-006; Statistics Canada, census
data, special tabulations (authors' calculations).

least five years. This was true for those living in reserve communities as well
as those living off reserve. The life expectancies at birth of Registered Indian
males and females living off reserve were 70.8 and 77.4 years, respectively,
while those for on-reserve males and females were 66.7 and 72.6 years.[6] In
contrast, reference population life expectancies were 75.5 and 81.3 years for
males and females, respectively.

Registered Indian females also scored better than Registered Indian males
in terms of educational attainment. As we have indicated, two measures were
used to calculate the educational attainment index for Registered Indians and
other Canadians. The proportions of the populations aged 19 and older that
had high school or higher educational attainment are compared in Figure 8.3
for males and females. In the Registered Indian population, females scored
higher than their male counterparts in 1996, while in the reference population, men were more likely than women to have completed higher education. As with the life expectancy index and the overall HDI scores, Registered
Indians living on reserve fared less well in educational attainment than those
living off reserve. Just over 71% of the total reference population aged 19 and
over had completed high school or higher in 1996, compared with 44% and
58% for Registered Indians living on and off reserve, respectively.

Figure 8.3 Proportion of the population aged 19 and over with high school or greater educational attainment, for the reference population and for Registered Indians living on and off reserve, males and females, 1996

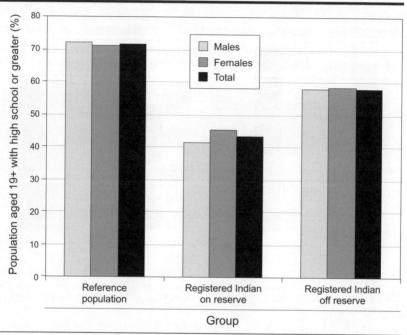

Sources: DIAND 1998; Statistics Canada, CANSIM Table 102-006; Statistics Canada, census data, special tabulations (authors' calculations).

Similar results hold for the other measure of educational attainment. The proportion of the on-reserve Registered Indian population aged 15 and over that had completed grade 9 was about 70%, compared with 85% for Registered Indians living off reserve and 88% for Canadians not registered under the Indian Act. While there were important differences between males and females in the proportion that had completed high school, the differences between males and females in the proportion that had completed grade 9 were only about 1%. As shown in Figure 8.4, this was the case for both Registered Indians and the reference population. This might be expected if early school leaving is generally not a problem at very young ages.

While Registered Indian women scored higher than their male counterparts in life expectancy and educational attainment, the opposite was true for average annual income. The comparison of 1995 average annual incomes for on- and off-reserve Registered Indians and the reference population reveals a wide gap, as well as gaps between men and women in both populations (Figure 8.5). Whereas the average total annual income for Canadian men not

Figure 8.4   Proportion of the population aged 15 and over, with grade 9, for the reference population and for Registered Indians living on and off reserve, males and females, 1995

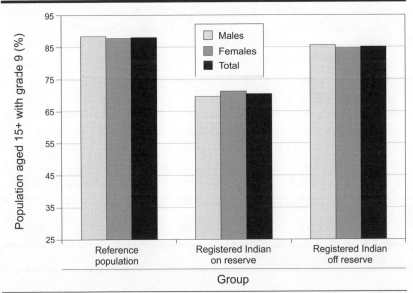

Sources: DIAND 1998; Statistics Canada, CANSIM Table 102-006; Statistics Canada, census data, special tabulations (authors' calculations).

Figure 8.5   Average annual income for the reference population and for Registered Indians living on and off reserve, males and females, 1995

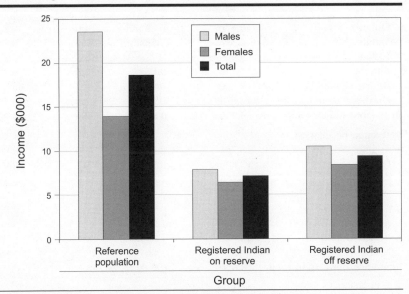

Sources: DIAND 1998; Statistics Canada, CANSIM Table 102-006; Statistics Canada, census data, special tabulations (authors' calculations).

registered under the Indian Act was about $23,500, the income for Registered
Indian men living off reserve was $10,500, and that for Registered Indian men
living in reserve communities was only $7,900. Registered Indian women
were more similar to other Canadian women in terms of their incomes than
Registered Indian men were to other Canadian men. Women in the reference
population had an average annual income of $13,900, while Registered In-
dian women living on and off reserve had average incomes of $6,400 and
$8,400, respectively.

Table 8.5 shows the index scores and average annual incomes for Registered Indians and the reference population by region. While scores on income, life expectancy, and educational attainment varied across regions, the
differences between Registered Indians and other Canadians were fairly consistent, with a nearly $10,000 difference in per capita income and about a six-
year difference in life expectancy. Life expectancy, income, and educational

Table 8.5 Regional breakdown of the Human Development Index for Registered Indians
and the reference population, 1995

Region	Average annual income ($)[a]	Educational attainment index	Life expectancy at birth (years)	Human Development Index
Registered Indian				
Atlantic Region	8,287	0.94	72.7	0.84
Quebec	9,776	0.73	72.6	0.78
Ontario	10,676	0.88	74.0	0.84
Manitoba	6,318	0.73	70.0	0.74
Saskatchewan	5,699	0.77	70.3	0.75
Alberta	7,170	0.85	70.8	0.79
British Columbia	9,402	0.89	70.7	0.82
Northern Region	10,861	0.78	71.9	0.79
Registered Indian total	**8,292**	**0.82**	**72.0**	**0.79**
Reference population				
Atlantic Region	15,267	0.94	78.0	0.90
Quebec	17,030	0.94	78.4	0.91
Ontario	20,155	1.01	78.9	0.95
Manitoba	17,427	0.97	78.7	0.92
Saskatchewan	17,194	0.95	79.1	0.92
Alberta	19,106	1.04	79.0	0.95
British Columbia	19,881	1.05	79.4	0.96
Northern Region	20,816	1.00	74.9	0.92
Reference population total	**18,650**	**0.99**	**78.8**	**0.93**

a 1995 dollars.
Sources: UNDP 1999; DIAND 1998; Statistics Canada CANSIM Table 102-006; Statistics
Canada custom tabulations of census data; authors' calculations.

attainment were lowest for Registered Indians in the Prairie provinces, and the differences in both life expectancy and educational attainment of the two populations were greatest on the Prairies. The differences in life expectancy and educational attainment between Registered Indians and the reference population appear to be the least in the Atlantic provinces.

Registered Indians living in reserve communities scored less well than those living off reserve, in all regions, on each of the three subindices as well as the overall Human Development Index (Table 8.6). Income and education were generally lowest on the Prairies, and the differences between on- and off-reserve Registered Indians was the lowest in Manitoba and Saskatchewan. In these provinces, the average per capita income for Registered Indians was less than $6,000 in 1996, compared with an average of $18,650 for other Canadians across all regions. Among Registered Indians, the largest differences in income between on- and off-reserve residents appear to have been

Table 8.6   Regional breakdown of the Human Development Index for Registered Indians living on and off reserve, 1996

Region	Average annual income ($)[a]	Educational attainment index	Life expectancy at birth (years)	Human Development Index
On reserve				
Atlantic Region	7,212	0.92	71.2	0.81
Quebec	8,611	0.64	71.2	0.73
Ontario	8,213	0.71	71.1	0.75
Manitoba	5,916	0.65	68.1	0.70
Saskatchewan	5,452	0.69	68.1	0.70
Alberta	6,029	0.77	68.1	0.74
British Columbia	8,545	0.84	68.0	0.78
Northern Region	9,696	0.69	70.6	0.75
On-reserve total	7,165	0.73	69.6	0.74
Off reserve				
Atlantic Region	10,165	0.98	75.8	0.88
Quebec	11,843	0.87	75.6	0.85
Ontario	11,995	0.95	75.7	0.88
Manitoba	6,864	0.83	73.2	0.79
Saskatchewan	5,964	0.85	73.2	0.79
Alberta	8,027	0.92	73.2	0.83
British Columbia	10,077	0.93	73.2	0.84
Northern Region	12,632	0.90	74.3	0.85
Off-reserve total	9,365	0.90	74.4	0.84

a 1995 dollars.
Sources: UNDP 1999; DIAND 1998; Statistics Canada CANSIM Table 102-006; Statistics Canada custom tabulations of census data; authors' calculations.

Table 8.7 Human Development Index scores of Registered Indians and the reference population, by region and gender, 1996

	Females				Males			
Region	Average annual income ($)ᵃ	Educational attainment subindex	Life expectancy at birth (years)	Human Development Index	Average annual income ($)ᵃ	Educational attainment subindex	Life expectancy at birth (years)	Human Development Index
Registered Indians								
Atlantic Region	7,430	0.87	76.4	0.826	9,196	0.86	69.1	0.795
Quebec	8,229	0.73	76.4	0.786	11,385	0.73	69.0	0.762
Ontario	9,517	0.88	77.7	0.851	11,971	0.87	70.1	0.817
Manitoba	5,918	0.74	73.0	0.752	6,739	0.71	67.3	0.718
Saskatchewan	5,684	0.79	73.3	0.768	5,716	0.74	67.6	0.719
Alberta	6,562	0.87	73.8	0.806	7,846	0.83	68.0	0.770
British Columbia	8,158	0.90	73.7	0.827	10,726	0.87	67.9	0.800
Northern Region	10,270	0.81	75.4	0.819	11,471	0.74	68.6	0.763
Total Registered Indians	**7,496**	**0.84**	**75.9**	**0.813**	**9,148**	**0.81**	**68.2**	**0.771**
Reference population								
Atlantic Region	11,043	0.96	80.8	0.901	19,519	0.93	74.7	0.890
Quebec	12,701	0.93	81.0	0.903	21,520	0.95	74.6	0.903
Ontario	15,257	1.01	81.3	0.939	25,246	1.02	75.9	0.942
Manitoba	13,191	0.97	81.1	0.918	21,781	0.96	75.7	0.913
Saskatchewan	12,775	0.97	82.1	0.921	21,677	0.94	76.0	0.907
Alberta	13,482	1.04	81.5	0.943	24,698	1.04	76.1	0.947
British Columbia	14,840	1.04	82.0	0.953	25,019	1.05	76.4	0.954
Northern Region	16,821	1.00	77.5	0.921	24,465	1.00	72.2	0.913
Total reference population	**13,906**	**0.99**	**81.3**	**0.927**	**23,538**	**0.99**	**75.8**	**0.928**

a 1995 dollars.

Sources: UNDP 1999; DIAND 1998; Statistics Canada CANSIM Table 102-006; Statistics Canada custom tabulations of census data; authors' calculations.

in Quebec, Ontario, and the North, where incomes for those living off reserve were higher relative to the Prairies.

Table 8.7 shows the HDI and subindex scores for Registered Indians and the reference population by region, for males and females. Regardless of region, female Registered Indians had lower per capita incomes in 1995, but had longer life expectancy at birth than males. Registered Indian women also had higher educational attainment scores than their male counterparts, regardless of region. While Canadians in Atlantic Canada and Quebec had the lowest scores on educational attainment, income, and life expectancy relative to other regions, the scores were lowest for Registered Indians on the Prairies, for both males and females.

Summary and Conclusions

In summary, this comparison shows that while Canada consistently scores near the top of the international HDI rankings, Registered Indians living both on and off reserve have not experienced the same level of human development, or "expansion of choices," as other Canadians. The Registered Indian population in all regions of Canada had lower life expectancy at birth, lower educational attainment, and lower average annual incomes in 1996 than the rest of the Canadian population. These gaps in well-being were most pronounced for those living in reserve communities, and on-reserve Registered Indians in Manitoba and Saskatchewan had particularly low HDI scores.

Overall, female Registered Indians tended to have higher levels of education and longer life expectancy than Registered Indian men. Longer life expectancy among women is common in developed countries, including Canada. However, the higher educational attainment of female Registered Indians is contrary to the overall pattern in Canada, where men generally have a slight advantage. This may indicate the existence of different sets of available opportunities for Aboriginal women and men. The work available for men in Aboriginal communities, such as in resource extraction, may require less formal education than the types of employment undertaken by women. Registered Indian women have also been found to migrate to urban areas at higher rates than Registered Indian men (Clatworthy 1996). High school or better education may be a more important requirement for employment in cities than in reserve communities, and might be more easily acquired there. Despite their advantage in educational attainment, Registered Indian women had considerably lower incomes than Registered Indian men, who themselves had much lower incomes than other Canadians. The relatively high proportion of female-headed lone-parent families in the Aboriginal population, particularly in urban areas, makes the low income of Registered Indian women an even greater problem (Statistics Canada 1998).

The United Nations Development Program Human Development Index is a useful tool for exploring the disparity between Registered Indians and other Canadians on the three dimensions included in the UNDP methodology. Although educational attainment, income, and life expectancy could of course be examined without the index, well-being or "quality of life" is in some ways a relative concept that can be understood only through comparison with other populations. The index provides a way of comparing the well-being of Aboriginal people in Canada with populations in developed and developing countries, in order to provide some understanding of their relative position on these indicators. Its wide use and general acceptance as an international measure may help refocus Canadian attention on the inequalities that continue to exist within Canada despite Canada's high level of development.

This chapter describes the use of data from the 1996 Census to examine the relative levels of human development among Canadians who are registered under the Indian Act. We plan to use the UNDP indices in future studies to measure the well-being of Canada's other Aboriginal populations, including Inuit, Métis, and Non-Status Indians. The changes in these indices over time will also be measured, in the hope of producing a more complete picture of the relative well-being of Canada's Aboriginal populations. It should be noted that the UNDP indices are not without their weaknesses; perhaps most importantly, the HDI is not able to address subjective or qualitative dimensions of well-being. Spirituality, relationships with family, freedom and human rights, the preservation of culture, and other aspects of well-being are not easily quantifiable but represent important benefits to living in particular communities. The findings presented in this chapter are intended to identify disparities between Aboriginal people and other Canadians on the measures included in the Human Development Index, but these should be understood in a broader social, political, and cultural context that recognizes the many other dimensions of well-being.

Notes

1 Written transcript of conversation, subject: Royal Commission on Aboriginal Peoples, National Press Theatre, Ottawa, 30 April 1997.
2 Cited in the *Red Deer Advocate,* 28 April 1997.
3 While we will briefly describe the construction of the indices here, the UNDP methodology as well as the modifications necessary to calculate the index for the Canadian Aboriginal populations in this chapter are described in more detail in an unpublished Technical Appendix available from the authors upon request.
4 Maxim and White (forthcoming) indicate in their study that missing data have little effect overall, given that the non- or under-enumerated communities have characteristics similar to those of communities actually enumerated.
5 A more detailed discussion of the adjustments made for international comparisons is available from the authors.

6 The Statistics Canada estimate of life expectancy at birth for Canadians in
   1996 is slightly different from that published in the 1999 *Human Development Report*.

References

Clatworthy, S.J. 1996. *The Migration and Mobility Patterns of Canada's Aboriginal
   Population*. Prepared for the Royal Commission on Aboriginal Peoples. Ottawa:
   Canada Mortgage and Housing Corporation, and the Royal Commission on Ab-
   original Peoples.
Chowdhury, Omar Haider. 1991. Human Development Index: A critique. *Bangladesh
   Development Studies* 19(3): 125-27.
Colcough, C., and K.W. Lewin. 1993. *Educating All the Children: Strategies for Pri-
   mary Education in the South*. Oxford: Clarendon Press.
DIAND. 1998. *Population projections of Registered Indians, 1996-2021*. Unpublished
   report. Ottawa: Indian and Northern Affairs Canada.
Estes, R.J. 1984. *The Social Progress of Nations*. New York: Praeger.
Hagell, Ann, and Jonathan Trudge. 1998. Illiterate adults in literate societies: Interac-
   tions with a social world. In *Literacy in Human Development,* edited by Marta Kohl
   de Oliveira and Jaan Valsiner. London: Ablex.
Insight Canada Research Inc. 1996. Perspectives on Aboriginal Conditions. *Perspectives Canada* 5(1), Ottawa.
Maxim, P., J. White, and P. Wilks. Forthcoming. *Missing Data Implications of the
   Under-Enumeration of First Nations Communities*. Population Studies Centre Work-
   ing Paper Series. London: University of Western Ontario.
McGillivray, Mark. 1991. The human development index: Yet another redundant
   composite development indicator? *World Development* 19(10): 1461-68.
Morris, M.D. 1979. *Measuring the Condition of the World's Poor: The Physical Quality
   of Life Index*. New York: Pergamon.
Rao, V.V.B. 1991. Human development report 1990: Review and assessment. *World
   Development* 19(10): 1451-60.
Saith, Ruhi, and Barbara Harris-White. 1999. The gender sensitivity of well-being
   indicators. *Development and Change* 30: 465-97.
Sivard, R.L. Annual. *World Military and Social Expenditures*. Washington, DC: World
   Priorities.
Statistics Canada. 1997. *1996 Census Dictionary*. Catalogue no. 92-351-XPE. Ottawa:
   Industry Canada.
–. 1998. 1996 Census: Aboriginal data. *The Daily,* 13 January, 2-7.
Stromquist, N.P. 1997. *Literacy for Citizenship: Gender and Grassroots Dynamics in
   Brazil*. Albany, NY: SUNY Press.
UNDP (United Nations Development Program). Annual. *Human Development Re-
   port*. New York: Oxford University Press.

9

Dispersion and Polarization of Income among Aboriginal and Non-Aboriginal Canadians

Paul S. Maxim, Jerry P. White, and Dan Beavon

It is well established that, as a group, Canadians of Aboriginal origin are economically disadvantaged (Frideres 1998; George et al. 1996; INAC 1989; Jankowski and Moazzami 1994).[1] Until recently, social scientists have paid little attention to the labour market behaviour or rewards of Aboriginal Canadians. The most recent works on the wage and income levels of persons of Aboriginal origin are based on data prior to 1991. The primary sources for this material are the Royal Commission on Aboriginal Peoples (George et al. 1996) and a recent article by De Silva (1999). Previous studies, using the 1986 and 1991 Censuses of Canada and the post-censal Aboriginal Peoples Survey (1991), identified a wage gap between Aboriginal Canadians and the general population.

Much of Canadian social policy over the past century has focused on removing barriers to economic success across social groups. There have been varying levels of success and, for some Aboriginal peoples, significant failures (Nixon 1990). The income differential across the Aboriginal and non-Aboriginal divide has received some attention (De Silva 1999; Bernier 1997; Gardiner 1994; George and Kuhn 1994), but not the disparity *within* the Aboriginal community and between Aboriginal groups.

The primary concern of this investigation is to use the latest available data to quantify the wage and income inequity for Registered (i.e., Status) Indians, Métis, Inuit, and Non-Status Indians and to compare the wage dispersion and polarization among these four subgroups of Aboriginal workers with that of non-Aboriginal Canadian workers. Measuring this inequality is important since dramatic social and political changes have affected these populations recently. We address five questions:

1 Why study intra-Aboriginal inequality?
2 What is the gap in wages and income between the general Canadian population and the different Aboriginal peoples?

3 How much inequality exists both within and among the Canadian non-Aboriginal population and the Aboriginal groups? Do transfer payments reduce inequality and, if so, by how much?
4 Has there been any change in inequality since previous studies were reported, notably the Royal Commission on Aboriginal Peoples?
5 What directions should future research in this area take?

Why Study Intra-Aboriginal Income Inequality?
Studies on income inequality and its relationship to well-being have shown that "SES [socio-economic status] is associated with lower life expectancy, higher overall mortality rates, [and] higher rates of infant and perinatal mortality. In fact, SES is correlated with all the major cause of death categories in the ICDD [International Compendium of Disease and Diagnosis], as well as other health outcomes such as measures of life expectancy" (Link and Phelan 1995, 81). Wolfson's studies (1995; also Wolfson and Murphy 1998) of the United States point to a significant association between income inequality and mortality.[2] The linkage of decreases in mortality and morbidity to increases in socio-economic status appears to be particularly strong (Brenner 1979; National Council of Welfare 1990; Wilkinson 1990).

Studies of Aboriginal health have pointed repeatedly to income disparities between the Aboriginal population and the general population in explaining the higher incidence of disease and excess early mortality (Anderson 1994). Researchers have also targeted income and wealth inequalities in relation to social maladies and problems of social cohesion (Royal Commission on Aboriginal Peoples 1996).

Despite this obvious linkage, there have been few studies of Aboriginal and non-Aboriginal inequalities, and virtually no investigations on the size or determinants of inequality among Aboriginal peoples in Canada. This is important because, as the US research suggests, differences in polarization and dispersion imply that the socio-economic characteristics responsible for inequality have a differential impact across social groups (Cloutier 1996, 287). Understanding intra-Aboriginal differences requires an investigation of the social, cultural, and historical roots of each Aboriginal subgroup, and a focused review of the causal factors behind their demographic and socio-economic situations. Too often, we view indigenous populations as homogeneous when they are actually distinct subpopulations of peoples with unique characteristics.

**Measuring Inequality: The Depth of Polarization
and Dispersion of Income**
The general Canadian population is currently experiencing what some have called "the best family income in a decade" (Little and Stinson 2000). While

Table 9.1   Gini coefficients for Canada using selected year's
pretax income, including transfers

Year	Gini coefficient	Increase over 1989
1989	0.329	–
1994	0.334	1.5%
1998	0.357	8.5%

Source: Statistics Canada 2000.

the average income has increased by 1.7% in the last decade, the data also show greater income polarization. The top quintile of Canadian families has experienced a 6.6% increase in adjusted income (1998 dollars) since 1989, whereas the lowest quintile has seen a 5.2% drop (Statistics Canada 2000).

When divided into quintiles, income provides an interesting picture of the relative distribution of the rewards in a population. We need other measures, however, to provide a more textured view of inequality. For example, international comparisons of income inequality have relied on comparisons of Gini coefficients using after-tax family incomes (World Bank 2000, 222).[3] Countries with the most developed welfare states, such as Sweden and Denmark, have lower Gini scores than countries such as the USA, which have less developed safety nets. In 1992, for example, the Gini value for Denmark was 0.239, whereas it was 0.408 for the US and 0.583 for South Africa (Atkinson 1996; World Bank 2000).

Statistics Canada reports Gini coefficients of income over time.[4] This allows us to gauge whether inequality is changing for the country as a whole. Table 9.1 shows temporal increases in inequality in Canada.

Aboriginal Canadians, 1985-96: A Review of Previous Studies of Income Inequality

First Nations communities experienced several dramatic changes between 1985 and 1996. Social, economic, and political forces within Canada as a whole have also affected these communities. This swirl of activity has brought considerable pressure to bear on Aboriginal peoples, both on and off reserves. The courts, for example, have created change with their clarifications of the evolving relationships between Canada's public and private institutions and First Nations.[5] Confrontation between First Nations and various levels of government in Canada has occurred over Aboriginal title and access to lands, resources, and governance.[6]

Changes have also taken place within First Nations communities. Bill C-31 (1985) resulted in more than 105,000 individuals gaining Indian status, a process that for many First Nations communities has meant increased pressures on resources such as housing. Intense debate over community membership has occasionally resulted in considerable political turmoil. In the midst of all these internal and external pressures, these communities have seen the transfer of many health and social programs from the federal government to the local community (Government of Canada 1999). These transfers have at times taxed community capacities while often broadening their horizons. Access to capital and the potential to break age-old cycles of dependency have emerged in some communities as private sector interests have become involved. Examples include resource companies and banks that have begun to work in partnership with First Nations (Sloan and Hill 1995).

Considering whether these forces have changed the circumstances for First Nations communities and for Aboriginals without status is important. Have there been changes in their labour market income? Have the dispersion and polarization in the wages of First Nations persons in their communities and other Aboriginal peoples become less pronounced?

Over the past decade, several studies have examined the mean earnings of Aboriginal peoples in comparison with the Canadian population of working age. The studies centre on the use of the 1986 Census Public Use Sample File (PUSF) (George and Kuhn 1994), the 1991 Census Public Use Microdata File (PUMF) (George et al. 1996; Pendakur and Pendakur 1996), and, more recently, the 1991 Census PUMF and the post-censal Aboriginal Peoples Survey (Clatworthy et al. 1995; Bernier 1997). The studies differ as to the precise population studied, but some find indications of considerable variation in wages and total income among Aboriginal groups, and between the Aboriginal groups and the non-Aboriginal population.

Clatworthy et al. (1995) find the mean income for workers of Aboriginal origin to be $17,367, but they also find variations between the various Aboriginal groups. Non-Status Indians, Registered Indians, Métis, and Inuit have mean incomes of $21,035, $15,791, $18,467, and $15,690, respectively. The authors conclude that, while the income gap for those with full-time/full-year employment (forty plus weeks) is smaller than for those with other employment statuses, the earnings of Registered Indians and Inuit lag behind those of other Aboriginals, and are even further behind the Canadian labour force as a whole.

George et al. (1996) draw similar conclusions in their report to the Royal Commission on Aboriginal Peoples. They argue that conditional on full-time/full-year work, earnings of Aboriginal persons are 10.4% below those of the non-Aboriginal population. This represents a slight improvement over their findings from the 1986 PUSF, where the differential was 11.0% (George and Kuhn 1994, 28). They find that for men, between 30% and 55% of the gap in the wages between Aboriginals and non-Aboriginals is attributable to differences in all the relevant observable characteristics of the Native and non-Native persons in the 1991 PUMF. For women, this accounts for 90% of the difference. Specifically, George and Kuhn (1994, 31) find that for men, education and training account for 30% of the wage gap, while for women educational differences explain up to 50% of the gap.

George et al. (1996) study rates of labour force participation based on whether a person "worked in the week of the census survey." They find that 58.7% of Aboriginal persons are employed while 70.4% of non-Aboriginal Canadians are employed, for a difference of 11.7%. Interestingly, George et al. (1996) disaggregate their data and find that for "those indicating *only* aboriginal origins" and those with multiple origins, the rates differ considerably. This 11.7% overall gap, however, consists of a 4% gap for those with multiple origins and a 25% gap for those of single Aboriginal ancestry (George et al. 1996, 22).[7]

Bernier (1997) reports that workers claiming Aboriginal origins earn $6,500 less than Canadians as a whole in 1990. For those who identify with a First Nation in the Aboriginal Peoples Survey, the earnings are lower by an additional $2,900. She attempts to adjust for differing taxation levels (Bernier 1997, 3-4), but we consider it unreliable to estimate the real effects of on-reserve exemptions.[8]

Bernier also reports a series of measures of inequality and concludes that all of the measures she uses show that there is a greater inequality and polarization in wages among Canadians reporting Aboriginal origins than among Canadian workers as a whole. She also finds that the more restrictive the definition of "Aboriginal," the greater the inequality and polarization of their distributions of wages (Bernier 1997, 4).[9]

In addition, Bernier conducts an analysis that includes persons with "zero wage and salary income" by adding into her sample those who had either a positive income from employment in 1995 or positive income from Employment Insurance (EI). She finds that inequality and polarization for Aboriginal peoples actually increases when EI benefits are added to wages. Greater polarization suggests that general government transfers are less effective in reducing inequality in Aboriginal communities than in the non-Aboriginal population. This has important policy implications, which we explore below.

Comparative Earnings and Wage Dispersion

The Population: Whom to Include?
To maintain continuity with previous research, we have identified four analytically distinct groups within the Census of Canada Aboriginal population: Status Indians, single-origin Non-Status North American Indians, Métis, and Inuit.[10] Studies have consistently assessed the Métis and Non-Status Indians as having less income disparity and less polarization than the Status Indians

who inhabit the First Nations communities.[11] Some research has also assessed Status Indian and Inuit populations as having the greatest inequities among all Aboriginal groups (Bernier 1997; Clatworthy et al. 1995). In terms of change, we had expected that given the recent policy interest in First Nations communities, and their relative deprivation, there would be the greatest change in this group.[12]

Assumptions and Guiding Questions

We divided the Aboriginal population into four constituent groups, which permits intra-Aboriginal comparisons and intergroup comparisons on four economic measures, including:

1 Positive reported wage and salary income for 1995, for all persons aged 18-64 years (labour force eligible)
2 Wage and salary income, including zero income, for 1995, for all persons aged 18-64 years
3 Positive total income (i.e., income from all sources) for 1995, for all persons aged 18-64 years
4 Total income, including zero income, for 1995, for all persons aged 18-64 years.

Results

Table 9.2 addresses the dispersion and polarization of income of those with positive wage and salary income (no zero-income reporters). It shows that, overall, Aboriginal Canadians report earnings that are lower than those of

Table 9.2 Positive wage and salary income for persons reporting income, ages 18-64, inclusive, 1995

	Non-Aboriginal	Registered under Indian Act (Status)	Non-registered Indians[a]	Métis	Inuit
Mean income[b]	$27,188	$16,863	$20,835	$19,529	$17,537
Coefficient of variation	83.9	94.8	90.6	89.5	101.3
Gini index	0.44	0.50	0.48	0.48	0.53
Thiel index	0.32	0.42	0.38	0.39	0.48
Atkinson index[c]	0.17	0.22	0.21	0.21	0.28
N	358,228	4,391	830	1,973	355

a Single-origin North American Indian as defined by the 1996 Census of Canada.
b Calculated from 1996 Census of Canada PUMF; Aboriginal status based on "Aboriginal Self-Reporting" variable and "Registered or Treaty Indian Indicator."
c Using a shape parameter of 0.5.

the non-Aboriginal population. Status Indians earn $10,325 less than non-Aboriginal individuals, and they have the lowest earnings of any of the Aboriginal subgroups. Non-Status Indians fare best, with a deficit of $6,353, but all the groups show a much lower level of wage and salary income than non-Aboriginal Canadians. Mean income (wages and salary only) includes those with a positive income for 1995.

All of the measures of inequality are consistent in direction and relative size, which is an important assurance if we are to have confidence in the analysis. Greater inequality of wage income exists within each subgroup of Aboriginal people than for non-Aboriginal Canadians. The measures of inequality among Registered Indians, Non-Status Indians, and Métis, however, are not significantly different from one another.[13] The most inequitable distribution of wages is among the Inuit. This finding is consistent with previous studies. Bernier (1997, 14) concludes that the Inuit work fewer hours for higher wages in the lower quintile of earners. She speculates that this may relate to an emphasis on artisan endeavours. While this may account for part of the difference, it cannot account for the entire gap. A more important factor is related but somewhat different: the geography of being Inuit, which we will discuss later.

Status Indians experience the next greatest inequality. Indeed, many Status Indians find themselves clearly disadvantaged in the labour market. First Nations communities are made up almost exclusively of Status Indians. The reserve is a key contributor to the kinds of inequities observed. The various indices suggest some interesting relationships. The coefficient of variation is most sensitive to the upper tail in the income distribution. It is also the measure that displays the greatest dispersion. All the indices show the same patterns but differ in magnitude. The non-Aboriginal/Aboriginal comparisons show serious inequity concerning polarization toward the bottom of the range for Aboriginals. There are smaller differences between categories of Aboriginal persons.

Table 9.3 addresses the question of whether measures of inequality produce a different result when they are calculated for the whole labour force population (18-64 years of age, inclusive), whether or not they report *any* wage income for 1995.[14] As expected, the mean income decreases for each category (since the analysis includes many people with no wage income), although the size of the decrease varies. We might expect that, because Status Indians report many more zero wage and salary incomes than non-Aboriginal Canadians, the decrease in mean income would be greater for Status Indians. This is not so. Only a much greater proportion of earners at the low end of the income distribution among Status Indians than among non-Aboriginals could produce this result.

Table 9.3 Wage and salary income, including zero incomes, for all persons aged 18-64, inclusive, 1995

	Non-Aboriginal	Registered under Indian Act (Status)	Non-registered Indians[a]	Métis	Inuit
Mean income[b]	$19,843	$9,747	$13,161	$12,956	$12,089
Coefficient of variation	115.5	151.1	137.2	130.9	139
Gini index	0.59	0.71	0.67	0.65	0.68
Thiel index	0.64	0.97	0.84	0.79	0.85
Atkinson index	0.40	0.55	0.50	0.47	0.48
Percent not reporting income	27%	42%	37%	34%	31%
N	490,816	7,597	1,314	2,974	515

a Single-origin North American Indian as defined by the 1996 Census of Canada.
b Calculated from 1996 Census of Canada PUMF; Aboriginal status based on "Aboriginal Self-Reporting" variable and "Registered or Treaty Indian Indicator."

A focus on the inequality measures leads to an interesting observation. Inequality rises dramatically for Status Indians particularly when the measures used are sensitive to the top of the income distribution. The Thiel (1967) entropy measure[15] and the coefficient of variation show the greatest proportional inequality with the non-Aboriginal population, and also the greatest relational inequality when compared with the other Aboriginal groups. The Gini index, which is sensitive to variations in the mid-range, and the Atkinson index[16] (Atkinson 1970), which is set to be sensitive to variations in the lower range, suggest that some income disparity also exists at the top end of the wage and salary distribution.

Another important difference across the groups is the percentage of the population not reporting any wage or salary income. While 27% of the non-Aboriginal group reported no wage or salary income, 42% of the Registered Indians reported no such income. The remaining three groups clustered between these two extremes – the Non-Status Indians at 37%, the Métis at 34%, and the Inuit at 31%.

How do government transfers and other sources of income influence polarization, dispersion, and the wage gap?[17] Table 9.4 reports total income for those between the ages of 18 and 64 reporting an income, and Table 9.5 includes all persons between the ages of 18 and 64, including those with zero income. Here the percentage of persons with zero income is small, as most people with zero income from work would qualify for a transfer payment of some sort.

Table 9.4   Total positive personal income for persons reporting income, ages 18-64, inclusive, 1995

	Non-Aboriginal	Registered under Indian Act (Status)	Non-registered Indians[a]	Métis	Inuit
Mean income[b]	$26,701	$15,056	$18,951	$18,512	$18,562
Coefficient of variation	90.4	100.5	95.6	94.1	95.4
Gini index	0.46	0.51	0.49	0.48	0.50
Thiel index	0.36	0.44	0.40	0.39	0.42
Atkinson index	0.19	0.23	0.21	0.21	0.22
N	461,147	7,191	1,233	2,819	474

a Single-origin North American Indian as defined by the 1996 Census of Canada.
b Calculated from 1996 Census of Canada PUMF; Aboriginal status based on "Aboriginal Self-Reporting" variable and "Registered or Treaty Indian Indicator."

Table 9.5   Total personal income, including zero incomes, for all persons aged 18-64, inclusive, 1995

	Non-Aboriginal	Registered under Indian Act (Status)	Non-registered Indians[a]	Métis	Inuit
Mean income[b]	$25,163	$14,261	$17,810	$17,607	$17,118
Coefficient of variation	96.3	105.9	101.8	99.1	103.5
Gini index	0.49	0.54	0.52	0.51	0.54
Thiel index	0.42	0.50	0.47	0.44	0.50
Atkinson index	0.24	0.27	0.26	0.25	0.28
Percent not reporting income	6	5	6	5	8
N	489,390	7,592	1,312	2,964	514

a Single-origin North American Indian as defined by the 1996 Census of Canada.
b Calculated from 1996 Census of Canada PUMF; Aboriginal status based on "Aboriginal Self-Reporting" variable and "Registered or Treaty Indian Indicator."

The wage gap decreases only slightly when total income, including the zero categories, is considered. This is the case for all the Aboriginal subgroups. This is because the percentage of zero incomes is relatively low due to the effect of transfer payments.

The indices of inequality show the same patterns here as in the other scenarios. What is unexpected is that analyzing total income appears to make the dispersion of income *slightly greater*. Ironically, the "top up" that results in total income consists primarily of government transfers. Other sources, such as investment income, comprise only a small proportion of the residual between total income and wage and salary income only. This does not mean that transfer income creates inequities, but it does appear to indicate that the structure of transfer income does not significantly adjust inequity as measured by dispersion and polarization. It could be that this result is created because so many incomes are clustered at the lower tail of the distribution, both before and after transfer income is considered. This is consistent with the patterns shown by the inequality indices. Given the prevailing understanding that transfers reduce inequality, however, this is a counterintuitive result that deserves further analysis.

In Figure 9.1, we present box plots of wage and salary income for each of the subpopulations. The lines represent the range of income. For example, the Registered North American Indians have a range from approximately zero to $170,000.[18] Each line is divided into four quartiles. In the case of Registered Indians, we see that the zero point to bottom of the first box contains the first quartile, or 25% of the population. Each of the two box segments contains another 25% of the cases, and the line above to the maximum represents the highest quartile of the cases. The cross within the box is

Figure 9.1   Wage and salary income by subpopulation, 1995

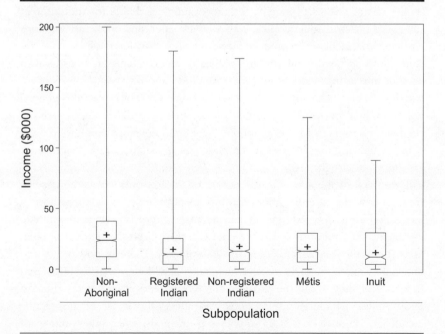

Source: 1996 Census of Canada PUMF.

the mean, and the line in the middle of the box separating the segments is the median. The box itself defines the interquartile range.

The box plots show that the non-Aboriginal population generally has a more equitable distribution of income (as indicated by lower levels of compression in the quartiles) relative to the other subgroups. Focusing on the Registered Indian and Inuit populations, we notice substantial income compression in the first quartile. The Inuit sample also indicates substantial compression in the second income quartile, but a relatively large dispersion in the third income quartile. Registered Indians have the smallest interquartile range among the five population groups. The higher level of income polarization among Registered Indians is illustrated by the relatively large income spread in the fourth income quartile relative to the first three quartiles.

Overall, Figure 9.1 graphically reinforces what the quantitative indicators of inequality are indicating: income inequality and polarization are primarily a consequence of a greater concentration of the population in the first two quartiles of their respective income distributions.

Assessing the Patterns of Inequality

Tables 9.2 to 9.5 make it clear that there is a gradient of inequality across the groups. All Aboriginal Canadians are disadvantaged compared with the non-Aboriginal Canadian population. The amount of disadvantage, as measured by the characteristics of income we are examining, differs for the different categories of Aboriginal peoples. It also varies depending on the assumptions we used to calculate income, namely, whether transfer payments are included and how we define the lower limit of income. This provides us with another interesting window into the magnitude and interrelationships of inequality. Table 9.6 compares our four Aboriginal groups with the general non-Aboriginal population in terms of the percentage difference in the Gini coefficient across our four assumptions.[19] Table 9.7 develops intra-group comparisons utilizing the different assumptions on transfers and the inclusion of zero-income earners.

If we think of the score for the non-Aboriginal population as the base or "norm," how do different Aboriginal groups vary from this basic pattern of inequality? Table 9.6 indicates that in all cases, there is greater measurable inequality for all groups when we compare them with the general population. This is the case regardless of the assumptions. There is, however, variation in the magnitude of the relative inequality. In all four scenarios, Registered Indians and Inuit show the greatest differences, and so are at the greatest disadvantage. Changing assumptions also affects the levels of measurable inequality. The inclusion of those with zero incomes, when other sources of income are not considered, increases the levels of inequality except in the

Table 9.6 Aboriginal income inequality as a percentage difference of non-Aboriginal income inequality (as measured by Gini coefficients), 1995

	Registered under Indian Act (Status)	Non-registered Indians[a]	Métis	Inuit
Wage and salary (no zero incomes)	13.6%	9.0%	9.0%	20.5%
Wage and salary (including zero incomes)	20.3%	13.6%	10.2%	15.3%
Total income (no zero incomes)	10.9%	6.5%	4.3%	8.7%
Total incomes (including zero incomes)	10.2%	6.1%	4.1%	10.2%

Note: See text for detailed explanation.
a Single-origin North American Indian as defined by the 1996 Census of Canada.

case of the Inuit. This may indicate that there are relatively fewer Inuit reporting zero incomes than non-Inuit Northerners doing so. The effect of using total income is that overall levels of relative inequality decrease in all cases. Transfers and other income sources appear to have the greatest impact on Registered Indians, with relative rates of measured inequality decreasing by approximately 50%. The case of the Inuit remains enigmatic, as the inequality actually increases with the introduction of earners of zero income even with the inclusion of transfer payments and other sources in the income calculations.

The last comparison is reported in Table 9.7. It examines changes in the relative inequality, but instead of using the non-Aboriginal population as a baseline, it addresses the question, "What is the intra-group effect as we apply our two basic scenarios?" For example, for non-Aboriginal people, the inclusion of zero wage and salary earners in the analysis results in a 31.1%

Table 9.7 Intra-group comparisons of income inequality with wage and salary income (excluding zeros) as base, 1995

	Non-Aboriginal	Registered under Indian Act (Status)	Non-registered Indians[a]	Métis	Inuit
Wage and salary with the introduction of zero incomes	34.1%	42.0%	39.6%	35.4%	28.3%
Total income in the absence of zero incomes	4.5%	2.0%	2.1%	0	−5.7%
Total income with zero incomes already included	11.4%	8.0%	8.3%	6.3%	1.9%

Note: See text for detailed explanation.
a Single-origin North American Indian as defined by the 1996 Census of Canada.

increase in the Gini coefficient compared with non-Aboriginals who have some wage and salary income.

Table 9.7 provides the clearest indication of the effect on inequality of considering other than wage and salary income. When extra wage and salary incomes are included, we see that the general pattern shows an increase in measured disparity and polarization in income for all groups. The reason for this is twofold. First, while some sources of income, such as government transfers, are designed to target low-income individuals, many non-wage and salary sources are nondiscriminatory. Thus, they serve to shift the mean income up slightly, but do little to reduce the overall gap. Furthermore, sources of income outside government transfers (such as investment income) are more accessible to upper-income earners. This serves to move the upper end of the distribution even higher, thus increasing income polarization.

Second, by looking beyond wage and salary income, we are invariably increasing the size of the target population. Almost all of those people outside the labour market either have no income at all or acquire small amounts primarily through government transfers. Very few people have substantial sources of income outside traditional wage labour. The "idle rich" are exceedingly rare.

The Determinants of Income Inequality

We wanted to explore the relative impact of factors that are known to affect income. We conducted two sets of regression analyses. The first analysis was on those identified as people with status in the PUMF, and the second included those who identified themselves as non-Aboriginal in origin. Table 9.8 presents a descriptive summary of the variables used, while Table 9.9 presents the results of the regression analysis, illustrating some of the possible reasons for variations in income.[20] As can be seen from Table 9.8, there are substantial differences in the profiles of those with status and the non-Aboriginal population.

The regression analyses are conducted on the data available for persons who are non-Aboriginal as well as for Registered Indians. The estimates enable a comparison of how education, skill level, job sector, gender, and geography influence income variations within each of those groups.[21]

Overall, both models are statistically significant according to most standard criteria of significance (alpha = 0.01). The variables considered account for a much larger proportion of the variance within the weekly wage and salary income of non-Aboriginal people as opposed to Registered Indians. The R^2 value for the non-Aboriginal sample is 0.304, indicating that 30.4% of the variance in log weekly wage and salary income is accounted for by the model. The corresponding R^2 value for the Registered Indian sample is 0.175,

Table 9.8   Descriptive summary of variables used in income analysis

Variable	Registered Indians	Non-Aboriginal
Mean log weekly income	5.83	6.11
Age	35.03	37.87
Weeks worked	34.34	42.76
Sex (percentages)		
Female	48.05	47.24
Male	51.95	52.76
Education (percentages)		
Less than grade 5	2.11	0.83
Grades 5-8	9.92	4.02
Grades 9-13	25.37	15.71
High school graduation	9.40	15.46
Trade certificate/diploma	4.96	3.95
Some university	32.77	29.62
University graduates	15.47	30.41
Work Status (percentages)		
Full-time work	78.88	79.90
Part-time work	21.12	20.30
Skill Level		
Level IV	22.33	12.93
Level III	35.07	35.76
Level II	26.65	27.58
Level I	15.95	23.74
Industrial Sector (percentages)		
Primary industries	9.59	4.28
Manufacturing	7.64	15.24
Construction	7.88	5.10
Transport and communications	6.19	7.61
Commercial activities	14.07	29.74
Government	21.14	6.95
Education	8.07	7.74
Health and social services	12.36	10.02
Accommodation	6.83	6.63
Other services	6.22	6.68
Region (percentages)		
Atlantic	4.98	7.879
Quebec	9.87	24.32
Ontario	21.55	38.387
Prairies	36.73	16.28
British Columbia	22.62	12.86
Yukon and Northwest Territories	4.25	0.26
N	4,214	70,491

Table 9.9 Wage and salary income regression results

Variables	Registered Indians		Non-Aboriginal people	
	Parameter estimates	t-value	Parameter estimates	t-value
Intercept	4.4785	27.02	4.3634	120.01
Age	0.0574	6.11	0.0732	38.83
Age-squared	−0.0005	4.49	−0.0007	31.06
Weeks worked	−0.0027	2.75	−0.0037	15.28
Sex				
Female	−0.0818	4.72	−0.1243	36.05
Male	0.0818	–	0.1243	–
Education				
Less than grade 5	−0.3161	3.31	−0.2085	7.21
Grades 5-8	−0.0439	0.93	−0.1504	10.01
Grades 9-13	0.0363	1.04	−0.0349	3.83
High school graduation	0.0084	0.17	0.0257	2.82
Trade certificate/diploma	0.0606	0.98	0.0761	5.26
Some university	0.0608	1.88	0.1018	12.77
University graduates	0.1939	–	0.1903	–
Work Status				
Full-time work	0.2912	14.67	0.3266	75.32
Part-time work	−0.2912	–	−0.3266	–
Skill Level				
Level IV	−0.1965	6.60	−0.2025	27.21
Level III	0.0976	3.87	−0.1225	23.56
Level II	0.0758	2.80	0.0449	8.07
Level I	0.2184	–	0.2801	–
Industrial Sector				
Primary industries	0.1498	3.02	−0.0060	0.42
Manufacturing	0.2711	5.08	0.1243	14.96
Construction	0.1105	2.05	0.0547	4.18
Transport and communications	0.1139	1.96	0.1932	17.76
Commercial activities	−0.0990	2.42	−0.0401	6.33
Government	0.0071	0.20	0.1848	16.26
Education	0.0103	0.20	0.0015	0.14
Health and social services	−0.0636	1.42	0.0568	5.70
Accommodation	−0.3221	5.79	−0.3259	27.76
Other services	−0.1780	–	−0.2433	–
Region				
Atlantic	−0.1909	3.21	−0.1519	10.91
Quebec	0.0713	1.60	−0.0514	4.37
Ontario	0.0538	1.57	0.0298	2.63
Prairies	−0.1344	4.61	−0.0635	5.18
British Columbia	0.0200	0.59	0.0675	5.31
Yukon and Northwest Territories	0.1801	–	0.1695	–
R^2	0.1810		0.305	
Adjusted R^2	0.1750		0.304	
N	4,213		70,491	

suggesting that 17.5% of the variance in log weekly wage and salary income is explained by the model. These R^2 values are within the typical range found in similar studies of individual income variability. The lower R^2 value for the First Nations sample indicates, however, that a larger proportion of the variation in the wage and salary income of First Nations peoples is accounted for by factors exogenous to the current model.

The models contain three classifications of variables. The first group consists of the ascribed characteristics of age and sex. Standard human capital theory (Mincer 1974; Becker 1975) suggests that, all else being equal, income displays a parabolic relationship with age. Personal income increases steeply in the early years of one's labour force life, flattens out in middle age, and then curves down slightly in one's later years. This pattern is reflected in the results of both regressions, with the parameters for both age and age-squared being statistically significant at a 0.01 level of significance.

The other ascribed characteristic, sex, is also statistically significant. First Nations counterparts earn approximately 16% less, based on gender.[2] This could indicate that there is slightly less gender discrimination in wages being experienced by First Nations women, but, more likely, it is due to there being generally less differential between men and women at the lower end of the income distribution. In other words, this is probably an income floor effect at work.

The second group of variables we consider are what might be termed human capital characteristics. Age is sometimes included in this category when it is used as a proxy variable for experience. In this study, however, we have chosen to consider age as an ascribed characteristic. On the other hand, education and occupational skill level have been identified as central indicators, and women earn approximately 24% less than men in the non-Aboriginal community, based on these indicators.

Education has been divided into seven categories. At the lower end of the educational scale, less than grade 5, there is a very high penalty in terms of wages – approximately 32% less than the average for all education levels. For those in the non-Aboriginal group, there is a lesser penalty (21%); however, the return to increased education is rapid for First Nations persons, where even small increments in education bring income up to the average for First Nations. Break-even income for non-Aboriginals does not occur until high school graduation. This pattern indicates two things. First, the educational levels in the First Nations population continue to be considerably lower than for non-Aboriginals (see George et al. 1996 for 1990 analysis), but their return for years of education is relatively high. The highest level of education, university graduation, returns about 19% above the average level of income for both the Aboriginal and non-Aboriginal populations. The gap in wages suggests that there may be some discrimination even at this level of training.

An examination of level of skill reveals that, at the lowest skill levels (Levels III and IV), there is a substantial, but slightly lower, penalty to First Nations compared with non-Aboriginals.[23] Income for the higher-skilled jobs produces a slightly lower return for Status Indians.

The third group of variables relate to structural factors. Here we have identified weeks worked, industrial sector, and region. The weeks-worked parameter is slightly negative, showing that, all else being equal, employers must pay a slight premium to workers who work fewer hours. Put another way, this parameter indicates that employers get a "quantity discount" when they purchase more rather than fewer of a worker's hours. This factor is significant for both samples, although the weeks-worked premium is slightly larger for First Nations employees compared with non-Aboriginal employees (−0.27% versus −0.37%).

The patterns of return across industrial sectors also varies a great deal between the groups. For example, compared with the average of non-Aboriginals in the primary sector, First Nations persons secure a 15% above average income in this sector. On the other hand, compared with the average of First Nations in the government sector, non-Aboriginals secure an 18% above average income in this sector. This latter finding indicates that government jobs for First Nations are less highly remunerated than government jobs being secured by members of the non-Aboriginal community. Employment in the areas of health and social services displays the same pattern.

Income advantages and disadvantages also differ by region. Both First Nations and non-Aboriginal people experience disadvantages in the Atlantic region, −19% and −15%, respectively. However, the most striking finding is for the Prairie region, where First Nations income is a full 13% below their mean while non-Aboriginals are only 6% below their mean. As Table 9.9 indicates, the overall profiles of First Nations and non-Aboriginal people differ significantly along several of the dimensions included in this analysis. One question we might pose is what the average income of Status Indians would be if they had the same profile as non-Aboriginal Canadians. One way of addressing this question is to apply the parameter estimates in the regression equation for First Nations people to the descriptive profile of non-Aboriginal people.

This exercise suggests that, overall, if Registered Indians had the same socio-demographic profiles as non-Aboriginal people, then their average *weekly* income would likely increase by about 15% above the current level. Based on the current data, non-Aboriginal Canadians earn approximately 29% more than Registered Indians. If Registered Indians had the same socio-demographic profile as non-Aboriginal Canadians, that gap in income would be reduced so that non-Aboriginal Canadians would earn just 14% more than Registered Indians.

This gives us some idea of the causes of the differences between the Status Indian and non-Aboriginal populations. However, it leaves a large variance unexplained, and it also leaves the cause of different socio-economic profiles unexplained. The outstanding difference and the cause of the difference have to be explored. Racism, ethnocentrism, geographic and market separations, educational quality, health differences, and any of a dozen other contributors need be consciously explored.

In this study, we are exploring the issues of intra-Aboriginal and inter-Aboriginal differences. Further research is necessary to identify and measure the main causes of intra-Aboriginal variations in income. It is, however, useful to consider the potential reasons for the differences.

Explaining the Intra-Aboriginal Variation

The data indicate that the Aboriginal groups rank from Inuit at the high end, through Status Indians, to Non-Status Indians, and, finally, to Métis having the lowest levels of inequality. It is interesting to note that the absolute wage gaps follow a similar pattern, with the exception of the Inuit, who are second to Status Indians on this measure. We would hypothesize that the spatial isolation of the Inuit and relative socio-spatial isolation of Status Indians compared with Non-Status Indians and Métis may provide a powerful explanation for the differences in inequality. Beginning with Park (1926), there has been a current in North American sociology arguing that successful minority groups move out from their settings with growing affluence (Park 1926, 9). This thread developed into theories equating social distance with physical separation, and finally proposing that separateness/segregation and economic difference are correlated (Massey 1981). Although these theories are usually related to urban residential segregation, they may offer important insight into our intra-Aboriginal differences. The often criticized "assimilation" thesis (Massey 1981) has posited that the more separate an ethnic group remains, the more economic inequality that group will experience as it is "excluded" from the reward structures of the market.

Recently, Flanagan (2000, 182-91) argued that a lack of integration into the wider economy is an important cause of unemployment and reduced wealth creation among First Nations. Leaving aside the extensive debate over structural discrimination and racism in market exclusion, separation is a powerful empirical correlate of variations in SES. The Inuit are clearly the most separated Aboriginal subgroup. The reserve community system functions in a similar way to the isolation of the North, creating socio-cultural distances and fractures in the market of opportunity. The Métis are, on the other hand, the least separate, given that they are the "least visible," live in close proximity to non-Aboriginal populations (Maxim and White 2000), and, as a minority, have the greatest levels of assimilation and market integration.

For both the Inuit and the Status Indians, labour market and social transfer issues might account for income inequality. The largest concentrations of Inuit are in the North, specifically in Nunavut, northern Quebec, and Labrador. An examination of rates of labour force participation in these geographic areas reveals that "living in the North raises the employment rates of non Aboriginal men and women and the non participation rates of Aboriginal Canadians" (George and Kuhn 1994, 6). Wage premiums are paid to non-Aboriginals for northern work, but they are not paid to Inuit in the region. The Inuit in the North report more "in-kind" income, from hunting and fishing, for example, but report fewer weeks of work for wages and salaries (George and Kuhn 1994, 6). Given that the northern areas are less attractive to migration for jobs, what we really are seeing is a geographical area that functions in some ways as do reserves in the south; that is, jobs are filled by those who live there, and if there are few jobs, rates of labour force participation will drop. Those working as artisans and in the marketing of artistic products report higher incomes, thus creating dispersion and polarization in income. The salaries paid to government employees who are Inuit also affects income dispersion in two ways. While these jobs may pay Inuit workers more than other types of employment they may obtain, they also pay the Inuit less than what people in the south receive. This is because the Inuit do not get northern differentials or a northern allowance to entice them to relocate.

Similar patterns appear on reserves, where certain occupations, such as elected office, are subject to salary grids that are insensitive to local market conditions. Many communities have a stratum of civil servants who are generally more highly paid. Furthermore, extreme educational level differentials may create a dual labour market where one is either limited to low-skill, low-paying jobs, or high-skill, high-remuneration positions in the government or in private sector industries such as utilities. This may account for some of the inequality of income and the hierarchy of inequality that we find. Certainly, this pattern is consistent with the findings of Massey et al. (1994), which show that geographic concentration and reduced out-migration possibilities are linked to lower SES and greater poverty in the US.

Existing theory and some empirical work argue that increased urban contact through increased size of community has the effect of reducing inequality. The major mechanisms at work here are increased access to capital and a greater dispersion of job skills with the attendant job market expansions

(Cloutier 1996, 288-89). The small communities of the North and the relatively small communities of the reserve system in the south make this an explanation consistent with our findings. The wage gap and the dispersion and polarization of income may also be explained in part by the devaluation of the occupations and job types concentrated within the Aboriginal population. Reid (1998, 512) argues, based on a rich sociological tradition, that jobs segregated by sex or ethnicity are characterized by discriminatory wage levels. Hirsch and Schumacher (1992) also confirm that, in the US, the proportion of African Americans in a job is negatively correlated with wages. Furthermore, we could argue that spatial and cultural segregation also results in Aboriginal wage levels being depressed, while the artificial connection with the wider market discussed above opens doors for very limited numbers of northern Inuit and First Nations people on reserves. These factors could increase the dispersion and polarization of income while holding down average income. Economic opportunities for Non-Status Indians and Métis, while certainly affected by discriminatory hiring and wage setting, are greater given the larger urban centres in which they reside.

If these hypothesized explanations are robust, why are reserves and the North not depleted of higher-income persons? The key to this question lies in a cluster of factors: the isolation of those communities, the structural discrimination that operates (Pendakur and Pendakur 1996), and the positive wage differentials created for these top earners.[24] For successful Inuit artisans, or those on tribal councils or in unique jobs such as reserve educational development officers, rewards are tied to the reserves and are often not mobile. This phenomenon is found in the US studies of ethnic residential concentrations (ghettoes), where the spatial connection of ethnicities remains even as the racial groups diversify economically. Erbe (1975) finds that intra-ethnic social connections remain even as class differences develop. His research indicates that the more economically successful African American is not always residentially separate from the poorer African American.

Conclusions

Several basic questions concerning income inequality are addressed in this chapter. The first deals with the importance of exploring the issues of inequality. The need for empirical research on which to assess the performance of past policy and the foundation for new programs and policies is self-evident. Given the relationship between inequality, health, and well-being, inequality has social impacts that should be addressed through research and policy initiatives. The differences we find suggest that there are many complexities to the issue and that there is a need to study inequality, particularly intra-Aboriginal inequality, in depth.

The second question concerns the gap in wages and income between the general Canadian population and different Aboriginal peoples. This gap exists for all the subgroups of Aboriginals identified in this study. Our results indicate that Registered or Status Indians and the Inuit are the furthest behind in terms of wage and salary income.

The third question addresses the extent of inequality within and between the Canadian non-Aboriginal population and the Aboriginal groups. We find that Aboriginal Canadians have more dispersion and polarization in income than non-Aboriginal Canadians, with Registered Indians and the Inuit having the greatest levels of inequality. These patterns hold regardless of our assumptions and different measurement scenarios. We find that transfer payments improve the situation for Aboriginal peoples in terms of reducing the magnitude of inequality.

Comparison of these results with previous analyses from 1986 and 1991 reveals very little change. In terms of the wage gap, both relative and absolute differences – for Aboriginal and non-Aboriginal and the intra-Aboriginal relationships – have remained. Even with the focus that the Royal Commission on Aboriginal Peoples created on issues of inequality, there is little, if any, progress. Our expectation that the attention focused on the First Nations and the potential improvements might have narrowed levels of inequality was not borne out.

The next step in the research will take four directions. The first is to determine why this inequality exists. What are the factors that influence inequality, and how do they interact to do so? Researchers should look at issues such as human capital, migration, fertility patterns, and social cohesion. The second direction is to model how income inequality interacts with other factors to influence health and social outcomes. A third area of research will include the examination of issues related to family income to see whether Aboriginal family income exhibits different patterns of inequality across Aboriginal groups and between Aboriginals and non-Aboriginals in Canada. Finally, the fourth research area will involve looking at the differences in the socio-economic characteristics, such as the relative prevalence of single-parent families or variations in education, that affect inequality. For future research on income, a reliable procedure is needed to control for the effects of on-reserve exemptions in taxation and the economic constraints of being located on a reserve.

Notes

1 Aboriginal peoples have been designated as one of the four economically disadvantaged target groups in Canada in the Employment Equity Act (1995).
2 There are other forces at work, but attempts to measure and model the other variables have not been well developed. An interesting development is found in the studies that examine community structure and community cohesion (Wilkinson 1996, 1997, 1998).

This view argues that structural forces related to income inequality, and relative and absolute poverty, are related to poor population outcomes. Whether it is international analyses (Wilkinson 1998), intranational analyses between regions (Kaplan et al. 1996; Kennedy et al. 1996; Kawachi and Kennedy 1997), or community-level investigations (Narayan 1997, 1999), the findings suggest that the more unequal the income distribution, the poorer the health and social outcomes. There is also mounting evidence that the cohesiveness of the community has structural origins (Kawachi et al. 1997; Kennedy et al. 1996; Narayan and Pritchett 1997; Wilkinson 1996, 1997, 1998).

3 Using after-tax family income often attenuates the Gini coefficients because it reduces the differences between individuals. Thus, the dispersion of family income appears smaller than the dispersion of individual income. To develop more precise explanations of the causes of inequality, it is important to examine individual data. Poverty and depth of poverty can be examined using family data, as families are the group that use income for consumption.

4 Studies of inequality have relied on the comparison of Gini coefficient values in the past. These are useful indices for exposing patterns of income distributions in the general population. Keeping in mind that a value of 0 implies complete equality (that is, where everyone has the same income) and a value of 1 represents complete inequality, the movement of the Gini coefficient from 0.329 in 1989 to 0.357 in 1998 indicates an increase in inequality.

5 These cases include, among others, *Guerin* v. *Attorney General of Canada* (1985), *Sparrow* v. *Attorney General of Canada* (1990), *Delgamuukw* v. *The Queen* (1997), and *Donald Marshall* v. *The Queen* (1999).

6 Kanesatake (Oka), Ipperwash, the New Brunswick Fishery, and Gustafsen Lake, for example.

7 This strongly suggests that data on persons reporting multiple Aboriginal origins should be separated from cases where only a single Aboriginal origin is reported.

8 Status Indians have a tax advantage if they live on reserve and collect their income from work on reserve. This advantage is estimated by Bernier (1997, 3) to be approximately $4,000 on $20,000 of income. We could not adjust for this because the data do not specify where income was earned.

9 Bernier used the Gini coefficient, the coefficient of variance, an exponential measure, and an index of polarization. Some of these measures differ from our own but indicate similar trends.

10 Any comparison between the 1991 and 1996 Censuses is difficult because the 1991 Census PUMF collapses the Inuit and Métis into a single category. We do not have access to the individual data in the adult file that would allow us to disaggregate this category. We experimented with creating proxy values based on proportions of Inuit and Métis populations by province, but found the results to be unreliable analytically. Attempts to use the Aboriginal Peoples Survey public use file were unsuccessful, since the income data are reported in categories rather than as a continuous variable. The use of means based on category midpoints would undermine any dispersion analysis. We have therefore resorted to reporting Métis and Inuit as separate categories in the analysis of the 1996 data. Previous analyses of data on the Inuit and Métis indicate that they are not similar groups. The Métis have patterns of dispersion that are similar to those of Non-Status Indians, and the Inuit display patterns closer to those of Status Indians living on reserve. Consequently, we have not produced tables based on the 1991 data and have chosen to just report the findings of previous studies.

11 When we speak of Registered Indians living in First Nations communities, we are using data for *all* Registered Indians. This was a common practice in earlier research (Bernier 1997, 11, fn. 14). See George et al. 1996 for an analysis of the 1991 Census PUMF, George and Kuhn 1994 for an analysis of the 1986 Census PUST, and Bernier 1997 for an analysis of the 1991 Census and the post-censal Aboriginal Peoples Survey.

12 The population studied here consists of those who identify themselves as being Registered Indians; Non-Status, single-origin North American Indians; Métis; or Inuit. We excluded categories of "multiple background" as it is unclear where these cases best fit. Furthermore, the numbers are small.

13 Based on bootstrapped 95% confidence levels.

14 This analysis is an attempt to focus on all labour force participants, including the unemployed. Some "slippage" is evident, however, since income is based on 1995 estimates while labour force participation is based on a reference week in 1996.

15 Thiel's measure of entropy gives more weight to differences in the upper tail of the distribution. The standard formula is given as:

$$T = (1/n) \sum_{i=1}^{n} (y_i/\mu) \log_{10}(y_i/\mu)$$

16 The Atkinson index is actually a family of indices based on a presumed social welfare transfer function. The index is influenced by a parameter, ε, where ε represents the proportionate value of $1.00 of income transferred from a higher income earner to a lower income earner. The appropriate formula is:

$$A_\varepsilon = 1 - [(1/n) \sum_{i=1}^{n} (Y_i/\mu)^{1-\varepsilon}]^{1/(1-\varepsilon)}, \text{ when } \varepsilon \neq 1, \varepsilon \geq 0, \text{ and}$$

$$A_\varepsilon = 1 - \exp[(1/n) \sum_{i=1}^{n} \ln(Y_i/n)], \text{ when } \varepsilon = 1.$$

17 Total income includes wages and salaries, income from self-employment, investment income, pensions and annuities, other cash income, family allowances, federal child tax credit, Old Age Supplement (OAS), Canada Pension Plan (CPP), Employment Insurance (EI) benefits, and other government transfers.

18 The upper limit of individual income is truncated by Statistics Canada to $180,000 in order to maintain confidentiality.

19 The non-Aboriginal population constitutes the base value for the Gini coefficient. Each of the aboriginal subgroup Gini values is subtracted from the base, then the percentage difference is calculated. In other words: $([Gini_{Aboriginal} - Gini_{non-Aboriginal}]/[Gini_{non-Aboriginal}]) \times 100$. The assumptions are zero incomes in or out, and non-wage and salary income included and excluded. For ease of interpretation, the sign denotes the direction of the relationship. Therefore, where the Gini coefficient is larger, the table indicates a positive value to denote an increase in inequality.

20 Only those with non-zero wage and salary incomes between the ages of 18 and 64 years of age, inclusive, were included in the analysis. Because of the large number of non-Aboriginal people in the PUMF, a further 20% random subset was selected to facilitate the analysis.

21 The dependent variable is the natural logarithm of average weekly income. The reasons for using a log are the following: (1) substantive parameters can be expressed as a percentage of income rather than absolute dollars, and (2) it reduces the technical problem of heteroscedasticity of the error terms.

22 All categorical variables were "effect"-coded. This means that the coefficients can be interpreted as percentage differences above or below the overall mean, ceteris paribus. Since the parameter for women in the non-Aboriginal sample is approximately −0.12, this means that women earn about 12% less than average while men earn approximately 12% more. Consequently, women earn about 24% less than men. A further consequence of "effect" coding is that all of the parameter values for a given categorical variable are constrained to sum to zero, i.e., $Eb_i = 0$.

23 This study uses the categories identified by Statistics Canada in its assessment of occupations (Statistics Canada 1994). Specifically these groupings are: Level I: senior managers, middle and other managers, and professionals; Level II: semi-professionals and technicians, supervisors, foremen/women, administrative and senior clerical workers, sales and service personnel, and skilled crafts and tradespeople; Level III: clerical workers, sales and service workers, and semi-skilled manual workers; Level IV: sales and service and other manual workers.

24 It should also be noted that income earned on reserve is not subject to taxation. This would allow employers to pay less for work done on reserve. It also means that incomes are actually higher than they seem in terms of purchasing power.

References

Atkinson, A.B. 1970. On the measurement of income inequality. *Journal of Economic Theory* 2: 244-63.

–. 1996. Income distribution in Europe and the United States. *Oxford Review of Economic Policy* 12: 15-28.

Becker, G. 1975. *Human Capital: A Theoretical and Empirical Analysis, with Special Reference to Education.* 2nd ed. New York: Columbia University Press.

Bernier, R. 1997. The dimensions of wage inequality among Aboriginal peoples. Research Paper Series No. 109. Ottawa: Analytical Studies Branch, Statistics Canada.

Brenner, M.H. 1979. Mortality and the national economy: A review and the experience of England and Wales. *Lancet* 2: 568-73.

Clatworthy, S., J. Hull, and N. Laughren. 1995. Patterns of employment, unemployment and poverty. *People to People, Nation to Nation,* the Royal Commission on Aboriginal Peoples. Ottawa: Minister of Supply and Services Canada.

Cloutier, N. 1996. Intra-racial income inequality: An examination of the metropolitan areas. *Review of Social Economy* 54: 285-301.

De Silva, S. 1999. Wage discrimination against Natives. *Canadian Public Policy* 25: 65-83.

Erbe, B. 1975. Race and socioeconomic segregation. *American Sociological Review* 40: 801-12.

Flanagan, T. 2000. *First Nations? Second Thoughts.* Montreal: McGill-Queen's University Press.

Frideres, J.M. 1998. *Aboriginal Peoples in Canada.* Scarborough, ON: Prentice-Hall.

Gardiner, P. 1994. Aboriginal community incomes and migration in the Northwest Territories: Policy issues and alternatives. *Canadian Public Policy* 20: 297-317.

George, P., and P. Kuhn. 1994. The size and structure of Native-white wage differentials. *Canadian Journal of Economics* 27: 20-42.

George, P., P. Kuhn, and A. Sweetman. 1996. Patterns of employment, unemployment and poverty: A comparative analysis of several aspects of the employment experience of Aboriginal and non-Aboriginal Canadians using 1991 PUMF. In *People to People, Nation to Nation,* the Royal Commission on Aboriginal Peoples. Ottawa: Minister of Supply and Services Canada.

Government of Canada. 1999. *Ten Years of Health Transfer First Nation and Inuit Control.* Ottawa: Health Canada.

Hirsch, B., and E. Schumacher. 1992. Labor earnings, discrimination and the racial composition of jobs. *Journal of Human Resources* 27: 602-28.

INAC (Indian and Northern Affairs Canada). 1989. *Highlights of Aboriginal Conditions, 1981-2001. Part 3, Economic Conditions.* Ottawa: Indian and Northern Affairs Canada.

Jankowski, W.B., and B. Moazzami. 1994. Size distribution of income and income inequality among the Native population of northwest Ontario. *Canadian Journal of Native Studies* 14: 47-60.

Kaplan, G.E., E. Pauk, J.W. Lynch, R. Cohen, and J. Balfour. 1996. Income inequality and mortality in the United States. *British Medical Journal* 312: 999-1003.

Kawachi, I., and B.P. Kennedy. 1997. Socioeconomic determinants of health: Health and social cohesion: Why care about inequality? *British Medical Journal* 314: 1037-46.

Kennedy, B., I. Kawachi, and D. Prothron-Smith. 1996. Income distribution and mortality. *British Medical Journal* 312: 1004-7.

Little, B., and M. Stinson. 2000. Average family enjoying best income in a decade. *Globe and Mail,* 13 June, A16.

Massey, D.S. 1981. Social class and ethnic segregation: A reconsideration of methods and conclusions. *American Sociological Review* 46: 641-50.

Massey, D.S., A. Gross, and K. Shibuya. 1994. Migration, segregation, and the geographic concentration of poverty. *American Sociological Review* 59: 425-45.

Mincer, J. 1974. *School Experience and Earnings.* New York: National Bureau of Economic Research.

Maxim, P., and J. White. 2000. *Patterns of Urban Residential Settlement among Canada's Aboriginal Peoples.* Population Studies Centre Discussion Paper Series 00-08. London: University of Western Ontario.

National Council of Welfare. 1990. *Health, Health Care and Medicine: A Report by the National Council of Welfare.* Ottawa: Minister of Supply and Services.

Narayan, D. 1997. *Designing Community Based Development.* Environmental Department Paper No. 7. Washington, DC: World Bank.

–. 1999. *Bonds and Bridges: Social Capital and Poverty.* Research Working Paper No. 1896. Washington, DC: World Bank.

Narayan, D., and L. Pritchett. 1997. *Cents and Sociability: Household Income and Social Capital in Rural Tanzania.* Working Paper No. 1796. Washington, DC: World Bank.

Nixon, P.G. 1990. The welfare state North: Early developments in the Inuit income security. *Journal of Canadian Studies* 25: 144-54.

Park, R.E. 1926. The urban community as a spatial pattern and moral order. In *The Urban Community,* edited by E.W. Burgess. Chicago: University of Chicago Press.

Pendakur, K., and R. Pendakur. 1996. *The Colour of Money: Earnings Differentials among Ethnic Groups in Canada.* Ottawa: Strategic Research Analysis, Department of Canadian Heritage.

Reid, L. 1998. Devaluing women and minorities: The effects of race/ethnic and sex composition of occupations on wage levels. *Work and Occupation* 25: 511-26.

Royal Commission on Aboriginal Peoples. 1996. *People to People, Nation to Nation.* Ottawa: Minister of Supply and Services Canada.

Sloan, P., and R. Hill. 1995. *Corporate Aboriginal Relations: Best Practice Case Studies.* Toronto: Hill Sloan Associates.

Statistics Canada. 1994. *User Documentation for Public Use Microdata File on Individuals, 1991 Census.* Catalogue no. 48-038E. Ottawa: Statistics Canada.

–. 2000. *Income in Canada.* Catalogue no. 75-202 XPE. Ottawa: Statistics Canada.

Thiel, Henri. 1967. *Economics and Information Theory.* Amsterdam: North-Holland.

Wilkinson, R.G. 1990. Income distribution and mortality: A natural experiment. *Sociology of Health and Illness* 12: 391-412.

–. 1996. *Unhealthy Societies: The Afflictions of Inequality.* London: Routledge.

–. 1997: Comment: Incomes, inequality and social cohesion. *American Journal of Public Health* 87: 1504-6.

–. 1998. What health tells us about society. *IDS Bulletin* 29(1): 77-84.

World Bank. 2000. *World Development Report: Selected World Development Indicators.* New York: Oxford University Press.

Wolfson, M. 1995. *Divergent Inequalities: Theory, Empirical Results and Prescriptions*. Research Paper Series No. 66. Ottawa: Analytical Studies Branch, Statistics Canada.

Wolfson, M., and B.B. Murphy. 1998. *New Views on Inequality Trends in Canada and the United States*. Research Paper Series No. 11F0019MPE-124. Ottawa: Analytical Studies Branch, Statistics Canada.

10
Toward an Index of Community Capacity: Predicting Community Potential for Successful Program Transfer

Paul S. Maxim and Jerry P. White

Since 1969, reaction to the Government of Canada White Paper (Canada 1975) has meant that the federal government has increasingly transferred the control of many programs to First Nations communities. The resulting negotiations have seen new relationships and commitments develop within policy frameworks for strengthening First Nations' oversight and influence of a variety of programs and services.[1] This evolutionary movement has been most obvious in the field of health and, sometimes, social services. Through the 1980s, the Berger and Penner reports encouraged First Nations and Inuit control of these types of programs.[2] By the 1990s, the Treasury Board had approved the financial authority to fund transfer activities and community-level management structures.[3]

This course of action was taken because First Nations occupy a distinct status in Canadian society. The more than 580 communities are unique culturally and politically compared with the rest of Canada. Their fifty-one languages, dispersed geography, particular histories, and specific identities distinguish them from one another and from the rest of Canadian society. Their uniqueness does not stop at language or social history. First Nations communities have developed differently across many economic and social indicators. For example, income levels, housing, educational attainment, governance structures, family characteristics, morbidity, and migration patterns have also evolved in different ways, depending on local conditions.

First Nations communities are demanding, and are being given, control of programs that have an impact on many areas of life. This chapter addresses a critical question: "Can we assess the capacity of communities to successfully implement and maintain transferred programs?" Resources of different types are not evenly distributed across First Nations communities. They have different capacities for accepting and successfully implementing transferred programs. Studies have suggested that the government has at times transferred programs to First Nations communities that have little capacity to maintain them effectively. All too often, the result has been frustration and failure to provide the communities with the services that they need (Whitehead and Hayes 1999). We have set out to conceptualize and develop a prototype tool designed to help identify the varying capacities of First Nations communities to accept and maintain transferred programs. This tool may also have implications for other aspects of self-determination.

The Components of the Community Capacity Index and the Underlying Assumptions in Its Construction

The development literature provides some insight into the elements that might be logically included in the assessment of a community's capacity to successfully accept and implement the transfer of programs. The World Bank has a substantial literature that assesses the success and failure of aid as displayed in the development it generates. This literature is of limited applicability to program transfer because it looks largely at "aid" and whether "aid" is going to "work." In spite of these limitations, there are some promising ideas. The World Bank and the United Nations have come to the conclusion that there must be a clear assessment of the environment of the receiving country. The questions they pose are, "What are the conditions that permit success?" and "What are the indicators of those conditions?" The World Bank argues that success is tied to the types of policies and institutions that the governments in these regions possess (World Bank Research Group on Social Capital 1999b). While this analysis is more applicable to programs of aid, it indicates that the ability of the community to benefit from a transfer is a factor in the success of the program. In brief, it suggests that the levels of human and social capital in a community can influence the success of transfer of programs. This is consistent with the model we presented in Chapter 1 of this book. We have argued that the combination of human, social, and physical capital operates through social cohesion at the community level to influence population outcomes. In this chapter, we look at how different elements of these core capitals may operate to define a community's general capacity.

This chapter takes only the first step in the creation of a Community Capacity Index (CCI). In that sense, it is a conceptual piece of work. We want to encourage dialogue on a new way of looking at the issues of transfer and the capacity to succeed. We also want to encourage the construction of data sets that would permit the actual index to be built. The completed Community Capacity Index would have two multiple-index-based components. These components would reflect the dual aspects of the strengths and resources that a community has at its disposal: human capital and social capital. This chapter discusses the construction of one component of the CCI, based on human resources, and identifies the dimensions of the second component, social capital,[4] which needs to be addressed in the future. Even using our single-index component, our test for validity indicates that the measure is robust. It predicts the capacity of communities to manage their financial affairs.

Constructing the Human Resources Component of the CCI

We use four subindices to measure human resources that reflect, *in toto,* the composite measure of the human resources that can be drawn upon to implement programs successfully. These subindices are: (1) education/human capital, (2) population size, (3) age-dependency ratio, and (4) occupational diversity.

Each of these components is based on a set of explicit assumptions and empirical evidence of their reliability and validity. The subindices are combined into a single Community Capacity Index (CCI) that measures the capacity of the 278 First Nations communities that we used as the basis for constructing this index.[5]

The Education/Human Capital Subindex

A central index in the construction of the human resources component would have to be educational attainment, or what is called human capital (Becker 1964). When investments are made in human resources, there is a return in the form of productivity of the population, and this is reflected in the income that is earned. Much of the investigation of human capital by economists asks, "Is the investment in human resources cost-effective?" We are not exploring that issue. Our concern is with the effects of increased education and training in terms of return at two levels: (1) a social (collective) return, and (2) an individual (income) return (Gunderson and Riddel 1988). There is considerable empirical support for looking at income returns to education (Hanson 1970; Dooley 1986; Ashenfelter 1978). Several Canadian studies of patterns of income among First Nations persons have verified the existence of a return for each year of education for Aboriginal Canadians (Maxim and White in Chapter 9 of this volume; Bernier 1997; George et al. 1996). If we know that there is a return, then we can assume that compensation is tied to capacity. This analysis assumes that levels of education are indicators of capacity to perform a variety of tasks, including those necessary to implement and manage programs at the level of the individual and the community.

Measurements of returns on human capital indicate that the incremental return on investment varies considerably. This depends on the labour market conditions facing the individual and also on the labour market conditions facing the social group to which that person belongs. Pendakur and Pendakur (1996) find evidence of discrimination in the labour market with respect to the income return on education for visible minorities. The same appears true for Aboriginal peoples (Clatworthy et al. 1995). This chapter focuses only on First Nations communities, so capacity is measured within communities. There is therefore shelter from the effects of external market discrimination for the purpose of constructing the index.[6] This is not to say that the incomes are not affected by discrimination, but there should be little variance in this by community.

The aggregate data for First Nations communities are employed for the population between 15 and 64 years of age.[7]

Population Size and the Age-Dependency Ratio
Both the size and structure of a population can affect the capacity of a community to implement transferred programs successfully. We have included a simple measure for predicting capacity based on size. For instance, logically a community with five people could not administer its own health program. The base of citizens could not provide the infrastructural labour needed to do the work. Cut points that make sense intuitively have been selected. They comprise wide enough population bands to give a reasonable, but crude, measure.

While size is important, the composition of a population is also a critical factor. It is a common and well-established practice in demographic analyses of regional or national labour market issues to calculate a dependency ratio from the statistics on population age, separate from actual economic involvement (Shryock et al. 1980, 358). The purpose of this age-dependency ratio (ADR) is to get a measure of the proportion of the population that is potentially economically active. In brief, this is a measure of the potential labour force in relation to those who are dependent on that base of potential workers. The ratio takes all persons in the age group 15 to 65 years and assumes them to be producers, while all those younger and those older are assumed to be dependent. The number can be greater than 1.0 if there are many young and old persons in relation to the "productive adults," but it is usually a fractional value.[8]

This can be used in the assessment of community capacity because it suggests the pool from which those who will administer programs will be drawn compared with those subpopulations that will almost exclusively draw on community resources. It is also a crude maximum measure because it does not take into account actual participation in the labour force. The measure has the advantage that it identifies the outside limits of capacity.

In First Nations communities, we assume that the age structure has a dramatic effect. The larger cohorts of young people, particularly those less than 15 years of age, will represent a negative pressure on the potential for successful program transfer. The younger cohorts are largely consumers of programs and services as they do not possess the training or education to be "productive," in terms of generating goods and services. Similarly, we assume that those aged 65 and older will be net consumers of services. This is borne out most clearly in the consumption of health care resources. Also, for First Nations persons, average educational levels are lower for those over the age of 60 years. This suggests that this group would have less formal education to contribute to the productive side of program transfer outcomes (George et al. 1996).[9]

The ADR cannot, by itself, be taken as a definitive indicator of the pool from which capacity derives. It taps potential, but needs to be supplemented by a measure of available human resources that is based on the desire and capacity for participation. This dimension of human resources can be approximated through an index that captures occupational diversity.[10]

Occupational Diversity Subindex

The occupational diversity subindex provides an indication of the distribution of workers across occupations. An index value of 0 indicates that everyone in the community is in a single occupation; an index value closer to 1 shows an even distribution across all occupations. The number of occupational categories determines the maximum value of the index used. Generally, the more categories included in the index, the larger the maximum value the Index of Diversity can have. With five categories, the index can have a maximum value of 0.8; with ten categories, the maximum value is 0.9. Because of this feature, it is essential that the same number of occupational categories be used for each community. Thus, it is the relative value of the index across communities that is important. The absolute value of the index is of less interest.

Formally, the Index of Diversity is $1 - \Sigma_{i=1}^{I} p_i^2$ where p_i is the proportion of people in a given occupation, i, and I is the total number of occupations. As an example, consider a community of 465 persons in the labour force, with

Table 10.1 Index of diversity for a labour force of 465 persons and seven occupational groups

Occupation	Number	Proportion	p_i^2
A	20	0.043	0.002
B	40	0.086	0.007
C	20	0.043	0.002
D	35	0.075	0.006
E	100	0.215	0.046
F	140	0.301	0.091
G	110	0.237	0.056
Total	465	1.000	0.210
Index			0.790

seven occupational groups labelled A through G. With the distribution illustrated in the accompanying table, the Index of Diversity would be (1 – 0.210), or 0.790 (see Table 10.1).

For our study of First Nations communities, we have taken the specific occupational groups from the 1996 Census of Canada.[11] Because of the small populations in most communities, occupations are aggregated at a crude level.[12]

The next step is to construct the Community Capacity Index. The simple combination of the subindices would be valid only if the amount of variance explained was roughly equal for each of the components. Review of the coefficients in Table 10.1 leads to the conclusion that this is the case. As the coefficients suggest, the subindices are of similar size, and they are therefore not weighted in the creation of the CCI.

Constructing and Testing the Community Capacity Index

To be useful, an index needs to have three properties:

1 It must provide a value that allows comparability between communities that is meaningful and robust.
2 It must be simple to use and understand.
3 It must be testable (i.e., falsifiable). (See also Appendix 10.1.)

Table 10.2 Subindices with assigned point values

Subindex	Number of points assigned	Subindex	Number of points assigned
Education subindex[a]		Age-dependency ratio	
0%-49% have postsecondary	0	0.75+	0
50%-64% have postsecondary	1	0.51-0.74	1
65%-74% have postsecondary	2	0.26-0.49	2
75% and above have		0.25 and less	3
postsecondary	3		
Population size		Occupational diversity	
100-499	0	0-0.69	0
500-999	1	0.70-0.74	1
999-1,999	2	0.75-0.84	2
2,000+	3	0.85+	3
Community Capacity Index			Points total

a Education is dichotomized into two categories: those with high school education or less, and those with some training beyond high school. In terms of the available data, this means that those with less than grade 9 and those with grades 9-13, with or without a secondary school graduation certificate, are collapsed into the first category. The second category consists of those with trade certificates or diplomas only, other non-university education (with or without a certificate or diploma), university without a bachelor's degree or higher, and university with a bachelor's degree or higher. This index is based on the percentage of the community with the postsecondary education. This is much more reliable as a predictor of variance than lower educational cut-offs.

Table 10.3 Counts of First Nations communities as ranked by subindices

Count	Cumulative count	Percent	Cumulative percent	Value
Size of community				
120	120	43.2	43.2	0
103	223	37.1	80.2	1
43	266	15.5	95.7	2
12	278	4.3	100.0	3
Education				
203	203	73.0	73.0	0
62	265	22.3	95.3	1
10	275	3.6	98.9	2
3	278	1.1	100.0	3
Age-dependency				
12	12	4.3	4.3	0
82	94	29.5	33.8	1
137	231	49.3	83.1	2
47	278	16.9	100.0	3
Occupational diversity				
9	9	3.2	3.2	0
34	43	12.2	15.5	1
221	264	79.5	95.0	2
14	278	5.0	100.0	3

The CCI has these three properties. Table 10.2 presents the subindices as categorical constructs that have values attached to them. Rather than creating a single index that must be applied in a complicated mathematical model, the index is simplified by having point values designated for each categorical condition based on predetermined cut points.

Table 10.3 presents the array of scores for the communities when they are rated on the individual subindices, one at a time. The table groups the results by each subindex, for example, education and population size. The first column shows the number of communities falling into each value category. For example, on the subindex of community size, 120, or 43.2%, of the 278 communities receive 0 points, and only 12, or 4.3%, get the maximum score of 3 points.

How Do First Nations Communities Score?

The result of applying the full CCI to First Nations communities appears in Table 10.4. The range on the CCI is 0 to a maximum of 12, and this represents a continuum on which the relative position of communities shows a level of potential to succeed or fail.

Table 10.4   Community Capacity Index: First Nations community scores

Community count	Cumulative count	Percentage	Cumulative percentage	CCI point level
1	1	0.4	0.4	0
8	9	2.9	3.2	1
9	18	3.2	6.5	2
35	53	12.6	19.1	3
77	130	27.7	46.8	4
65	195	23.4	70.1	5
45	240	16.2	86.3	6
19	259	6.8	93.2	7
9	268	3.2	96.4	8
8	276	2.9	99.3	9
2	278	0.7	100.0	10+

Figure 10.1 describes how one should view the values generated by the index. The results suggest that there is a wide range in capacity among First Nations communities. Transition or cut points where communities would more likely fail or more likely succeed are identified in the following section, where the analysis was performed on all First Nations communities that participated in the Census. Because of the current demographics of the communities, we can see that the distribution of these 278 communities is clustered around the low scores on the scale.

Mapping the First Nations Communities by Capacity

In previous work, Armstrong (1999) explored regional differences in patterns of well-being. His aim was to illustrate how a series of indicators of well-being could be used to rank communities by mapping those communities with similar scores on the index of well-being so that geographic patterns could be identified. Figure 10.2 maps the communities by their score on the composite Community Capacity Index. The values for this figure come from Table 10.5.

Figure 10.1   Capacity continuum

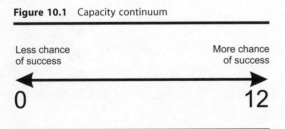

Less chance of success

More chance of success

0   12

Figure 10.2 Distribution of First Nations communities based on their Community Capacity Index scores

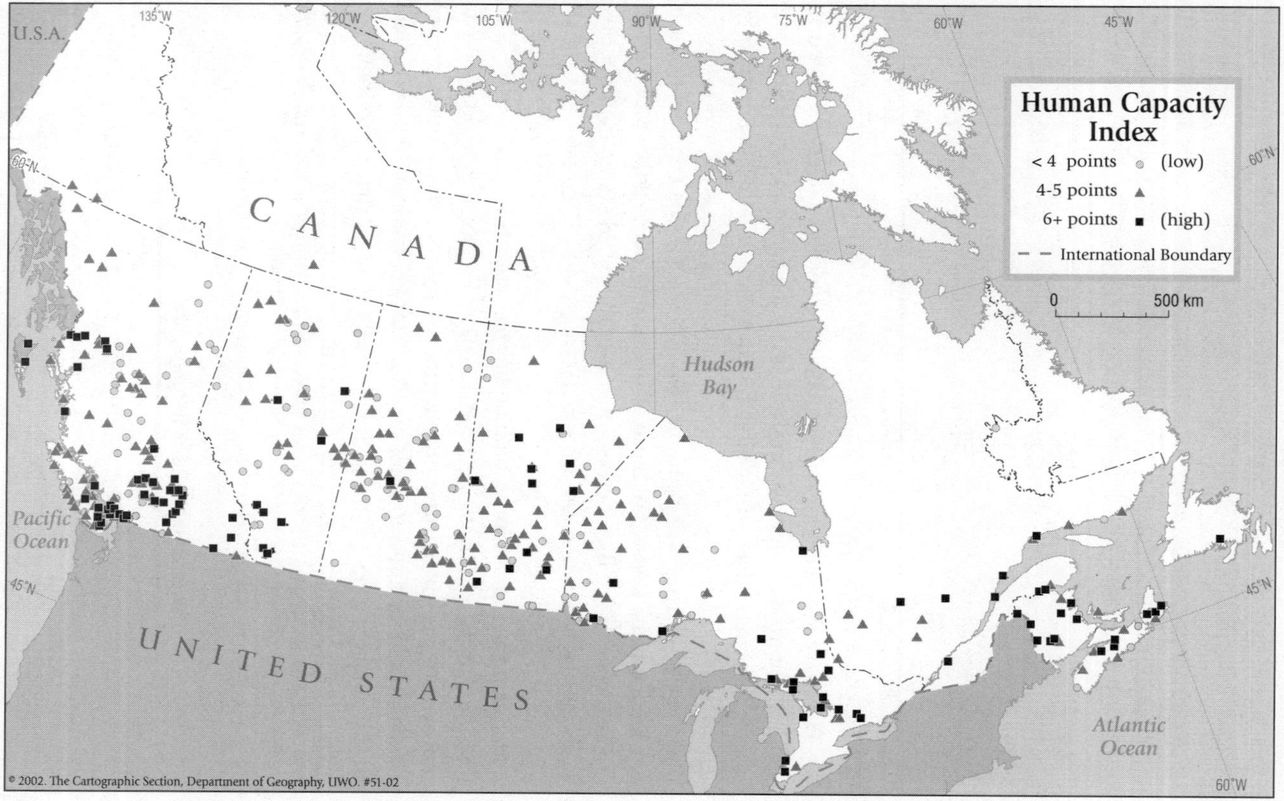

Human Capacity
Index

< 4 points ○ (low)
4-5 points ▲
6+ points ■ (high)
— — International Boundary

0   500 km

60°N
45°W
60°W
75°W
90°W
105°W
120°W
135°W
60°N
45°N

U.S.A.

C A N A D A

U N I T E D   S T A T E S

Hudson
Bay

Pacific
Ocean

Atlantic
Ocean

45°N
60°W

© 2002. The Cartographic Section, Department of Geography, UWO #51-02

Table 10.5 Counts of First Nations communities as ranked by subindices and the Community Capacity Index (CCI)

Count	Cumulative count	Percentage	Cumulative %	Size
341	341	68.3	68.3	0
103	444	20.6	89.0	1
43	487	8.6	97.6	2
12	499	2.4	100.0	3

Count	Cumulative count	Percentage	Cumulative %	Education
337	337	67.5	67.5	0
117	454	23.4	91.0	1
37	491	7.4	98.4	2
8	499	1.6	100.0	3

Count	Cumulative count	Percentage	Cumulative %	Age-dependency
35	35	7.0	7.0	0
110	145	22.0	29.1	1
208	353	41.7	70.7	2
146	499	29.3	100.0	3

Count	Cumulative count	Percentage	Cumulative %	Occupational diversity
92	92	18.4	18.4	0
86	178	17.2	35.7	1
303	481	60.7	96.4	2
18	499	3.6	100.0	3

Count	Cumulative count	Percentage	Cumulative %	Scale
		CLUSTER 1		
8	8	1.6	1.6	0
25	33	5.0	6.6	1
32	65	6.4	13.0	2
87	152	17.4	30.5	3
		CLUSTER 2		
128	280	25.7	56.1	4
105	385	21.0	77.2	5
		CLUSTER 3		
67	452	13.4	90.6	6
27	479	5.4	96.0	7
10	489	2.0	98.0	8
8	497	1.6	99.6	9
2	499	0.4	100.0	10

Table 10.5 reports on the 499 communities that have the necessary data for all of the subindices to be applied.[13] Communities display a value from 0 to 3 according to their score on the particular subindex. For the mapping of the CCI shown in Figure 10.2, the communities fall on a longer scale, with values ranging from 0 to 10. We have clustered the communities based on our assessment of capacity and the distribution of communities. Table 10.5 provides details for the clusters. Cluster 1 groups 152 communities (30.5%) with 0 to 3 points. This represents communities that have the lowest chance of successfully implementing transferred programs, and we predict that failure would be likely.

Cluster 2 groups 233 communities (47.1%) with 4-5 points. These communities would have to be assessed on a case-by-case basis. Using the results of subindices might identify particular weaknesses that could be addressed, such as size, where outside personnel would remedy the situation, or clustering with neighbouring small reserves with political and cultural compatibility. Cluster 3 groups 114 communities (22.8%) that would be highly likely to succeed.

If we look at the distribution of communities by the full index, we can see an interesting pattern. In general, the Prairie provinces and Northern communities show patterns of lower capacity, whereas communities in the British Columbia Lower Mainland, the Maritimes, and areas of Ontario show some clustering of higher capacity.

Validating the Community Capacity Index

Constructing a capacity index is one task; validating it is another. The primary objective of this exercise was to see whether it is possible to distinguish among communities in their ability to develop, implement, or manage various programs. The primary assumption we made was that communities that had the most capital, human and otherwise, would, all things being equal, be more likely to succeed in their programmatic endeavours than communities with less capital.

One test of the index and its underlying rationale is to determine how well communities are managing resources provided by the federal government to administer various programs under their control. Because public monies are provided to First Nations communities, the Department of Indian Affairs and Northern Development (DIAND) conducts audits to determine whether or not the bands' financial resources are being managed in a fashion consistent with standard accounting and managerial practices.

Communities were initially identified by whether or not their financial practices were acceptable or whether some form of remedial action was required. Table 10.6 shows a distribution of communities by their ranking on the CCI.

Table 10.6 Financial management status of First Nations communities by ranking on the Community Capacity Index

Community Capacity Index	No action required	Remedial action required	Sample size
Low	28%	72%	43
Medium	60%	40%	178
High	91%	9%	47

Data were obtained for 208 communities for the 2000 fiscal year. Among communities that scored low on the CCI, 72% required some remedial action in terms of third-party supervision, co-management, or, in the extreme, receivership. Forty percent of the communities scoring in the medium range of the CCI required remedial action, while only 9% of those scoring in the high range required remedial action. (See also Appendix 10.2.)

Conclusions

If it is possible to decide, within reasonable bounds of predictive accuracy, whether a community has the quality and quantity of human resources to successfully accept and implement downloaded programs, there can be a more reasoned strategic approach to carrying out the current mandate of bringing control of policy into the hands of those affected. The tool developed here cannot answer all questions, nor is it capable of exact prediction. It is only one component of a broader index of community capacity. A second component cannot be built until the data necessary for its construction are available. Fortunately, the First Nations Cohesion Project at the University of Western Ontario is constructing the very information base needed to complete this Community Capacity Index tool.[14] As it stands now, the CCI can suggest the kind of shortfall that potentially exists, and therefore indicate what preparatory action may be necessary. It can be used to estimate where communities fall relative to one another, and provides some opportunity to assess the relative strengths of the community and the relative potential for successful program transfer. It can also be diagnostic in cases where there has been difficulty in successful transfer, by pointing out the areas where the community may wish to improve its level of capacity for the future.[15]

This CCI, as presented, is only one component of a complete Community Capacity Index. The data are simply not available to construct the social capital side of the tool. When that is done, the CCI will be a more powerful predictor and diagnostic tool than it is now.

In the future, when reports are available on the success or failure of program transfers, the CCI could be used as a diagnostic tool to detect those aspects of the structural relationships within the community that enhance or hinder the likelihood of successful program implementation.

Appendix 10.1
Constructing the Indices of the Community Capacity Index

Each index is developed through a series of steps:

1 Determine potential measures for a subindex and calculate descriptive statistics.
2 Determine a test of capacity by selecting a proxy that reflects a community's success in matters similar to or related to program transfer. We had to choose from readily available data and therefore chose income, taking its mean and then using a log transformation to reduce heteroscedasticity and enhance reliability.
3 Determine whether the subindex is robust in explaining the variance in capacity. We regressed the log of the average income in the community on the individual subindices to find their individual contribution, and to find whether they needed to be weighted in the final CCI. Table 10.7 in Appendix 10.2 shows that all the subindices are statistically significant, and the size of the coefficients suggests that leaving the components of the CCI unweighted is reasonable.

Appendix 10.2
Alternate Measures of Effectiveness

An alternative measure of effectiveness, for the purposes of testing the subindex, would be a proxy that is clearly identifiable as related to community success. We are constrained by the nature of the data that are available at the community level. The test we apply is based on average income in the community. For analytical purposes, its natural logarithm is used. Table 10.7 displays the results of a regression analysis conducted to assess the CCI. All of the measures are significant, and cumulatively they account for about 23% of the variance in the community's ability to secure income.[16]

Table 10.7 Regression analysis of Community Capacity Index subindices on the dependent variable log of mean community income

Effect	Coefficient	Std. error	Std. coefficient	t-value	P (2-tail)
Constant	8.936	0.062	0.000	143.831	0.000
Size	0.077	0.018	0.227	4.215	0.000
Education	0.096	0.030	0.199	3.226	0.001
Age-dependency	0.085	0.023	0.228	3.637	0.000
Occupational diversity	0.053	0.030	0.098	1.755	0.080

Source	Sum-of-squares	df	Mean-square	F-ratio	P
Analysis of variance					
Regression	5.282	4	1.321	20.282	0.000
Residual	17.774	273	0.065		

Notes: Dependent variable: LOGWAGE; N = 278; Multiple R = 0.479; Squared multiple R = 0.229; Adjusted squared multiple R = 0.218; Standard error of estimate = 0.255

We feel that the significant results give an indication of the potential of the index. The next stage is to construct the CCI. The simple combination of the subindices would only be valid if the amount of variance explained was roughly equal for each of the components. Review of the coefficients in Table 10.7 leads to the conclusion that this is the case. As the coefficients suggest, the subindices are of similar size, and they are therefore not weighted in the creation of the CCI.

Notes

1 See Government of Canada 1975.
2 See Government of Canada 1980, 1983.
3 See Government of Canada 1999.
4 The data for constructing the social capital component is being created by the First Nations Cohesion Project at the University of Western Ontario. While the concept of social capital is very likely a key aspect of any attempt to create a predictive tool, it is not easy to operationalize. "Measuring social capital may be very difficult, but not impossible and several excellent studies have identified useful proxies for social capital ... Trust, civic engagement and community involvement are generally seen as ways to measure social capital" (World Bank Research Group on Social Capital 1999a, 1). We hypothesized in Chapter 1 that the development of human capital and establishment of a physical resources infrastructure need to be complemented by social capital, which in turn allows institutionalized development in order to reap the full benefits of all these investments. The problem is that, at this time, we cannot measure these types of relationships in ways that are conducive to quantitative analysis. We are working on this problem, and it is likely that two subindices will be added in the future to create the social capital component of the CCI. The first will be a measure of "institutional completeness." This takes account of the existence of structures and services that show the vitality and potential for growth of a community (existence of a school and health clinic, for example). The second subindex would focus on governance. This would assess the political cohesion and effectiveness of the community. The subindex may focus on the frequency and extent of change ("churn") of political leadership and the ability of local political leadership to deal effectively with other levels of government.
5 For this process, we could use only 278 of the 530 census communities because income data were not available for the other 252.
6 This is the same reasoning used to assess protected occupational labour market segments, referred to as labour market sheltering. For a discussion, see Freedman 1976.
7 All the data used in calculating the various subindex values come from the 1996 Census of Canada data (community-level data files, or CSD). In 1996, Statistics Canada collected data from 751 populated geographical units that qualified as First Nations communities as defined in this study. We assumed that communities with populations of fewer than sixty-five adults aged 15 to 64 years would likely have an inadequate population to sustain program transfer. We concluded that these communities would have to be clustered by considering geography, culture, and governance structures. These communities would automatically be classified as having lower capacity until they are actually linked with others to form a minimum basic population level. These small communities comprise less than 5% of the Registered Indian population of enumerated First Nations communities. This is similar to the methods employed in previous studies (see Armstrong and Rogers 1996). We should note that some government agencies (e.g., Medical Services Branch of Health Canada) are developing some basic clustering procedures that may be ready for analysis later in 2004. Statistics Canada applies random rounding procedures to data retrieval from the Census database, to maintain confidentiality. They randomly assign zero values to counts of 0, 1, 2, 8, and

9, and 5 to counts of 3, 4, 5, 6, and 7. This problem confounds the counts for the smallest communities and contributes to overall error due to rounding. It is possible, therefore, that anomalies might appear in the study when communities have small populations. In the end, we processed the characteristics for 278 communities, representing approximately 80% of the First Nations population.

8 The age-dependency ratio (ADR) is calculated as follows: ADR = (population under 15 years + population 65 years and over)/(population 15-64 years of age).

9 This should be tempered with the understanding that the elderly have a lot of experience and contribute through the sound advice and direction that come from that experience.

10 Not all persons between the ages of 15 and 64 show an equal ability or willingness to be productive in the community. This unevenness affects the capacity of the community. The economic dependency ratio gives a measure of this. The economic dependency ratio is also a well-established demographic indicator. Shryock et al. (1980, 335) define it as "the ratio of the economically inactive population to the active population over all ages" – simply put, non-workers to workers. For the present purpose, we are not concerned with those less than 15 years of age or those more than 65 years of age, because a measure of their effect is at the heart of the age-dependency ratio. The economic dependency ratio, based on rates of participation, includes all those persons employed or seeking employment, over the total population 15-65 years of age. This provides a measure of the capacity to work. However, the explanatory power of the variable is not strong in accounting for variation in income. Therefore, no strong case exists for its inclusion and, instead, we chose to use a different index that has a window on the labour market, an occupational diversity index.

11 Table 95f0246xdb96001.csd.

12 The following groupings were used: management occupations; business, finance, and administrative occupations; occupations in the natural and applied sciences; health occupations; occupations in social science, education, government service, and religion; occupations in art, culture, recreation, and sport; sales and service supervisors; trades, transport and equipment operators, and related occupations; occupations unique to primary industry; and occupations unique to processing, manufacturing, and utilities.

13 The 530 communities in the census minus the 31 where no data on occupation are reported.

14 The next component will include elements of a social cohesion/social capital set of subindices, such as family types, children in care, and social and recreational infrastructure.

15 Another use for the index is to diagnose potential underlying reasons for apparent failure in the implementation of a program. The CCI can be used in two stages to effect such a diagnosis. First, the community could be assessed using the CCI itself. It could then be compared with the distribution of communities reported in Table 10.3, which would indicate the relative capacity of the communities. The second stage of analysis would be to examine each of the component subindices for the community to determine which of the underlying factors indicates the greatest problem.

16 This phase of the project is testing the validity of the indices by correlating them with the log of average income of the community. For this process we were forced to use only 278 of the 530 census communities because data on income were unavailable for the other 252.

References

Armstrong, Robin. 1999. Mapping the conditions of First Nations communities. *Canadian Social Trends* 55 (Winter): 14-18.

Armstrong, Robin, and Tim Rogers. 1996. *A First Nations Topology: Patterns of Socio-Economic Well-Being.* Ottawa: Research and Analysis Directorate, Department of Indian Affairs and Northern Development.

Ashenfelter, O. 1978. Estimating the effect of training on earnings. *R.E. Stats* 63 (February): 47-57.

Becker G. 1964. *Human Capital.* New York: National Bureau of Economic Research.

Bernier, R. 1997. *The Dimensions of Wage Inequality among Aboriginal Peoples.* Research Paper Series No. 109. Ottawa: Analytical Studies Branch, Statistics Canada.

Clatworthy, S., J. Hull, and N. Laughren. 1995. Patterns of employment, unemployment and poverty. In *People to People, Nation to Nation,* the Royal Commission on Aboriginal Peoples. Ottawa: Minister of Supply and Services Canada.

Dooley, M. 1986. The overeducated Canadian? Changes in the relationships between earnings, education and age. *Canadian Journal of Economics* 19 (February): 142-59.

Freedman, Marcia K. 1976. *Labour Markets: Segments and Shelters.* New York: Allenhead Osman.

George, P., P. Kuhn, and A. Sweetman. 1996. Patterns of employment, unemployment and poverty: A comparative analysis of several aspects of the employment experience of Aboriginal and non-Aboriginal Canadians using 1991 PUMF. In *People to People, Nation to Nation,* the Royal Commission on Aboriginal Peoples. Ottawa: Minister of Supply and Services Canada.

Government of Canada. 1975. *The Canadian Government – The Canadian Indian Relationships Paper.* Ottawa: Minister of Supply and Services Canada.

–. 1980. *The Report of the Advisory Committee on Indian and Inuit Health Consultation (The Berger Report).* Ottawa: Minister of Supply and Services Canada.

–. 1983. *Report of the Special Committee on Indian Self-Government (The Penner Report).* Ottawa: Minister of Supply and Services Canada.

–. 1999. *Ten Years of Health Transfer First Nation and Inuit Control.* Ottawa: Health Canada.

Gunderson, M.J., and W. Riddel. 1988. *Labour Market Economics: Theory, Evidence and Policy in Canada.* 2nd ed. Toronto: McGraw-Hill Ryerson.

Hanson, W.L. 1970. *Education, Income and Human Capital.* New York: National Bureau of Economic Research.

Pendakur, K., and R. Pendakur. 1996. *The Colour of Money: Earnings Differentials among Ethnic Groups in Canada.* Ottawa: Strategic Research Analysis, Department of Canadian Heritage.

Shryock, H., J. Siegal, and E. Lyman. 1980. *The Methods and Materials of Demography.* 4th ed. Washington, DC: Bureau of the Census, Department of Commerce.

Whitehead, P.C., and M.J. Hayes. 1999. *The Insanity of Alcohol: Social Problems in Canada's First Nations Communities.* Toronto: Canadian Scholars' Press.

World Bank Research Group on Social Capital 1999a. Social capital methods and tools. <http://www.worldbank.org/poverty/scapital/methods/index.htm>.

–. 1999b. *Assessing Aid – What Works, What Doesn't, and Why.* Report of the Assessment Commission. Washington, DC: World Bank.

Conclusion:
The Research-Policy Nexus –
What Have We Learned?
Jerry P. White

We began this book with the identification of a problem: the need, in Canada, to build a research-policy nexus. Such a relationship and approach should be aimed at improving research and developing evidence-based policy making in our country. We argued that, now more than ever, answering the simple pair of questions, "What is the situation?" and "Why has it developed?" is the foundation of public policy. The crafting of policy that addresses social problems and builds on the social successes of Aboriginal peoples requires a refined scientific investigation of the true conditions facing the community.

There needs to be a dynamic strategic relationship between three types of stakeholders: governmental, Aboriginal, and academic. This is based on the recognition that both the government and Aboriginal stakeholders conduct research as well as make policy. Scholars may also be engaged in determining policy directions through a secondment, but primarily our responsibility has to be the development of the research skills and actual scholarship that provides a solid foundation for policy development.

The studies in this book are a direct product of private and public researchers working in tandem to uncover the key elements of the current and future conditions that set the parameters around policy. Our aim is to promote policy making that is evidence-based.

This book set out to speak to three important constituencies and therefore has three purposes. We write for scientists, both Aboriginal and non-Aboriginal, with the aim of presenting findings from our recent research and thereby pushing forward the research agenda on issues of relevance to Aboriginal Canadians. We hope that this scientific interest will contribute eventually to positive social development. *Aboriginal Conditions* speaks to policy makers in government and in Aboriginal leadership positions, with the aim of promoting evidence-based policy making, encouraging a greater link with the scientific and external research community, and demonstrating the types of research necessary as a foundation for public policy. We also want to speak as scientists to the Aboriginal communities about research and how to proceed on issues of data collection and analysis. We wanted this to be a call for more cooperation between scientists and Aboriginal organizations, to ensure that the decisions about who will conduct research and how they will do it serve both the community directly and the long-term interests of finding truth.

This book also set out to explain how capacity is built in Aboriginal communities. It was not to be a litany of problems but rather a compilation of some trends and objective conditions that could serve as a way to understand both how to move forward and what obstacles might very well impede such development.

What Was Presented and What Are the Policy Implications?

The research chapters began with the proposal that policy in the future has to be based on communities of people. The movement toward more sovereignty, and the continuation and development of collectivities of Aboriginal Canadians as nations with boundaries and rights, presupposes that the collective level is critical in terms of building capacity and success. Chapter 1 challenged researchers to look not only at the characteristics of the individuals in a community but also at the characteristics of the community, and encouraged the use of more innovative models. We took this to the level of measurement with a simple look at a Community Capacity Index in Chapter 10, in which we began the process of examining how different forms of resources can combine to yield different capacities at the community level. We argued that, in the future, resources will have to be directed toward, and developed within, communities based on a more scientific assessment of how productive they will be, given the configuration of existing forms of social, human, and physical capital. Perhaps this means that all the stakeholders in this enterprise will develop and refine their approaches. Aboriginal policy makers and politicians can pinpoint their demands, researchers will employ an innovative range of theory and methods to enhance the focus on reality, and government departments can rationalize in order to bring the Canadian public on-side through a better explication of what results from investments.

In Part 2, we examined the population projections, definitions of who is First Nation, and the implications of the choices being made about both. For scientists in and out of government, there is much to learn, from the discussion of population projections, about weaknesses and strengths in our recent attempts to forecast population growth. For policy makers, this book holds other very critical lessons. First, population projections are at the centre of many planning processes. Modest differences between actual and projected numbers can throw health, education, infrastructure, and social planning seriously off the mark. In Chapter 2, Kerr and co-authors found that the Royal

Commission on Aboriginal Peoples projections were so far off the mark that they could not be used for policy development. They did concur that it was safe to conclude that there will be a rapid but declining rate of growth in the Aboriginal population. However, the problems they pointed to in the projections mean that policy makers may be basing their decisions on very incorrect assumptions.

One of the key problems that scientists and policy makers will have to wrestle with is that projections that assume that ethnicity is inherited and permanent are outdated. Chapters 3 and 4 examined this and other related issues that impact Aboriginal conditions directly. Clatworthy explored the nature and implications of the many changes introduced by the 1985 changes to the Indian Act. He pointed out that the choices that First Nations persons are making combine with the changes in the rules about who is or is not a member of the community, and this will dramatically change the numbers of those who are entitled to resources and programs. This interaction of law and choice will also dramatically change the social and the political structures in First Nations communities. For example, the new rules are projected to result in a larger population entitled to Indian registration for about five more generations, but they will also disenfranchise a growing number of descendants. Within two generations, most of the children born to First Nations people are not going to qualify for registration, and within four generations only one in six children will be registered First Nations. Clatworthy commented that the demographic changes will be accompanied by political and social change as the communities begin to develop "classes of citizens" with different rights and entitlements. Regardless of whether First Nations communities adopt one-parent, two-parent, or Indian Act rules, they will have socially difficult times ahead. Significant governance policy reform is needed. For the Department of Indian Affairs and Northern Development (DIAND) the question of who its constituency will be is on the table, as is the issue of how resources are going to be allocated.

If we put this in the frame of the model from Chapter 1, we have to ask: "Will this undermine the cohesion of communities? Will it lead to lesser social capital?" It will certainly dramatically impact the policies that are to be developed by both Aboriginal leaders and the Canadian government.

Aboriginal Conditions then added another layer to the analysis and confronts the issue of identity and ethnicity. Guimond's study (Chapter 4) explored ethnic mobility, which is the shift of one's identity from one ethnicity to another. Through the three illustrations of the compositional effect, he took us to some potential explanations of the mobility and finally to some inescapable policy effects. For example, Guimond is correct when he says that those who congratulate the system for increasing the number of Aboriginal persons with higher education are fooling themselves. It is the ethnic mobility of formerly non-Aboriginal, highly educated persons who now claim Aboriginal identity that is increasing these numbers. The same is true for life expectancy. Some policy makers report that there is a significant improvement in life expectancy. This, however, is a statistical artifact, not an actual improvement. There has been an influx of persons who have longer lifespans into the group defined as Aboriginal. These are people who self-identify (drifters) and those included due to the 1985 changes to the Indian Act. Again, we have a responsibility to improve the science and base the policy development on an evidentiary foundation.

Part 2 of *Aboriginal Conditions* concluded with a study of migration between reserves and cities. Norris and co-authors found in their examination of the actual flows of persons that, contrary to common belief, there is not a net flow to the cities. In fact, there is a net positive flow of people to the reserves. They found that there is a dramatic churn in population where a sizeable proportion of First Nations people are leaving First Nations communities for the cities while others are returning home. This churn migration has implications for further research on community cohesion and the generation and utilization of different forms of capital. Studies are now underway to examine the effect of this migrational pattern on the generation of community capacity using models developed at the University of Western Ontario (Chapter 1). This churn also has implications for the policy around governance, for both Aboriginal leaders and the federal government.

The other set of policy implications involves intergovernmental affairs and cost sharing. Provinces have long complained that the federal government was downloading the costs of First Nations programs because there was a net outflow from the reserves to the cities, which would mean from federal to provincial jurisdiction. Our study dispels this particular belief about outflow to the cities.

Part 3 of *Aboriginal Conditions* explored a very complex and charged issue: language. The studies looked at two distinct but related issues. In Chapter 7, Norris and MacCon presented a study of how languages are maintained, as well as why some are disappearing while some appear relatively robust. Many of the traditional Aboriginal languages are in serious decay or are virtually extinct. However, some are quite vital because of the development of intergenerational transmission mechanisms. Part of the difference depends on the decisions being made by the people themselves. For example, the decision to out-marry and take a partner that does not speak the traditional language is having a devastating effect on intergenerational transmission. The Norris and MacCon study points to some clear indicators of which languages are salvageable and even what the mechanisms might be to do that. Clearly, indiscriminate support of any and all languages is not the evidence-based decision, just as it is mistaken to assume that languages will live on without intervention.

In Chapter 6, O'Sullivan described two important relationships that are very complex to deal with from a policy perspective. Her primary policy target involved assessing a long-standing debate. On the one hand, if a people isolate themselves from the dominant culture and economy through language and cultural separatism, there will be a reduction in socio-economic development. This is a sort of development penalty. On the other hand, the argument is made that maintaining a people's identity through language and cultural continuance builds pride, self-worth, and capacity in the group. The enhancement of cohesion and the reciprocal trust and social interrelationships will lead to the enhancement of well-being and eventually increased socio-economic development.

Because this is a complex issue, O'Sullivan developed the chapter with a lot of discussion about the role and place of language. It is necessary to contextualize any study of a factor that is core to national identity. First, O'Sullivan did not find that high traditional language use is a guarantee of either socio-economic failure or success. She did find that maintenance of language is correlated with lower socio-economic development in many cases. She also found that traditional language saturation is high in communities with low human capital. She was careful not to draw conclusions, but the work certainly points to resource allocation issues. If we think in terms of the theoretical model presented by White and Maxim in Chapter 1, it seems logical that the maintenance of traditional language and/or its reintroduction should help build social capital. The findings are mixed, however. The reintroduction of language appears to be correlated with positive indicators, but not the maintenance of language. The conclusion we may draw is that communities that reintroduce language do so in an environment of higher human capital, and therefore building human capital is key. This has an important policy implication. The First Nations Cohesion Project at the University of Western Ontario is currently looking at differences in educational attainment in band-controlled and public-controlled schools for First Nations children. It is also conducting more general studies of educational attainment in First Nations communities (White and Maxim 2002). These should further elucidate the relationships we are examining here.

When we look at the two studies together (Chapters 6 and 7), we have many important policy issues. Can we marshal resources effectively to maintain traditional languages? Should we even try if there seems little chance of any positive outcomes? Should we view the language maintenance issue as an issue of maintaining nations and ethnic identity, and not see it as an issue of building success in communities? Perhaps resources must be targeted toward building human capital, and the issue of language will be decided by the practices and decisions that the ethnic group makes for itself. First Nations want to chart their own futures and these questions are for both Aboriginal and non-Aboriginal policy makers.

Part 4 looked at capacity issues. In the Beavon and Cooke research (Chapter 8), the United Nations Development Program Human Development Index was adapted to the evaluation of First Nations in Canada. The Canadian government's policy focus on eliminating differences between different collectivities in Canada was implicitly under scrutiny. There can be no doubt that resources and energy have been expended. Why, then, do First Nations people place well below Canada as a whole? The answer may lie in part in the study of income by Maxim, White, and Beavon (Chapter 9) and the Community Capacity Index research presented by Maxim and White in Chapter 10.

There is a consistency between the work of Beavon and Cooke and our work. Each of the studies indicated that there are differential capacities to succeed in First Nation communities. They indicated from very different directions that communities in the Prairies have significantly less success than communities in some other areas of Canada. This is important for policy makers to take into consideration. When we add in the dimension of income inequality, there are further levels of complexity, but greater possibilities for better policy. Our studies of income found that there is still a much larger gap between Aboriginal and non-Aboriginal Canadians than could ever be acceptable, despite the fact that the gap is closing. That is, there is a high relative income disparity that is diminishing very slowly. We also found that there are important inequalities among the non-Aboriginal population, which is to be expected. What was more unusual was the finding that differences between Aboriginal groups are quite large and that the measured intra-group differences are actually much larger than for non-Aboriginal society. The First Nations have the greatest intra-group inequality, followed by Inuit, Non-Status Indians, and then Métis.

The policy implications are manifold. Are we creating great inequities in the communities through our policy action or inaction? Do the transfer systems actually build capacity, or are they creating divisions in the communities? Is the capacity of the communities to build cohesion and develop being undermined by income inequality? Should we be worried at all, or is this inequality simply going to encourage more success seekers?

We saw earlier that classes of citizens are being created in the reserve communities due to the changes in the Indian Act and people's marriage choices. Geographic and community-level differences are differentiating the population according to the Human Development Index and community capacity work presented here. We now see that income is so polarized and dispersed that the communities are also polarized along these lines. Will these reinforcing tendencies create dramatic differences and promote the disintegration of cohesion?

These and other questions require exploration, based on the same kind of scientific approaches that are advocated by the scientists in this book. In each of the chapters, the teams themselves make cases for answers, suggest directions, and clarify what their research indicates, but many, many issues remain to guide research for the future.

Can researchers in and out of government work together to develop important joint projects? Can we create the nexus of research and policy that will take strides forward in confronting the roots of Aboriginal conditions?

These questions are, in the end, empirical queries. We will see what happens. One thing that is clear is that we must improve our scientific rigour, improve the link between evidence and policy, and improve the communication among ourselves. Only by building a research-policy nexus can we bring Aboriginal and non-Aboriginal policy makers and researchers together to truly make social progress on the difficult issues that face us all.

References
White, J., and P. Maxim. 2002. The Correlates of Educational Attainment in First Nation Communities. Paper presented at the Aboriginal Policy Research Conference, November 2002, Ottawa.

Notes on Contributors

Dan Beavon is Director of Strategic Research and Analysis Directorate, Indian Affairs and Northern Affairs Canada. His research looks at how the quality of life can be improved for First Nations peoples and their communities. His latest book is *Hidden in Plain Sight: The Contributions of Aboriginal Peoples to Canadian Identity and Society* (forthcoming). He co-organized and co-chaired the 2002 Aboriginal Policy Research Conference.

Stewart Clatworthy operates Four Directions Project Consultants, a management consulting company specializing in socio-economic and demographic research, program evaluation, and information management. He has been conducting Aboriginal research for more than twenty-three years and has completed numerous studies of Aboriginal socio-economic and demographic circumstances, migration patterns, and population projections.

Martin Cooke is a PhD candidate in the Department of Sociology at the University of Western Ontario. He currently holds a SSHRC Doctoral Fellowship and is a winner of the 2000 Canadian Policy Research Awards Graduate Prize.

Eric Guimond is a senior research manager at Indian and Northern Affairs Canada (INAC), Strategic Research and Analysis Directorate. He currently heads a number of demographic research projects on the issue of the definitions and transmission of Aboriginal identities. Before joining INAC, he was a research analyst at Statistics Canada and Hydro-Québec.

Don Kerr received his PhD in Social Demography at the University of Western Ontario. He currently teaches at King's College at Western. Prior to 2000, he worked for several years as a population analyst for Demography Division at Statistics Canada. His research interests lie in the area of population studies, with a particular interest in Canadian demography.

Karen MacCon is a PhD candidate in the Department of Sociology at the University of Western Ontario. She served a research apprenticeship at the Department of Indian Affairs and Northern Development in 2000-2001.

Paul Maxim is currently a professor in the Department of Sociology at the University of Western Ontario. He obtained his MA at the University of Ottawa and his PhD from the University of Pennsylvania. His current research interests focus on the relationship between demographic factors and socio-economic development. His most recent book is *Quantitative Research Methods in the Social Sciences*.

Mary Jane Norris is a senior research manager with the Research and Analysis Directorate, Indian and Northern Affairs Canada. Prior to her current position, she also concentrated in Aboriginal research in the Demography Division of Statistics Canada. She is of Aboriginal ancestry, with family roots in the Algonquins of Pikwàkanagán (Golden Lake), in the Ottawa Valley.

Erin O'Sullivan completed her masters degree in Sociology at the University of Western Ontario. She currently holds a research position at the Department of Indian Affairs and Northern Development.

Jerry P. White is Chair of the Sociology Department at the University of Western Ontario. He is former Deputy Chair of the Health Professions Regulatory Advisory Council of Ontario and a holder of the Pleva Professorship for teaching excellence. From 1998 to the present he has been co-director of the First Nations Cohesion Research Project with Paul Maxim at UWO. He co-organized and co-chaired the 2002 Aboriginal Policy Research Conference.

Index

182(f), 190(t); knowledge of, 166(t), 168, 175, 176(t), 188(t); mother tongue population, 166(t), 169, 176(t), 184(t)

Avison, W., 12

Backlund, E. (co-author with Wolfson, M.), 12

band membership: blood quantum rules, 79, 80(t), 82-84, 87; Indian Act or equivalent rules, 79, 80(t), 81, 87; marriage patterns and, 79, 81-86; political rights of, 78, 88; rules, impact of, 36, 78-79, 80(t), 81-86, 87-88; two-parent rules, 79, 80(t), 84-86, 87; unequal rights, 36, 78, 79, 81, 87-88, 266; unlimited one-parent rules, 79, 80(t), 81-82, 83(f), 87; vs. entitlement to Indian registration, 78

Barsh, R.L., 126

Beavon, N. (co-author with Norris, M.J.), 120

Benediktsson, H., 12

Bernier, R., 226

Bill C-31. *See* Indian Act, 1985 (Bill C-31)

birth rates. *See* fertility

blood quantum rules, 79, 80(t), 82-84, 87

British Columbia: CCI for region, 256(f), 258; HDI data for Status Indians, 217, 218(t), 219; income, Aboriginals vs. non-Aboriginals, 234, 235(t)-236(t), 238

Cairns, A.C., 151

Canadian Institutes of Health Research (CIHR), xvii

Catalano, R., 12

causes of death: and socio-economic status, 11-12, 223

CCI. *See* Community Capacity Index (CCI)

Census of Canada: 1991 data on Aboriginal peoples, 42; 1996 census

vs. RCAP projections, 35-36, 52-55, 59; Aboriginal identity concept, 52-53, 92; Aboriginal language questions, 171-73; access to data, problems, xix; First Nations data, problems with, 11; historical comparability of data, 59, 243n10; migration data, 110-11; modelling social capital, 9; undercoverage, 94-96, 105n4, 127n1, 206

Census Public Use Microdata File (PUMF), 225

Census Public Use Sample File (PUSF), 225

Chandler, M.J., 20

Clatworthy, S., 72-73, 126, 225-26

cohesion. *See* social cohesion

cohort-survival model, 72-78

Coleman, J., 13, 14

communities: definition, 7

community-based models, 3-5. *See also* population outcomes model

Community Capacity Index (CCI): construction/testing, 253-54, 260, 261n7; description, 199, 249-50, 265; education/human capital subindex, 250-51, 253(t); effectiveness measures, alternate, 260-61; occupational diversity subindex, 252-53, 262n10; policy implications, 260, 269; population size/age-dependency ratio subindex, 251-52, 253(t), 262n8; scoring First Nations communities, 254-55, 256(f), 257(t), 258; social capital component, 249-50, 259-60, 261n4; validating index, 258-59

community cohesion. *See* social cohesion

community development: intra-group inequalities, impact of, 198; transfer policies, impact of, 198, 225-26, 229-31, 233, 248-49. *See also* Community Capacity Index (CCI)

Constitution Act (1982), 40, 109

Printed and bound in Canada by Friesens

Set in Garamond and Myriad by Artegraphica Design Co. Ltd.

Copy editor: Francis Chow

Proofreader: Gail Copeland

Indexer: Patricia Buchanan